Claude de Passioné

Revelations and Peace

The sequel to the dramatic and romantic adventures of Claude de Passioné

A novel by John H. Gray

Other works by John H Gray

Journey of Betrayals

Journey to Unknown Consequences

Claude de Passioné

Rosita's Way

Children's Books

The Adventures of Tutu and Tula. Lost

The Adventures of Tutu and Tula. Perdu (French)

The Adventures of Tutu and Tula. Christmas.

The Adventures of Tutu and Tula. Noel (French)

The Adventures of Tutu and Tula. Rescue

The Adventures of Tutu and Tula. Brave

The Adventures of Tutu and Tula. Farewell

All rights reserved. In accordance with the U.S. Copyright Act of 1976, the scanning, uploading, and electronic sharing of any part of this book

without permission of the publisher is unlawful piracy and theft of the

Thank you for your support of the author's rights

All characters and events in this book are fictitious. Any similarity to real persons, living or dead, is coincidental and not intended by the author.

.

       Website: www.johnsnovels.com

       Email: thestory@myself.com

© **Copyright registered (2020) John H Gray**

ISBN Number: **978-1-7777978-5-0**

Part 1

Mysterious Happenings

Chapter 1

de Passioné Estates, Napa Valley, California.

The sound of gunshots echoed through the still air of the late morning. Barry Jones, Claude's rough and ready Australian business partner, and friend rushed through the vineyard in the direction of where he had heard the shots. He came upon the inert body of Claude de Passioné lying on the ground. He looked down at the still smoking shotgun in Claude's hand. He knelt and gently placed his fingers against Claude's neck and felt the weak pulse. Claude was not dead. Gingerly, he rolled Claude onto his back. As he did so, from the corner of his eye he saw a movement. Barry turned toward the movement. A figure dressed in black clothing raced up the incline through the rows of grapevines. Barry was torn. He wondered whether he should pursue the running figure or stay with Claude and summon help. He did not need to think for long. Two of the migrant workers of the vineyard arrived at the scene. They dropped to their knees. Barry watched as one withdrew an evil-looking knife and quickly thrust it forward in the direction of Claude's chest. The worker grabbed at Claude's shirt and slashed a huge tear. He ripped the shirt apart, exposing a neat round hole from which blood was seeping. Barry instantly realized that Claude had been shot, but the wound he observed was not a wound from a shotgun. He spun and ran with all his strength toward the figure who was now almost to the road at the top of the field. He was too late. Barry was still running when a black Mercedes arrived at high speed and screeched to a halt. The person in the dark clothing jumped into the car. It sped off, scattering stones at the side of the road. Tires screeched as they spun and smoked on the asphalt road surface. Barry was unable to catch a glimpse of any identifying marks on the car or its registration. He turned away and ran back to where Claude lay wounded.

The migrant workers had used a part of Claude's shirt to make a tourniquet and tied it around an area of his arm where blood was rushing from a large gash. There was another bullet wound and Barry could see the embedded bullet in his upper arm.

Barry cursed and used some of his best Australian swearings. He looked at the migrant workers and in a very broken Spanish asked them to wait while he called for help.

Chapter 2

Emergency vehicles had been summoned and after applying life-saving treatment at the scene, they transported Claude to the area hospital.

Later that day, back at the estate's Mansion, Barry thought back over the past weeks. He pieced together the events of those weeks. He wondered whether Claude's amorous infatuation with Misty Moon and the unsavory dealings she had had with Dr. Stanley Stubbs had in any way contributed to the attempted killing of Claude. He thought of the information that the police had shared with them. Dr. Stanley Stubbs had cared for several elderly men and most had died under suspicious circumstances and left huge estates to Misty Moon. The police further disclosed that she was also involved in international drug smuggling, human trafficking, money laundering, and other highly illegal activities. Barry had been shocked when the police had revealed Misty's real name…Wendy Wong.

The thought of Claude caught up and in trouble with a Chinese Triad gang worried him. The Chinese Triad gangs were powerful, international, and reckless.

Barry wandered over to a wine cooler in the kitchen of the estate and found a bottle of cold Chablis. He poured a large glass and sat thinking.

"What had Claude uncovered? Had he accidentally stumbled upon some critical information? Who had tried to kill Claude? Was it Lise Victor, the crooked international art and antique dealer with whom Claude had been involved years earlier? Claude had certainly been intimate enough with her. Was she now seeking revenge?

He wondered about the family Claude had met in New Zealand during his travels."

Barry's gloomy mood further increased and black thoughts of the situation intensified. Then it dawned on him.

He recalled the times that Claude had spoken of his trip in the South Pacific and his romances there. In particular, his romance with the Polynesian beauty called Atarangi. Was it her family seeking revenge for his deserting her and leaving her heartbroken?

Barry considered this possibility and then dismissed it. He decided that it was not constructive to sit and imagine the possible reasons. He decided to visit Claude at the hospital. He swore that when Claude recovered, they would search for the culprits.

Barry walked to the kitchen and retrieved the keys to his old pickup truck and his weather-beaten old Australian digger's hat. He left the Mansion and crunched his way across the white stones of the path to where he kept his old truck. He reached the rusted old relic, and after jumping into it, fired up the engine. As normal, clouds of bluish-grey smoke billowed from its exhaust. Barry crunched the manual transmission into reverse and backed out onto the grassy area beside the tool shed where he kept the truck. He dropped it into first gear and with a throbbing roar from the truck's collapsing exhaust system, he roared off to visit his best friend, Claude.

Barry drove at speed to the hospital, where he parked haphazardly and went into the emergency area.

"Good afternoon. I'm here to assist with my friend and business partner, Claude de Passioné."

The triage nurse looked at him.

"Sir, I can't allow you to see him. He is in surgery and there are police waiting for him to recover. I am under instruction from the police that no one is to visit him or have any access to his room."

"I'm his bloody partner and I'm going in there come hell or high water. Who is the goddamned cop? They could have prevented all this."

Barry continued to fume at the staff until a firm hand clamped down on his shoulder. He spun to face the hand's owner, expecting to see a scrawny hospital security guard, instead, he was face to face with the young cop who had attended the accident at the restaurant in Bodega Bay where Claude's fiancé, Clare had died in that tragic car accident.

"Come on now, Barry. Calm down. You being like this isn't going to help. The staff has been given instructions to follow and you are not helping them and just upsetting the situation. When Claude is lucid you can join me. We have a lot of questions. Do you have any idea who shot Claude?"

"No, but I think that Wendy Wong, or as she calls herself, Misty Moon is involved. I also suspect that Lise Victor may be involved as well."

"We will need to question you as well. Did you shoot Claude and then come up with an elaborate story to throw us off the trail?"

"I'll knock your fucking head off if you continue with that, mate. Cop or no cop you'll be wearing blue that isn't part of any fucking uniform."

The young cop stepped back from Barry's menacing approach.

"Barry, be reasonable. I am required to ask you that. I have my superiors to answer to. It's all just part of the initial investigation process. Please calm down. I suggest you call that lawyer friend of Claudes. What was his name?"

"His name is Al Pine."

Barry and the cop continued talking. Initially, they didn't notice the tall Chinese man enter the Emergency waiting area. It was the young cop who noticed his presence. The man stopped at the desk and asked several questions before turning and walking out of the exit.

The young cop ran to the desk.

"Who was that? What was he asking?"

"He said he was a family friend. He simply asked if the patient was alive, then he turned and left."

The young cop ran out the door and watched as a black Mercedes sped from the parking area.

Back inside the hospital, the cop returned to speak to Barry.

"I will need you to come to the station and tell us all you know. I am required to wait until Claude regains consciousness. There is no need for you to stay. We will be in contact."

Barry looked at the cop and realized from the cop's confused look that he was mentally grappling with the few clues he had gathered. It seemed hopeless to proceed without further information.

"You know where to find me, mate. Happy to help you, anytime."

Barry slapped his old Australian digger's hat back on and headed out the exit.

Chapter 3

That evening, Barry sat alone relaxing with a glass of fine wine. In his mind, he worked through the major events of the last two years. He thought of the situations in which Claude had been embroiled, either through his own stupidity or as an unwitting victim. It seemed there were plenty who probably wished to exact revenge on Claude.

Barry's thoughts drifted back to that morning in the vineyard. He recalled the sound of the gunshots and the curl of gunsmoke as it had risen into the air, filtered by the sun's rays. There was something about the scene Barry had witnessed that worried him. He played the images through his mind over and over.

The loud jangling of the phone snapped Barry back into reality. He grabbed the receiver.

"Barry Jones, here. Who's bloody disturbing me?"

He listened intently to the caller, a nurse at the hospital. Claude was to be released the next day at noon. Barry thanked her and, after assuring her that he would be there to pick up Claude, he hung up and returned to his wine and thoughts.

He slumped back into the huge chair and rested his head against the firmly upholstered headrest. He continued to think of the scene. He closed his eyes, recalling the crack of the shot from a rifle and remembering the black-clad figure racing up through the grapevines to the road and that black Mercedes. There was something he was missing.

The air in the room was warm and Barry was drifting asleep when he sat up with a jolt. He realized what he had been overlooking. The dark-clad figure with the rifle was slim and small. It was the figure of a woman who was fleeing. Barry smiled. This would reduce the number of possible events to check, but knowing Claude and all of his romantic escapades, there would still be plenty.

There was one thing troubling Barry. Who was the tall Chinese man at the hospital with the black Mercedes? He decided to call Al Pine, Claude's lawyer, in the morning and ask him to employ 'Snoops' Dugan, one of the greasiest and sleaziest private investigators in San Francisco. If anyone could sniff out the ownership of that car, it would be 'Snoops'.

Barry decided to turn in for the night. He stood and walked over to the desk in the living room and switched off the lamp. He hit the wall switch and the overhead lights went dark. As he turned to leave the room he saw a glint of light shine from a car parked at the driveway entrance into the estate. He moved back from the window and concealed his presence behind the thick heavy drapes.

The car was in total darkness, except for its outline cast in the light from the moon. Barry attempted to identify the car. It appeared to be a Mercedes. While Barry was deciding whether to take a rifle and confront the occupants or to call the police, there was a small flash and flicker in the car as someone lit a cigarette.

"Whoever is in that car is no bloody professional at the surveillance game," Barry muttered. He decided to confront whoever was in the car.

Barry went to the estate's kitchen and opened the door to a small closet. He reached in and unlocked a gun rack before removing the rifle that looked the most menacing and slid out of the back door.

He crouched and ran into the small orchard and made his way down the side of the estate toward the driveway entrance. The ground in the orchard was lower than the raised driveway and allowed Barry to approach undetected. Barry guessed at the approximate location of the Mercedes before running up the incline and onto the stone drive.

It was not the black Mercedes. This one was dark grey.

He swung the rifle at the front window. He heard a piercing scream from inside the car. The driver's door flew open and a young woman called to him.

"Okay, dearie. Get your arse out of there and tell me what the fuck you're doing here on private property with the lights turned off and spying on the house."

Barry kept the rifle trained on her as she crawled out of the car.

"You got anyone else in there? Stand here where I can see you. I will check."

Barry pulled open the rear door of the car while keeping the rifle aimed inside. The car was empty.

"Let's hear your story before I call the cops."

"My name is Crystal Moon. I am Misty Moon's sister. She asked me to come and see Claude de Passioné. She is worried that he is in grave danger. He has information that some people are very eager to get or to ensure he doesn't live."

"We are going to walk down this drive to the house. Inside you will explain everything. If you try to run or do anything stupid, I will shoot you. Are there any others here on the property?"

"No, I came alone."

Barry walked her to the house at a fast pace. He wanted her safely inside. He did not believe she was alone.

Inside the house and in the light, he examined her. She seemed to be young, and maybe in her late twenties. Her hair was long and dark and she closely resembled the features of her sister Misty.

"I'd like it if you could tell me what the hell this is all about."

"I came to speak to Mr. Claude directly. I am not to speak to anyone else."

Barry picked up the phone.

"Well then, I'm calling in the cops. I'm sure they will be intrigued."

"No, please. Just get Mr. Claude. Let me speak to him and I will leave."

Barry set the phone back down.

"Did you think he was here? Did you expect to speak to him tonight?"

"Yes. Tomorrow morning I must leave for Hong Kong. I wished to deliver the message to him early and return to my hotel tonight so I could pack and be ready to leave for the airport early."

"Claude is not here. Do you know where he is?"

Barry watched her as she frowned. She seemed to be confused.

"No. I expected to see him. I was waiting and watching to see if he was alone and then I would come to the house. I wanted you to leave."

"Claude was shot today. He is in hospital."

Crystal gasped and started shaking.

"How? Who did it? Is he alright?"

"He will recover. Now sit down and explain everything to me."

Chapter 4

It was just before noon when Barry picked Claude up from the hospital. Claude was in surprisingly good spirits.

"Barry, I don't want to go back to the estate yet. The police were here this morning asking all sorts of questions. They were not particularly sociable. I need a change of environment. Please drive us down to Bodega Bay and my favorite restaurant. There are things we need to discuss. Why was I shot? We need to work out what is happening. I don't want to get my mother, Marie-France, involved at this time. Her mental state gets worse each day."

Claude sat back and tried to relax as the old pickup roared onto the freeway entrance. Horrified motorists gave wide berth to the lumbering, noisy, smoke emitting machine. Claude had offered on many occasions to provide Barry with a new truck purchased by the vineyards, but he had steadfastly refused. The local cops recognized the truck and knew better than to stop Barry and receive the torrent of Australian slang and swearing. Barry and his truck were accepted items.

Claude wondered how fate had brought him into a business partnership with the gruff Australian. Claude had been with Barry long enough to recognize that it was a façade and all bluster.

Claude thought back on his life. His family, the de Passionés were from a long line of wealthy French aristocrats. They had huge ownership of vineyards and wineries. He wondered how his parents could have been so abnormal. His father, the Marquis, and his insatiable appetite for beautiful women led to his ultimate demise and death. His mother, Marie-France, a woman lost in the past with visions of never-ending youth and still suffering the extremes of the continuous drug use during her days as a hippie. Each day Claude was unsure what new adventure Marie-France would unleash, still, he loved her. He smiled to himself at the image of her in his head. He remembered her failed membership in the motorcycle gang he had come home to find on the front garden of their French Chateau. He recalled the bikes and their noise, and of her dressed in motorcycle leathers. The bright and unmatched dress of her hippie days she still wore caused him to laugh on occasion. The purple bell-bottoms with those lime green shoes and the tie-dyed shirts. The collection of beaded necklaces and the giant peace and love rings that adorned her fingers. What he did not like about Marie-France, was her infatuation and desire for young men. He had talked to her about this on many occasions, but it was all in vain.

Claude's memories drifted to his travels after he left the Sorbonne. He thought of his many affairs, but only one remained forceful in his mind and heart. It was his love for Atarangi, a beautiful Polynesian woman he had met during his stay in the Cook Islands. He wondered if one day he could live in the islands with her, but dismissed the idea.

The trip to Bodega Bay seemed to take only a few minutes, though, in reality, it had taken over forty-five minutes. Barry had watched Claude dozing during the trip, and had not spoken to him. He figured the medications were still working.

The tree-lined road wound down through farmland and finally dropped to the shore and the black sands of Bodega Bay. Barry turned right and drove along toward The Tides Restaurant. He was apprehensive, uncertain how Claude would react. It had only been a few months since Claude's fiancé had been run over and killed as they had been leaving at The Tides. It had been the lunch when Claude had proposed marriage.

Barry drove further than was needed to park. He did not want to stop at the exact location where Claire had been killed, but Claude insisted.

"Stop now. I wish to go back to where she died. I will pray for her."

Barry was even more shocked. It was the first time he had heard the words 'pray' uttered by Claude. He slammed on the rusty brakes that squealed at their arrival. He backed up to the area.

Claude took the wrench from the floor and used it on the shaft of the broken door lock. The handle had fallen off years earlier. With the old door open, he jumped down to the pavement and walked back to where the accident had happened. Claude stood with his head bent and his hands clasped in front of him. Barry stood back and waited.

After a couple of minutes, Claude turned and motioned to Barry to cross over to the restaurant. Inside they were seated at one of the large windows that overlooked the bay. The restaurant was busy with patrons enjoying a late lunch.

Several of the staff recognized Claude from the fatal accident and their embarrassment and concern were obvious.

Claude placed his order for his favorite hot crab sandwich. Barry wanted steak and eggs but was told it was a seafood-only restaurant. He wasn't amused and ordered a seafood platter.

"I dunno how the Yanks live on the crap they eat. This isn't a real man's food."

Claude smiled at his comment. He knew it was all bravado.

"Barry, we need to talk, I have no idea why I was shot. Do you have any ideas?"

"Last night we had a visitor at the estate. Came and parked in the dark driveway. I went out to see what was happening. It was a young lady. She claims to be Crystal Moon, the sister of Misty Moon. I took her into the house and we had a long chat. It turns out that you, my friend, are in some serious trouble."

Claude was about to ask Barry to elaborate when the young cop who had attended the accident came over to their table.

"I am pleased to see you are up and about, Claude. I am wondering if you and Barry could come by tomorrow morning. We have some information we would like to discuss with you."

"Do I need to bring legal counsel ?"

"It is not necessary, but it might be advisable given the information we have uncovered. It seems that you have become involved with some very nasty people. I understand that last night you received a visitor at your home. We want to know more about that person and that visit. I hope you are not involved with these people, Claude."

"I have no idea what you are talking about. We will meet you at ten tomorrow. Please come to the house. I am still uncomfortable and would prefer that.

"It can be arranged. There will be detectives and others with me."

The young cop left Claude and Barry as the waitress returned with their meals.

"Barry, what the hell is going on?

Chapter 5

When Barry and Claude arrived back at the estate, Marie-France was entertaining some rather unusual visitors. The two men wore shabby black clothes and sported long white beards. Claude had never seen the men before.

"Mother, I see you have friends visiting. Who are these gentlemen?"

"Xavier and Heinrich, meet my clever son, Claude. He is so good to me."

"Who are these men?"

"Claude, these are the founders of that new church on the road into the village. They are the pastors of The Church of Happy Glory. They need money to buy the land. I am thinking of helping them. They tell me I will be a saint in their church and that they will put a statue of me in the church. Isn't that nice?"

Claude immediately thought of Marie-France's earlier contribution to join the motorcycle gang. He had no tolerance for the scammers.

"Gentlemen, it is nice to meet you, but I must ask you to leave. We have some important family matters to discuss. Someone from our office will be in contact. Now, Goodbye."

The men appeared confused but realized they had been dismissed.

"Barry, please escort these men off our property and gentlemen do not return here unless either Barry or I invite you. If you attempt to return, I will have you both arrested and charged with trespassing."

Marie-France didn't understand what had just transpired.

"Aren't they nice men, Claude?"

Claude did not respond but watched as Barry held the arm of each man on either side and marched them from the room.

"Mother, why don't you go and take a nap before dinner? Barry and I have some boring old work to do and phone calls to make. I look forward to seeing you all sparkling and refreshed for dinner."

"Oh, Claude. You tease me."

In reality, Marie-France felt great pride and believed she had retained her looks like a twenty-year-old. She preened in front of the living room mirror and left to take a rest.

With Marie-France gone and Barry back from dismissing the churchmen, Claude got down to business.

"Barry, I need you to tell me about last night."

"I will in a minute Claude but first you should know that I called Al Pine early this morning after I had heard Crystal's account of why you are in trouble. I think we should call him to attend tomorrow and bring 'Snoops' Dugan. We are going to need him."

Claude considered this for a moment.

"Why do we need him?"

"According to Crystal Moon, you are being pursued by two different Triad gangs. She did not have the identity of the man at the hospital but said he is based in San Francisco. I do not know how he is related to these gangs."

"I am confused, Barry. I have never had any business dealings in China or with the Chinese. The only relationship was with Misty Moon."

"So Claude, either the issue is related to her or some dealing you have had. I remember when we first met Misty at the hospital with Dr. Stubbs. I told you then that there was something I sensed about her and did not trust. I did not trust that doctor either. I think you have stumbled into some strange situation. Did Misty Moon ever give you any gifts or ask you to look after anything for her? For two Triad gangs to be pursuing you means it must be something of great value, whether it's information or an object. Think carefully, as your life may be in danger."

"Barry, the first time I met Misty Moon was in that hospital when Dr. Stubbs recommended her to me. I had never met her before then. I admit that I became quite infatuated with her, but I cannot recall ever receiving any gifts from her."

"It's final then. We are going to see Al Pine and 'Snoops' Dugan. We need to get to the bottom of this immediately."

"Why don't we try to just go and meet the Chinese? I am sure there is some mistake here. We will explain that I have nothing of any interest to them."

Claude had barely finished speaking when the large picture window in the living shattered as a hail of bullets smashed through it and into the walls of the room. Claude and Barry dropped to the floor. An extreme silence followed the shooting. As they lay there, Marie-France arrived in the room. She had heard the breaking of the glass and decided to investigate. She looked at Barry and Claude on the floor and frowned.

"Why are you two lying on the floor. It was just some birds that flew into the window. I'll call Russell the handyman to come and fix it. Those damned birds."

It was too much for Barry. He was unable to stand up as he rocked back and forth with laughter. Claude looked at Barry and then at Marie-France before he too started to laugh.

"You are correct, Mother. Those damned birds."

Marie-France turned to leave the room but hesitated at the door.

"I think we need to celebrate the day. I'm going to get some wine from the cellar."

Claude was again confused. He looked at Barry and frowned.

"Mother, what are we celebrating?"

"I think I have a new lover. He's a nice oriental man. He came earlier to see you. I told him you were out on business. He had a package for you. I offered to take it, but he said it could only be given to you. He was very charming and wanted to take me to dinner. A very nice man. He told me I was a gorgeous woman. I am so impressed that I am going to learn Chinese cooking."

"Barry, contact Al Pine. Ask him to come here to the house. They will need to interview Mother. I do not wish to take her into San Francisco. What the hell is going on? Who are these people?"

Claude thought some more about the situation.

"Mother, is that man returning? What was his name?"

Marie-France looked vacantly at Claude. She grappled for the name the man had used. It took a few moments for her to recall the name.

"He introduced himself as Wee Hoe. Tall, good-looking, and seemed very strong. He's my kind of man."

"Mother, he may be involved in some bad things. Do not go anywhere with him nor allow him in our house. Do you understand?"

"Claude, you are my son and you will not dictate who my friends are or where I go."

"Mother, that window was not broken by birds flying into it. Someone fired shots at it. That is how it broke. There seem to be some nasty things happening to us. I want you to be safe. Do you understand? You are not to see him again and you are not to go anywhere with him."

He watched as Marie-France pursed her lips and her expression showed she was starting to sulk. Claude went to her and hugged her.

"You must trust me. It is for the best. I am having a meeting with our lawyer in the morning. Please join us. I am sure he will want your information on Mr. Hoe."

When Marie-France left the room, Claude called the police station and asked to speak to the young cop. He was advised that he was not at the station. Claude explained to the person who answered the phone that he needed to reschedule the planned morning meeting.

Part 2

The Investigation starts

Chapter 6

It was mid-morning when Al Pine and 'Snoops' Dugan arrived at the estate. It had been a long drive up from San Francisco in snarled and heavy traffic.

One of the servants escorted them to the living room with its large picture window replaced. The servant offered them coffee and pastries while they waited for Claude and Barry.

'Snoops' looked around at the expensive furnishings and paintings. He had never been in such an opulent home before.

"Al, how long have you been counsel to the de Passioné family?" 'Snoops' asked.

"I was hired by Claude's father, the Marquis, and his wife Marie-France when they were acquiring other vineyards. You might find Marie-France a bit different, but she means well."

The words had no sooner left his lips when Claude walked in accompanied by Barry and Marie-France.

Marie-France had dressed in her finest 'business attire' after learning of Al Pine's visit. She seductively glided up to him with her hand outstretched for the assumed kiss. Al obliged, and Marie-France feigned a blush and embarrassment.

"Al, welcome back to the estate. It has been a long time since you last visited. I believe the Marquis was still alive."

"It is a pleasure to be here and I must say you look as ravenous as ever."

The compliment was not wasted. Marie-France swooned and displayed as much of her draping cleavage as she considered appropriate.

"Mother, I'm sure that Al has other important business in San Francisco, so we must start our meeting now."

Marie-France pouted and sank back into her favorite chaise lounge.

Al Pine turned to Claude and Barry.

"I think I should introduce 'Snoops'. He does all my investigative work and can be fully trusted. 'Snoops' spent close to twenty years with the San Francisco police department. There isn't much he hasn't seen or experienced. Anything you have to discuss with me can be shared with 'Snoops', so please tell me what is so important for you to request this meeting."

Claude discussed the shooting, the strange visit at the hospital, and then the arrival of Crystal Moon at the house, followed by the visit of a man who named himself Wee Hoe and wanted to deliver a package to Claude directly.

Barry took over and told Al and 'Snoops' of the conversation he had with Crystal Moon. He mentioned the Triad gangs and her claim that Claude's life was in danger.

'Snoops' sat quietly making notes.

"I'd like to speak. When I was in the police, I spent several years working in the Chinatown district. I know many of the 'actors' there. The illegal gambling, the counterfeiters, the opium dens, the extortionists, all the lovely characters. They can be a brutal bunch. Claude, I need you to tell me how you came into contact with these people."

Claude described the events that had hospitalized him and how he had been introduced to Misty Moon by his doctor as a physiotherapist who could assist him in recovering from the car accident that claimed the life of his fiancé. He went on to detail the evolution of the relationship and the romance that followed.

'Snoops' frequently jotted down entries into the battered notebook he had fished from his jacket pocket.

When Claude had finished, 'Snoops' asked Marie-France about her encounter with Wee Hoe. She was only too happy to oblige and described him as one would an old-time Hollywood star.

When Marie-France was finished, 'Snoops' scanned back through his notes before speaking.

"Claude, my initial analysis of what is happening is that you have in your possession something of great importance. You mentioned that two Triad gangs are pursuing you. That means it is of real value to one gang, and if the other was to get it they would then have some power or control over the other. I know these gangs and how they operate. It may be something as simple as a list of names of associates in crime, drug deal information, or information on other underworld gangs. I can assure you that they will not give up the pursuit until they get whatever it is."

"I do not have anything. I never received any gifts or items from Misty Moon. Do you think we should contact her?"

"No, and I advise you not to open any package delivered to you by Wee Hoe or any other of the Chinese. It is possibly a booby-trapped bomb, anthrax, or other device intended to harm you. If you receive such a package, call me and I will have it taken to the bomb disposal unit. I still have friends there."

Barry had, until now, been a passive observer. Finally, his patience had run out.

"Are you guys just going to let Claude take his chances with these buggers running around after him? Typical bloody Yanks. I tell you that I'm not going to wait. I got some buddies in San Francisco as well. It seems it's time for me to enlist some help. Jesus, you are all a hopeless bunch. A bloody bunch of wankers"

"Barry, listen to Al and 'Snoops'. They know the city and the underworld contacts. If you interfere you may create more problems."

"You're all a bunch of bloody pansies. I'll get some results real fast."

Al Pine turned to Barry, whose tanned face was now a shade of crimson. Al recognized the true anger that Barry was expressing.

"Barry, I have an idea. I know you are upset about the shooting of Claude and the actions of these Triad gangs. Instead of going it alone, why don't you work with 'Snoops'? I think you would make a great pair."

Suddenly, Marie-France addressed the small group.

"Mr. Pine, I want to join with 'Snoops' and Barry. I'm sure I can get more out of those men than those two."

Al tried hard to suppress a laugh.

"No, Marie-France. It will be way too dangerous for an esteemed woman of your standing. Leave the dirty work to the professionals."

Barry had been eyeing 'Snoops' and finally made a decision.

"I'll work with 'Snoops', but I expect him to investigate my ideas and leads. I'm not there to be his bloody office boy."

Claude was becoming annoyed with Barry's attitude.

"Barry, I appreciate your frustration, but we must all work together as a team. This is not the time for a case of one-man bravado. While Crystal Moon claimed the Triad is after me, it could well be that all of us are in danger."

The red veins at the end of Barry's nose pulsated. He was furious at being admonished by Claude.

'Snoops' broke the awkward silence that had descended in the room.

"Claude, I have a question. Has the winery done any business with any Chinese company, either here or in China?"

"We have an arrangement with a trading and export company in San Jose. We have very little communication with them. We receive orders and ship them to their address in Oakland. Executives from the firm may visit once or twice a year. The management group we deal with are not all Chinese, there are several Russians involved in that company."

'Snoops' listened. The news of Russian involvement surprised him, but not totally. He recalled raids he had made on Triad groups when he was a cop. Many of the gangs were equipped with high-end Russian-made weapons. He rubbed his scarred elbow and recalled the round from the Kalashnikov AK-12 that had shattered the bone and ripped the surface skin and flesh away during a botched drug bust.

'Snoops' had no love for either the Triads or the Russian mob.

Chapter 7

Chinatown, San Francisco

It was late in the afternoon in San Francisco when 'Snoops' stopped into his old police precinct. As he climbed up the worn concrete stairs, he recalled the years he had served on the police force and the friends and adventures he had experienced during his time there.

His visit today was to chat with his old friend, Paddy O'Regan, a crusty Irish cop who had transferred from Boston to San Francisco. If anyone had information on the Chinese gangs, it would be Paddy.

'Snoops' took the old wooden stairs up to the second floor where the detectives worked. He pushed the battered metal door open and walked into the office. There was a jumble of desks stacked with files and papers. Phones jangled and men stood in small groups talking and arguing. It was a scene of organized chaos.

'Snoops' had barely entered when the booming voice of Paddy echoed across the room.

"Jesus, Mary, and Joseph. Look what the bleeding cat dragged in. Are you here to surrender for some nefarious deed?"

'Snoops' smiled to himself. He knew that behind the heavy Irish accent act, there was a brilliant mind that had solved many cold cases. Paddy was one of the best.

"Good afternoon to you as well, Paddy. I'm here to ask you for some information."

"Now, why the hell would I want to give you information that you will probably turn around and sell to some attorney or client for an exorbitant sum of money. Typical private gumshoe. Why don't you go get an honest job delivering rubber dogshit in boxes for Amazon?"

"Well, Paddy, when you hear what the situation is I think you will be most interested."

"Are we going to talk in here or should we take a walk?"

"I think we should walk. It's already mid-afternoon so let me buy you a cold one while we chat."

"You poor bugger. Must be desperate if you are going to reach into your pocket to buy me a beer."

"Paddy, this is big. If you solve this one you will be promoted high enough to retire like a king."

Paddy reached his desk and picked up his worn police uniform jacket. He was going to make this trip with 'Snoops' an official event.

The pair left the police precinct and headed out along Grant Street and toward the famous Dragon's Gate. Suddenly, behind them, there was the sound of explosions, like gunshots. Paddy grabbed his service pistol and spun around to witness a group of young teenage boys laughing and running away. On the ground was the debris of the fireworks the boys had thrown at them. People walking on the sidewalk were laughing but Paddy didn't see the humor and shouted at them.

"You little bastards. If I catch you then you better pray that Saint Patrick and all his helpers are there to save you."

In Chinatown, Paddy was often the target of practical jokes. He was both feared and ridiculed. The police were not held in high regard amongst the Chinese residents.

"Let's get out of here. I feel like mingling amongst all those tourists, so let's go down the O'Malleys near Fishermans Wharf."

'Snoops' loved O'Malleys, where they had beers from around the world and some of the best Whiskey he had ever tasted. This was going to be an expensive afternoon, but he didn't care. His client would pay.

Paddy hailed a taxi and as they drove down into the bay, light fog and mist were forming off the water. Late afternoon in San Francisco was 'Snoops' favorite time.

The taxi stopped near the fish market stalls selling fresh steamed crab and other delicacies. The air was filled with the aroma of the crab and other delicacies.

They walked along past buskers performing for small groups of tourists and past barking sea lions lazing on the pilings of the wharves. After five minutes they crossed over the road and approached the entrance to O'Malleys. The squat long bar was situated away from the main area of the Wharf and tucked against a hilly cliff.

As they entered the bar, the noise of the patrons' conversations hit them. Paddy was greeted by the ruddy-faced genial barman. He was a frequent customer. Paddy spied a table in a corner next to the huge plate glass window that offered a magnificent view of the Bay. The sun was starting to set behind the Golden Gate Bridge and over the Pacific. The late afternoon light took on a golden glow.

After they were seated, drinks were brought to their table before they could order. Paddy grinned at the pint of Harp Ale and the side of Jamesons. "Snoops' was served a local Anchor Steam Beer.

"Ok 'Snoops'…spill the beans. What's going on?"

'Snoops' described in detail the strange events that had occurred at the de Passioné estate and the involvement of the Chinese. He told Paddy of Claude's earlier romantic involvement with Misty Moon and the subsequent visit by Crystal Moon and of the shooting and the curious presence of the tall Chinese man who claimed his name to be We Hoe.

Paddy listened silently while 'Snoops' spoke. He did not interrupt. When he had finished, Paddy asked.

"What do you want from me?"

"Paddy, you know who the mob players are in Chinatown and beyond. Can you try and find out who these people are and what they are looking for?"

"It won't be easy. Get me more information. Maybe a meeting with Claude de Passioné himself and his business friend Barry Jones. Call me when we can meet. In the meantime, I will make some gentle inquiries. From what you have described there is something of great importance that they are trying to retrieve or alternately silence your client. I suggest your employer, the attorney, review all of the wineries' recent dealings. I will try and find this We Hoe character. It doesn't sound like he is with the Triads after the actions of those who are after Claude. We Hoe could have taken advantage during Claude's hospital stay. It sounds to me that you've got yourself into a messy one."

Chapter 8

By the time Paddy and 'Snoops' finished discussing the mystery surrounding the attack on Claude, the sun had set and a light mist had settled in over the bay. Several yachts made their way down the harbor. Foghorns started to sound as the fog increased.

The crowd in O'Malleys had steadily grown, and the noise from the conversations had increased. Paddy and 'Snoops' decided to leave and order dinner at a quieter restaurant. Paddy suggested a restaurant not far from his precinct in Chinatown. 'Snoops' knew the place and quickly agreed as the food was always excellent.

The taxi ride was short. As 'Snoops' was paying the driver, he looked out at the crowded street and recognized someone who did not seem to belong. It was Barry Jones.

'Snoops' initial thoughts were to call out to Barry but decided he could learn more by following him. He recalled the meeting at the estate and the instructions Claude had given that Barry was to work with 'Snoops' and not to go off alone trying to solve the mystery.

"Paddy. That is Barry Jones. He is Claude's close partner. I am not sure why he is here, but he is not going to help in solving things alone. He's a bit rough and I'm not sure that will get much cooperation from any of the Chinese here. He will make things harder for me."

"OK. Let's follow him for a few minutes and observe what he is doing."

They trailed behind Barry from a distance where they would not easily be seen. The street was crowded. Merchants had stands of fruit and other items organized on the sidewalk. They followed

Barry past the busy stores. Sounds of haunting Oriental music played from speakers mounted outside some of the stores. The smell of incense and burning joss sticks wafted out the front doors of others. The people on the street chattered loudly and the scene was one of a busy carnival-like setting.

Paddy was watching closely and memorizing the various men that Barry approached. Paddy knew most of them. They were small-time crooks involved in car thefts, gambling, and petty drug deals. He did not observe Barry speak to anyone who was a major Triad player.

" 'Snoops', I think it's time we accidentally run into Barry. Tell him you're having dinner with an old friend. Invite him to join us. I want to know more about this lad."

'Snoops' immediately realized that Paddy had decided to take an active interest in the case. He wondered how Barry would react to his friend and old police partner. He had read Barry's character at their meeting and did not expect a friendly reaction from Barry.

They watched as Barry entered a store selling all types of Oriental items, including urns, paintings, electronics, hardware, and clothing. It was the ideal opportunity to stage an accidental encounter as Barry exited the store. They didn't have to wait long.

"Barry? Barry Jones? Well, it's great to see you here. I was just visiting my former colleague and friend Paddy O'Regan. What are you doing in Chinatown?"

"Just taking a quick look around. Never know what might show up."

"Barry, you might remember that Claude asked us to work together. Come and meet my old friend here, Paddy. I think he can help us."

Paddy lunged forward and grabbed the stocky Australian's hand and vigorously pumped it.

"Good to meet you. Always great to meet someone from Aussie. Most of that country was filled with convicts from my Ireland, so I have a special place in my heart for an Aussie."

'Snoops' could barely contain a laugh. He knew that Paddy was turning on his fake Irish act.

"Nice to meet you mate, but I'm not from bloody Ireland. Try Wales if you would, and none of my ancestors were like those Irish who were sent to Australia for stealing a loaf of bread or starting bar fights. We, Jones, are a proud lot."

Paddy nodded. He knew that he had met his match in Barry and instinctively liked him.

"Barry, we are about to have an early dinner at Chop Chings. They make the best Peking duck and other dishes. Please join us."

"Don't mind if I do, mate."

The trio slowly walked the garbage-lined streets of Chinatown until they arrived at Chop Chings with its extravagantly decorated façade of lions and dragons. Upon entering the restaurant, they were treated to the aromas of the exotic and tantalizing dishes.

The restaurant was crowded. A slim Chinese waiter greeted them and at Paddy's request showed them to a quiet table near the rear of the main dining area.

They had no sooner sat when waiters arrived with pots of tea and stood back quietly to take their orders. Paddy was first to order.

"Bring us the best Peking Duck you have, and order of Schezwuan shrimp, sweet and sour beef strips, and a bowl of the famous corn and shrimp soup. Tsingtao beers for all of us.."

The waiters hurried away to place their orders. As they did, Paddy surveyed the restaurant looking for any diners he may know. He did not want to draw the attention of anyone. When he was satisfied it was safe he removed his cop jacket and lit up a Marlboro cigarette and turned his attention to Barry.

"OK, now Barry. Before I have to go and kiss the Blarney Stone, what the story with your Claude boy?"

"Well, there is no story. In Claude's younger days he was a free spirit and a very wealthy young man. He spent his life wandering the world. Naturally, he had romantic adventures but none lasted and some were total disasters. He got himself into a bad situation during his years at the Sorbonne when he took up a job with an art and antique dealer. He had no idea that the company was involved in international art smuggling. After that, he traveled to the South Pacific where he developed strong relationships with the people of Rarotonga in the Cook Islands. There he met the girl of his dreams. It's a pity he left as he always talks about those days. His subsequent affair with a woman named Misty Moon never seemed right. It turned out she was heavily involved with Hong Kong-based crime. After the romance collapsed, he returned to the family business of the vineyards and wineries. He met a girl here and was planning to marry before an accident in Bodega Bay took her life. He has been somewhat introverted since that accident. There is nothing I can think of that would make him a target for any gang. I cannot think of any deal or issue that has led to this situation."

"Barry, there is something major for these guys to go after him. It is not a case of kidnapping for a ransom. They could have snatched him from the vineyard and demanded money. There is a reason why they want him silenced. Claude would be worth a lot of money, and the Triad gangs are experts at extortion. No, this was an attempt to kill him and silence him forever."

"But there is nothing he or the business has been involved in that would create this situation.".

"Barry, I have worked with the gangs here for many years. At times I wonder what makes them react the way they do. Several Triad gangs operate in the Bay area. Their methods are brutal and barely human. For years I have been dealing with them and involved in cleaning up the messes they leave behind. I caution you not to go digging around. It will soon be known you are with Claude de Passioné and you will find yourself facing many troubles."

"Nothing I cant take care of mate. Never run away from any fight yet."

"Barry, I have been working the streets of Chinatown for years now. I know these gangs and their brutality. They are inhumane. Trust me when I tell you that you are no match for them. Please work with 'Snoops' and me. We have the experience and knowledge."

Barry was not pleased with the comments.

"I can't see what problem there is just visiting and asking a few simple questions."

"You do not understand these people. The gangs are tightly protected."

"Snoops' decided it was time to intervene as he could sense Bary's agitation building."

"Let's consider what we know:

Firstly, there is no plan to kidnap Claude.

Secondly, they are not after an item or money. They want him silenced.

Thirdly, we have another unknown party in the person of We Hoe sniffing around.

"Then we have the mysterious Black Mercedes."

For several minutes, they sat in silence sipping on their beers and considering the situation. Their meals arrived with a great flourish of fanfare. The Peking Duck was on an enormous platter. Two young girls followed carrying plates containing the other foods.

The food was laid on the table and the waiter immediately began to carve and serve the duck.

'Snoops' was watching in amazement as the waiter skillfully sliced the duck. He was watching it intently when Barry spoke.

"What's that fella over there staring at? I guess he's never seen a production like this."

'Snoops' looked in the direction that Barry indicated and gasped. Sitting alone at a table near the door was Little Jimmy Deng. He was the last person 'Snoops' wished to run into. He recalled the year before his retirement when he had accepted a huge bribe from Little Jimmy Deng to lose the evidence of a gang hit that left six opposing gang members dead. He had hidden the materials deeply and ensured that Paddy never knew of his betrayal to the force.

Little Jimmy Deng was staring at 'Snoops' with intensity. After a few minutes, he got up and left without ordering. 'Snoops' realized they were already being warned.

'Snoops' was surprised how quickly his presence with Paddy had been observed, and the fact that Little Jimmy Deng himself had arrived to give them the warning to back off.

Barry was confused as he had watched the interchange between 'Snoops' and Little Jimmy.

" So, Snoops, who was that evil-looking fella. He didn't seem too happy to see your face in here."

"Paddy and I had some dealings with him when I was on the force here. He's not a particularly nice person."

Paddy was troubled. Why had Little Jimmy arrived to warn them? Obviously, there was something big involved. Paddy decided it was time to speak with his informants in the three most powerful Triads in San Francisco. He considered the reality of the situation. Paddy recognized given the fact that Claude lived in the Napa Valley, where the attempted assassination had occurred, the matter was probably outside his jurisdiction, and would probably involve the FBI and other police forces. If he could keep the focus on the gangs in San Francisco, he could take the lead in the investigation.

"Shit," he thought. "I don't need this just a year from my retirement."

Part 3

An unlikely love

Chapter 9

Russian River Community Hall, Napa Valley, California.

The parking lot at the hall was filled. Marie-France watched as couples in country and western outfits walked from their cars and pickup trucks into the hall. She drove around the parking area and finally found a space and tucked her new Mini Cooper tightly between an old Ford Fairlane, in pristine condition, and a 1950's rusty red Chevy pickup.

She looked in the car's rear vision mirror to ensure her heavily made-up face was perfect. When satisfied, she fluffed up her risqué top, adjusted her breasts, and started off for the Annual County Fall Fair Square dance night. She has been waiting for this event for weeks. She cursed that she did not have a partner to accompany her, but happily considered the alternative. Surely, there would be men who would be only too eager to capture her with all her beauty and fortune.

The twanging sound of country and western guitars drifted out the open doors of the hall and created a surreal feeling in the tree-lined parking lot which was bordered by tall trees and grasses. It all seemed to fit.

Marie-Frane entered the packed smoky and warm hall. Her entrance drew gasps from the crowd. She had spared no expense to be the best dressed that evening. She had dressed in the best of cowgirl outfits. She was dressed in a frilly white off-the-shoulder blouse and skin-tight blue jeans with a huge belt buckle, hot pink hand monogrammed cowboy boots that matched her pink cowboy hat. Blue turquoise jewelry in long silver chains hung around her neck. Gigantic silver engraved earrings hung inches below her ears. Her hair was stacked high in a beehive, held firmly in place with excessive amounts of hairspray. The generous dousing of perfume she had applied could not be ignored. She was a sight.

Wolf whistles erupted from a group of men standing against the wall with beer bottles in hand.

Marie-France acted demure and feigned embarrassment, but silently she was loving every minute of the attention. She moved through the crowd to a table where she recognized some other women from the area. They greeted Marie-France, though each one wished she had chosen another table.

Clare Singer, who was the heiress to the largest vineyard in Napa welcomed her.

"Why, Marie-France you certainly look the part this evening. How do you do it"

The sarcasm was wasted on Marie-France, who took it as a compliment.

"I try so hard, and of course I have my fashion consultant in San Francisco. He never fails me."

The other women at the table snickered. Marie-France was confused.

"Did I miss a joke?"

"No, we were talking about that handsome man who is the emcee tonight."

Marie-France looked up to the small stage at the muscular tanned man with the microphone who was announcing the music and events of the night. He was dressed in a black satin shirt with white epaulets and sparkling rhinestones that ran down the sleeves, each of which was stylishly turned back at the cuff. The shirt was tightly tucked into his black jeans. On his feet were expensive Baron Lucchese cowboy boots. She was immediately attracted to him.

"Clare, do you know who he is?"

"Yes, Marie-France. His name is Buzz Kutz. He has his own business and emcees these dances as a hobby. He has been in the area for at least 5 years I know of, though I have never personally met him."

Marie-France fixed her eyes on him. She had found her catch of the evening. She thought of the time she could enjoy with him at the Mansion, given that Claude and Barry were away in the city on business. Her mind was filled with passionate scenes.

The band stopped playing. Dancers left the floor to return to their tables. Buzz took over.

"Ladies and Gentlemen, Cowgirls and Cowboys, we are going to take a brief break before we kick off the first line dancing event of the night. Enjoy a refreshment or two and be ready for the fun."

Buzz jumped down from the stage and was heading to the men's washroom when Marie-France intercepted him.

"Buzz, I would be delighted if you would be my partner for the line dance. My name is Marie-France de Passioné from the vineyards of the same name. Maybe you have heard of us."

"Why, yes Ma'am. I am well aware of the de Passioné estates. I have had several meetings with Claude de Passioné. Nice guy."

"Yes, he is my son. I am very proud of him."

As they spoke, Marie-France observed the muscular chest and arms that flexed and rippled beneath the satin shirt. She mentally imagined the flesh that the shirt was covering. She intended to conquer this fine specimen of a man. The other women at the table looked on aghast at her brazen approach to Buzz.

"Please excuse me. I need to visit the men's room before I go back on the stage. I will come and accompany you after I announce the dance. Jerold will be calling the song tonight. That is one thing I do not do."

As Buzz moved away, the eyes of all the women at the table followed him.

Again, it was Clare who spoke.

"Marie-France! How could you be so forward with that man?"

"Clare, I have nothing to lose and everything to gain."

Marie-France sensed disappointment and some mild jealousy amongst them. She didn't care.

Minutes passed before Buzz returned to the stage. He was accompanied by a large overweight man.

"Everyone take your partners. We are ready to start. First, I will call the do-si-do. My friend here, Jerold will follow and call the dances and provide the vocal accompaniment. The first dance is that old Roy Rogers favorite 'Birdie in the Cage and Three Rail Pen', followed by the line dance 'Achy Breaky Heart."

Buzz jumped down from the stage after his performance as the band broke into music. He headed straight toward Marie-France. She was ready.

Dancers flocked to the floor. The music filled the Hall and Jerold's deep voice boomed out the tunes.

Marie-France was in heaven. Buzz was an excellent dancer. As they swirled and changed partners, she was scheming on how to get him to return to the Mansion with her that night.

When not on stage, Buzz spent time with Marie-France. She was flattered and curious about the man. She decided to take a direct approach and invited him back to the Mansion.

"Buzz, I would like to invite you to the Estate for a glass or two of our finest wine. The night is still early and I could use some company as I am alone there, except for some servants. I would like to get to know you better."

"That would be nice. I am not flying tomorrow so I can be up later tonight."

With that comment, Marie-France's curiosity leaped.

Chapter 10

Sausalito, California.

Claude and Barry had decided on an early lunch at a beautiful dockside restaurant, Les Jardin of Sausalito. The owners knew Claude well and often traveled to de Passioné Estates to sample and order the finest wines for the restaurant.

Emile, the proprietor greeted them warmly.

"Claude, Barry I am so pleased you are joining us for lunch. Today we have some fine specials. Please come and let me seat you."

They were seated next to the window offering a panoramic view of the San Francisco Bay and Golden Gate Bridge.

"Barry, I am starved. I left the Mansion early this morning for that meeting with our exporters. I am pleased with the outcome of the meeting. Now, tell me about your trip yesterday afternoon and what you have found out."

"I was unable to have the freedom to do much at all. I ran into 'Snoops' and his cop friend Paddy. His friend seemed somewhat reserved, but I think he knows far more than he is letting on. We went to a restaurant, Chop Ching. While we were waiting for our meal, a man entered and sat staring at us. 'Snoops' called him Little Jimmy Deng. I couldn't find out much about him, but he seems to be some sort of leader in Chinatown. The fella watched us then got up and left. Very bloody strange."

"Did you ask 'Snoops' about him?"

"Yes, but he was in no mood to answer. Something strange there."

"OK. I'm going back to the Mansion later after I meet our security company. I want to bring them up to date on all that has happened. What are your plans?"

"I think a little more investigating is needed. I also ran into an old Aussie friend of mine. He is working here for the Australian Lamb export company. We had some great times together in Sydney. Might look him up and have dinner with him."

"Barry, remember what we discussed. I don't want you to investigate this alone. You do not know these gangs and could inadvertently cause us some problems. Please work with 'Snoops' as we agreed."

"Look mate, I don't fully trust that bugger. I sensed something was wrong between him and his pal Paddy when that Little Jimmy Deng walked in. Trust me on this. The guys hiding something."

"Please be careful. I will see you back home in the morning. Now let's order."

In silence, they studied the menu. Emile had been discreetly watching them and approached.

"Gentlemen, I highly recommend the Dungeness Crab Cioppino. Chef Luigi has spent the whole morning preparing it. The aroma alone is intoxicating."

Barry was unfamiliar with high-end foods and was unsure. Emile noticed his frown.

"Barry, you will like it. It is a broth that is infused with fresh basil and fresh tomatoes. In the broth, a stew of fresh crab, clams, and shrimp are simmered. It is one of Luigi's finest creations."

"Sounds pretty bloody good to me then. I reckon I'll go for one of those."

Claude ordered the same and a bottle of the de Passioné 1986 Sancerre.

Claude and Barry sat immersed in conversation, attempting to understand what had motivated the attack on Claude and failed to notice the arrival of the young Oriental woman. She chose a table in a corner to be discreet and yet observe them.

Their meals arrived and were accompanied by fresh crispy Italian bread.

Barry was amazed at the meal and sipped a small portion of the broth as a test.

"Struth mate. This is a bloody marvelous concoction. Gotta remember this one for me next date."

Claude smiled. He knew that Barry's next date was nowhere close to San Francisco. He wondered whether Barry's love life still existed. Claude knew better than to pry into that issue.

They sat in silence and gazed at the yachts and ships plying the Bay.

"I think I will go and meet our security people and then start the drive back home. Please remember our agreement and try to work with 'Snoops."

Claude pushed back his chair and stood. Emile came to their table.

"I hope all was well. I look forward to seeing you again. I think we will need to visit you at the vineyard as we will need to order new wines for the upcoming summer season."

"Please let us know when you wish to visit. I will be sure to be there."

Claude and Barry walked out and onto the wooden planks of the dock, where Claude had parked his Ferrari 250LM. It was his pride and joy.

As he slid into the driver's seat, Claude noticed a black Mercedes parked several buildings away. There was a sole occupant in the car.

"Barry! There's that black Mercedes. Let's try to find out who it is."

Throwing caution to the wind Claude and Barry raced toward the car. The engine revved and the tires squealed as the driver pulled a U-turn and sped off into the distance.

"Were you able to see the license plate?"

"No Claude. Whoever was driving the car seemed to be waiting for us and made a hasty retreat. I should come with you back to the Mansion."

"No. I will be fine. Besides, there is the matter of 'Snoops' and investigating for information in Chinatown."

Claude returned to the Ferrari, which he fired up. The cackle and throb from the exhausts expressed the power of the machine. He slipped the car into gear and accelerated away in the direction the Mercedes had gone.

Barry decided to leave his rented car at the restaurant and returned inside to ask Emile to call him a taxi. He did not want his presence in Chinatown to be too obvious.

As he walked in the entrance, he came face to face with the young Oriental woman. She smiled and brushed past him.

She seemed familiar to Barry, but he could not place her. He shrugged and then asked Emile to order a taxi for him.

A bright yellow Bay Taxi Service car swooped into the entranceway of the restaurant. Barry climbed into the back and asked the driver to take him into Chinatown. The driver grinned and thanked Barry. It would be a nice fare.

The taxi climbed up the hill from Sausalito to the highway and entrance to the Golden Gate Bridge for the trip back into San Francisco.

Barry relaxed in the back seat as they crossed over the bridge. He looked to the left at the city and wondered what evils were hidden in such a beautiful place.

Minutes passed and soon they were amongst traffic in the downtown. Horns blared and angry drivers cursed and attempted to cut each other off. Barry was pleased he was not driving.

The driver pulled to a halt at Dragon's Gate. Barry handed the driver a wad of money and exited the cab.

Chapter 11

The Mansion, de Passioné Estates, Napa Valley, California.

Buzz Kutz followed Marie-France back to the Estate in his old rusted Chevy pickup truck. He pulled in through the gates and onto the long driveway to the Mansion. He was not impressed. He had been in many similar homes in the area.

Marie-France was waiting at the door.

'Buzz, welcome to my home. Come in and I will get us a nice nightcap."

Marie-France showed Buzz into the spacious drawing-room.

"Buzz, what would you like to drink. We have lots of wine, but maybe a Whiskey or something else?"

"If you don't mind, I'll just have a cold beer. Being an emcee at those dances dries out my throat and makes me thirsty."

Marie-France left the room and returned several minutes later with wine for herself and a tall glass of beer for Buzz.

They sat and toasted until she spoke.

"Buzz, are you from around this area? I thought I knew most people here."

"Yes I live not too far from here, but I am very seldom home as my business often takes me away"

"Please tell me. I am most interested."

Buzz relaxed back into the oversized couch and flicked open his top shirt buttons. Marie-France ogled his muscular tanned chest and saw a small tattoo.

"Buzz, what is that tattoo?

"It's in memory of a long-ago romance when I was in the Marines and posted overseas. She was my first real true love. Unfortunately, she was killed during an enemy ambush of her village. It's been hard for me to forget her and establish any other relationship with a woman."

"What did you do as a Marine?"

"As a young guy, I had gotten myself into trouble several times with the law. It was a judge who one day recommended that I apply and try to clean my act up. I thought anything to keep that old bird of a judge happy I would try. Little did I know that I would like the Marines and soon got involved in several training programs. I trained as a paratrooper and enjoyed the thrill of the jump. Later an opportunity arose for me to enter into flight training. Since then I have never looked back."

Marie-France was intrigued. Sitting across from her was what she considered a real man. A man of action and excitement.

"What do you do now?"

"I left the Marines with a pilot's license so I decided to find work as a pilot. In those days there were not many jobs available, so I decided to invest everything I owned or had inherited and start my own aircraft operation. I started with an old leased Cessna plane. It was a workhorse and never let me down. I had seen some of the crop dusters at work and decided to get the plane outfitted for crop dusting. The business grew and soon I need another pilot and plane. I asked an old pal from the Marines to join me. The business continued to grow and I was looking for ways to expand and offer some different services. I decided to purchase a helicopter and offered aerial surveys and other services. I believe that's how I met your son Claude when he wanted an aerial survey and photos taken during the time he was looking to purchase that vineyard nearby. Now we offer crop dusting and work with the chopper. I never lost the thrill of parachuting, so I trained as a skydiver, and later as an instructor. We started a little skydiving company we called 'The Descenders.' It's busy every weekend. I love the feel of jumping from the plane and the feeling of free-falling until the chute opens and the last slow glide to the ground."

At this point, Marie-France decided that this was the man she had wanted to capture for many years. She was about to ask Buzz another question when the wall of the drawing-room lit up with the headlights of a car turning into the driveway.

"I wasn't expecting anyone this evening. I wonder who could be coming here so late?"

She went to the large window and looked out at a non-descript Chrysler driving toward the house.

"Buzz, I don't recognize that car. It's not Claude as he left to go to the city in his favorite Ferrari."

The beige Chrysler turned near the entrance to the Mansion and exited to the right of the mansion, where it was out of sight.

Someone was soon going to be ringing the bell. She was concerned.

"I am worried. I am here alone as our servants and help took time off this weekend."

"Don't you go worrying about anything. I'll soon protect you from any nastiness. Just let them try."

Buzz reached behind him and pulled out a menacing pistol. He stood near the door of the drawing-room and awaited any intruder. The main door creaked open.

"What the hell? Who are you and what are you doing here?" shouted Claude.

"Claude, you scared me. Where is your car? Why are you driving that thing?"

"Mother, let me get a coffee and I will explain. What on earth is Buzz Kutz doing here?

Claude strode into the room with an extended hand and shook Buzz's hand.

"It's been a while Buzz. How have you been keeping? I will be back in a minute and we can chat."

Claude disappeared and headed in the direction of the kitchen. He reappeared 10 minutes later with a large mug of coffee.

Marie-France was confused.

"Claude, why don't you join us in a glass of wine?"

"No mother, I have a very early appointment in the city, so I am driving back tonight to avoid the heavy traffic in the morning."

"But you have just arrived."

"I need to retrieve some business papers for the meeting. Barry is also spending the night in the city and will be with me at the meeting."

"Claude, where is your car, and what is that thing you are driving?"

"I don't want to concern you, but it seems someone wants to either hurt or kill me. I met with our security firm this afternoon. They are going to be placing some security people here disguised as workers. They insisted I do not drive the Ferrari until this is over. The car you refer to as 'that thing' is an armored car. The tires are made of solid rubber so they cannot be shot out, the windows are polycarbonate laminate and bulletproof. The engine is a highly modified V8 and coupled with other enhancements allows the car to outperform most high-performance cars available. The interior is a cage inside the car with its own air circulation system in case of a gas attack."

Buzz was impressed and asked Claude to show him the car.

"Well, if you boys are going to go and play with a stupid car, I'm going to get changed into my sleepwear."

Claude grabbed his coffee and led Buzz out to the car.

Before they reached the car and out of hearing range of the house, Buzz grabbed Claude's arm and demanded to know what was happening.

"Claude, what the fuck is going on that you need extra security and a tank like that to drive?"

"In all honesty Buzz, I have no idea. I was shot in the vineyard and the police have no ideas as to who or why. There have also been strange things happening. My old girlfriend's sister showed up here to warn me, and we have had several incidents of being watched by someone unknown in a black Mercedes. It seems that someone wants me killed. I have no idea why. The security experts say it is not a possible kidnapping or a form of extortion for money."

"What can I do to assist you? If you wish I can spend some time here and ensure your mother is safe."

"I appreciate that offer very much, Buzz. Now, let's go back inside. I am sure Marie-France is getting more than curious. We have tried to keep as much of this as possible away from her. She doesn't know the full story of all that is happening."

Claude and Buzz returned to the Mansion and went back into the drawing-room. Marie-France was sitting and awaiting their return. She was dressed in a short black frilly negligee and wore a bright yellow bath robe. She looked like a giant bumblebee perched on the couch and about to attack.

" I will leave you to enjoy your evening, but I must go and get those papers from my office and drive back into the city. Good night."

Claude walked from the room and up the stairs to his office. He re-emerged several minutes later with several folders and descended the stairs. He looked into the drawing-room.

"Good night Mother. Good night Buzz. I will be back tomorrow afternoon."

Claude left and Marie-France was alone with Buzz. Secretly, Marie-France was thrilled to be in a romantic setting with Buzz.

Chapter 12

The lobby bar, The Hyatt Hotel, San Francisco.

After checking into the hotel and dropping his case in his room, Barry decided to wait for his meeting with Paddy O'Regan in the open bar area off the lobby.

As Barry sat in the low-slung chairs, waiting for Paddy to join him, he watched in amusement as people walked into the hotel to check in. A pianist played soft music to entertain the guests sitting in the lobby bar area. He watched couples walk from the elevator arm-in-arm, and he guessed which ones were having secret affairs. He loved to watch the little glass pods that were the elevator cars as they rode up to the exposed balconies of floors above. He found it fascinating to watch the pods as they arose from the inside center foyer of the hotel, festooned with decorative lights.

Barry was curious about 'Snoops' and had phoned Paddy to join him so he could learn more about 'Snoops'. In Barry's mind, something about 'Snoops' was not right.

Initially, Barry did not recognize Paddy when he arrived dressed in civilian clothes. He wore a stylish leather jacket and tailored denim jeans. Barry waved to him and Paddy wove his way through the groups of chairs and tables until he reached Barry.

"What a day, Barry. I'm more than ready for a stiff drink. Seems all the problems arrive at once. It's time for me to retire and leave it up to the younger cops."

Paddy dropped himself into the chair next to Barry and a waitress arrived in minutes.

"Paddy, I asked you to join me, so it's on me. What would you like?"

"I think I'd like a double Jamesons."

They sat and made small talk until the drinks were delivered.

"OK, Barry, what's on your mind? Must be important for you to call me down here for a chat.?"

"There is something about "Snoops" that I can't quite work out. I am not comfortable with him. I suspect he knows a lot more than he's letting on. What was that all about with Little Jimmy Deng? He never explained that. I sensed that a strong message was being sent. Who is Little Jimmy Deng?"

"Little Jimmy Deng is a powerful gang boss. Several Triad gangs operate here in San Francisco and Oakland. The gangs are primarily comprised of young men and are extremely violent. There have been wars between the various gangs. Recently a Vietnamese gang has emerged and has been active in attempting to take over another of the Triad's territories. The assaults they make on each other are brutal. They range from shootings to kidnappings and torture. We have attempted to obtain enough evidence on the role Little Jimmy Deng plays, but somehow he manages to elude us. We do know he is tied in with the international 14-K Triad gang which has chapters in many countries. They are particularly active in drug and human trafficking, extortion, counterfeiting, and money laundering. Several years ago, we had almost enough evidence to proceed against him but a series of unexplainable events occurred. There was a massive war between the gangs that we traced to financing from Little Jimmy Deng. We had amassed confidential information in conjunction with the FBI and were preparing to make mass arrests. Somehow, information was leaked to Little Jimmy Deng and his people and he simply disappeared for months. Besides, key gang members could not be found and there was a massacre of about a dozen gang members who were suspected of cooperating with the police. It was a particularly violent and bloody time. Interestingly, it was a project that was in part headed up by 'Snoops'. Within months of the massacre, 'Snoops' resigned. It was strange as he forfeited a full police pension, yet was close to retiring with a full pension. We were all suspicious and wondered whether he had tipped off the gangs as we moved closer to arresting many key members and busting the gangs."

Barry sat quietly for a few minutes digesting the information.

"Paddy, was there an internal investigation? "

"Yes. The Feds took it over. For months they probed his records and contacts. They even had him tailed. They got a sealed order for wiretaps. He was too clever and eluded us and left no trace of criminal activity. I remain in contact with him, in case one day he slips up. I tell you all this in the strictest confidence."

"I knew it. I can generally tell when a person is hiding something. Now I am wondering if he is involved in whatever is going on with Claude. I think I'm going to pretend to become his buddy and confidante."

"I suggest you forget that idea. He will smell a rat."

"How do you suggest I work with him? I am meant to cooperate in investigating some of the individuals and try to trace the black Mercedes?"

"I suggest you keep anything you find quiet and not share it with him. Bring any info to me personally. Be careful he does not find out we are working together. He is dangerous. I suspect he has some deal with Little Jimmy Deng and it would give me great pleasure to get the evidence so we can bust him."

"What about his personal life? Is he married? Does he have kids?"

"No, he was in a particularly nasty divorce around five years ago. Shortly after it was settled his former wife passed away from suicide. It was always too coincidental in my mind. I believe he killed her."

"How has he gotten away with so much?"

"I believe he has someone on the inside within the department. Do not communicate anything you find with anyone except me. I suggest you leave a note in a sealed envelope at the front desk for me. I will check daily."

Paddy stood up to leave. As he did, Barry noticed a figure across the bar also stand. He was shocked when she turned and he realized it was the woman he had seen at Les Jardin restaurant in Sausalito. He reached out his hand and grabbed Paddy's arm.

"Paddy, I think you are being watched. That woman over there. I saw her at lunch with Claude and here she is now. She stood at the same time you did. I think she is following you."

Paddy looked in her direction and then laughed.

"Relax Barry. She is my junior assistant, Jenny Chin. Yes, she followed you to the restaurant. I wanted to be sure about you and also know you were safe."

"You really are one devious bastard."

"Enjoy your evening Barry. What are your plans?"

'Snoops' had left a message suggesting dinner and a walk through Chinatown."

"Be careful, and remember, you have no authority here. Nor does 'Snoops' so please stay out of trouble."

Paddy turned and walked across the lobby looking like any visiting businessman. At a discrete distance behind him, Jenny Chin followed.

Barry waited a while longer. He ordered another beer and when he was convinced that no one was watching him, he left and returned to his room to call 'Snoops'.

Arrangements were made to meet at Tony's Pizzeria, a busy and popular restaurant where 'Snoops' and Barry could blend into the crowd.

Chapter 13

de Passioné Mansion, Napa Valley. California.

Marie-France awoke, freshened, and invigorated after their passionate and wild night of lovemaking. Even though they had stayed up talking and drinking until the wee hours of the morning she felt alert and happy.

Buzz lay in the crumpled pink satin bedsheets and with his head buried under two oversize baby blue pillows. He was snoring lightly. Marie-France nuzzled up beside him and was aroused by his scent and that of their lovemaking. She nibbled at his ear and he slowly turned towards her.

"Good morning, Buzz. Little Buzzy Bee certainly knows how to satisfy a woman."

Buzz smiled and threw back the sheets. Marie-France glanced down at his manhood and knew he was primed for action.

The giant four-poster bed creaked and groaned as they engaged in the most acrobatic of lovemaking. Marie-France emitted a howl that echoed through the Mansion.

After forty-five minutes of intense passion, they both collapsed and lay quietly. Buzz started to laugh.

"You devil. I'm going to need more than a handful of vitamins for breakfast."

"Should we stay here and eat, or would you like to go somewhere for a nice brunch?"

"Do you have any plans for today, Marie-France?"

"No, I was going to have a quiet day. What are your plans?"

"I was going to take a nice flight in our new helicopter and try it out. It has been equipped with a special camera and location recording devices for when we do surveys. We have also been requested by the police and coast guard to have it available if needed and participate in search or rescue operations. Today I was going to test the systems. Would you like to join me?"

"I have never been in a helicopter before. I'd love to join you."

"OK. We will take quick showers and then we will head to the airport. There is a great fly-in restaurant within 20 minutes of flying time. We will have a nice brunch there."

Marie-France was excited. She showed Buzz to a guest bathroom with an enormous shower for his use and then returned to shower and dress for the occasion. She decided that for this special day she would need to dress in the attire that was most appropriate for her inaugural helicopter flight.

Buzz, who was showered and dressed, waited downstairs in the kitchen for Marie-France. He was enjoying a strong coffee made by a kitchen staff member when she arrived all dressed for the occasion.

Marie-France was a rainbow of color. She wore a lime green blouse tucked into lilac-colored jeans with sequined legs and navy sneakers. In her desire to look young and an aviatrix, she had put her hair in ponytails. Buzz was dumbstruck and misjudged as he placed his coffee on the kitchen counter. The mug tumbled to the floor spraying coffee in the air as it did so. Marie-France was in the firing line. Coffee sprayed her blouse and face. Heavy mascara ran down her face in streaks. Buzz did not know whether to laugh, cry or apologize.

Marie-France ran from the kitchen and back to her room to change. Fifteen minutes later she reemerged. She had changed her outfit and now was dressed in leopard skin jeans and a fluorescent orange blouse. The navy sneakers remained, and to repair the damage done to her makeup, she had glued on a set of huge false eyelashes. She kept these in case of any makeup crisis.

"OK my dear, let's pile into my old truck there and head out to the little airfield where we have our flight operations."

"Is it far? I'm starved for both food and more of you, and after last night I need more than your weenie or a pretzel."

Buzz grabbed her playfully and whisked her towards the door and out to his rusty old red pickup. He opened the passenger door, and before assisting her onto the seat he brushed off old hamburger wrappings and drink cans from the seat and onto the floor. The pickup had the distinctive aroma of a fast food joint and musty stale fruit.

Buzz revved the pickup and spun its wheels in the loose gravel before bouncing onto the sealed driveway. Marie-France was enjoying every minute.

They continued on county back roads passing fields of hay and other vineyards until they reached a major highway. Buzz turned onto the highway and gunned the old pickup. It surged ahead leaving a huge cloud of bluish grey exhaust smoke behind it. As they sped along the highway, Marie-France burst into 'Oh, What a Beautiful Morning'. Buzz grinned and joined in. They continued their blissful trip singing at the top of their voices until a group of low white buildings appeared. A billboard at the entrance road proclaimed 'The Descenders Skydive and Flying School'.

Buzz pulled up to the nearest building. The signs indicated it was the office. The pickup had no sooner stopped when a buxom peroxide blonde with a drawling accent came out to greet them.

"Welcome, y'all. What brings you here today Buzz? It's your day off from this place."

"Marie-France, meet Cynthia Honeysucker, our delightful office and everything else manager."

Marie-France immediately sensed competition and put on her best airs.

"I'm delighted to meet you. Are you a real blonde?"

"Yes, and I must say you are a kaleidoscope of color. Never quite seen a fashion statement like that."

"I dressed for the occasion. My first helicopter trip."

Cynthia shook her head.

"Buzz, please come into the office. There have been several calls from the State Police. Seems they are urgently wanting to speak with you."

Cynthia turned her head in the direction of Marie-France.

"Where on earth did you find that specimen?"

Buzz ignored her. He was aware of her desire for him but had no interest in any relationship with her.

"Where is the number for the State Police? I will call them now and see what it is all about."

He entered the office and Cynthia handed him a sheet with the name and number of the officer who had been trying to reach Buzz.

Chapter 14

Chinatown, San Francisco.

Tony's Pizzeria was busy when Barry arrived. He spotted 'Snoops' sitting staring out the window with a tall beer on the table in front of him. Barry looked around at the patrons, looking for something or someone who didn't quite fit. He detected nothing and proceeded over to 'Snoops' table.

'Snoops' was startled by Barry's greeting. He visibly jumped when Barry spoke his name. Barry wondered why he was so nervous.

"Sorry. I didn't mean to startle you. Is everything OK? You seem nervous."

"Yeah. I was reflecting on my days with the force here. I sort of miss those days and the guys. Being a private investigator in this town isn't too thrilling. Most work requires me to be a keyhole peeper investigating husbands and wives in their adulterous relationships. It pays OK but is as exciting as watching the grass grow."

"Why don't you just retire? Throw it in. Go traveling or fishing?"

"I need the money, plus I'd just get bored."

" Let's eat and then cruise through the streets and see if we can find out anything."

They ordered an all-dressed pizza and made small talk while eating.

Darkness was setting in as Barry and 'Snoops' left to walk through Chinatown. The streets were surprisingly busy. Barry was intrigued by the selection of goods displayed in many of the store windows. He stepped out off the dirty sidewalk and onto the street to avoid piles of garbage and empty cardboard boxes.

'Snoops' tapped Barry on his arm and pointed up a little side street.

"There is a place up there I want to visit. When I was a cop I had a lot of dealing with an informant there. I think we will get some useful info. Just follow my lead."

Barry was intrigued by this development. They walked down the narrow street and 'Snoops' pointed out the building. There was a dark doorway that contrasted against the yellow façade of the building. Painted red lions stood at either side of the doorway. A sign hung overhead the door reading 'Hung Lo Culture Club'.

As they went to enter, a muscular man appeared and stopped them.

'Snoops' stood close to the man and spoke with authority.

"Let us pass Benny. I am here to see Little Jimmy Deng. I believe he has some information for me. Tell him we are here. We will wait here until you return and admit us. Remember, you and Little Jimmy owe me."

While they waited, Barry noticed a sweet smell rising from the stairway that led down to a floor below. He could not identify the smell.

'Snoops', what is that smell?"

"That is the smell of opium. I can guarantee there will be guys down there smoking it. This place is a known opium den. It claims to be a cultural center for the men to have coffee and play board games and gamble, but there is a lot more that happens here. Little Jimmy has an office down there with an escape exit. When we raided this place we could never catch him as he bolted through that exit."

"Why are we here and why do you think Little Jimmy will see you?"

"Little Jimmy owes me. He will see us. You be quiet and let me talk."

Benny returned with another burly thug. His face was thunder.

"Come. I will take you to him. First, wait. I need to check you for weapons."

Benny searched both 'Snoops' and Barry in a very rough manner. It took every ounce of restraint for Barry to remain calm.

They descended the narrow stairway into a hazy smoke-filled den. Several old men lay on straw mats with dirty stained cushions pushed up against the walls to act as pillows. Half-naked young women were draped over the beds in a comatose state. Barry watched an older oriental man in loose baggy pants as he plugged an opium pill into his pipe. A small group of men sat at a table playing a game similar to dominoes. Other men sat in euphoric trances.

Benny shoved Barry forward.

"Not for you to see. Move now."

'Snoops' lead the way into a narrow corridor and to the door of Little Jimmy Deng's office. Benny thumped on the door before a voice called out in Cantonese to enter.

They entered Little Jimmy's office. There were ornate jade figurines on every piece of furniture and the walls were covered in Oriental art. A large mahogany desk was strategically arranged in front of a door that exited into a narrow lane that then snaked past the rear of a vintage laundry.

"What you want 'Snoops'? I no like you. You bring trouble. Who is he?"

Little Jimmy stared at Barry. It was an evil, cold and penetrating stare.

"This is the partner of a man that seems to have some problems with the Triad gangs. I need your help with information, and don't forget you owe me for a past transaction."

" I have no information for you. Now go."

"Not so fast Jimmy. I still have those police files and I am sure some of the other gangs would pay for them. They will be willing to do anything to get that information. You are in no position to bargain with me."

Little Jimmy Deng looked down at his desk and waited minutes before answering.

"Who is this man in trouble?"

"His name is Claude de Passioné. His family owns vineyards and wineries in the Napa Valley. What do you know?"

"I cannot help you. Very powerful men in China seek this man. I do not know why. Please leave now."

"I think you know a lot more Jimmy. Remember, I can make your life difficult."

" 'Snoops', these are very powerful men in Hong Kong. I am just a very simple merchant. Now, please go. I am certain you were seen coming in here."

'Snoops' realized that Little Jimmy Deng was truly nervous and scared. He knew something of importance and was afraid that by talking to others who were not gang members he could be betraying other members of the Triad. 'Snoops' was convinced that Little Jimmy was involved.

"Come on, Barry. Let's get out of here."

Benny grabbed Barry and pushed him out of Little Jimmy's office.

"Hey fella, touch me again like that and you'll be eating dirt for dinner. Forget your chow mein."

Benny grunted and spat on the floor in front of Barry.

They slowly made their way back through the hazy den and were starting up the staircase when the sound of gunfire from an automatic weapon pierced the air.

Benny pulled a large automatic pistol from inside his vest and sprinted at amazing speed back to Little Jimmy Deng's office. 'Snoops' and Barry ran after him. They burst through the door into the office. It was empty. The exit door behind the desk was open and papers and books had spilled out into the laneway. The mahogany desk had white splintered wood from where the bullets had torn into it. Smashed jade figurines lay on the floor. Little Jimmy Deng was gone. He had been snatched. Someone was making sure Little Jimmy Deng didn't talk.

Chapter 15

Hyatt Hotel, San Francisco.

Back at his hotel, Barry sat with 'Snoops', trying to piece together the events that had happened since Claude had been shot. None of it was making sense, and he considered that the lawyer, Al Pine, and his private eye, 'Snoops', were now suspects in his mind.

They sat in the inside courtyard and Barry ordered some Jamesons. He was hoping that the strong drinks may result in 'Snoops' opening up and revealing what he knew about the shooting, the Chinese influence, and Little Jimmy Deng in particular.

They had quickly left the 'Hung Lo Cultural Center'. Neither Barry nor 'Snoops' wished to be present when the police showed up to investigate the shooting and snatching of Jimmy

Barry watched as 'Snoops' quickly drank the whiskey. As Barry had expected he became more talkative after the third glass.

" ' Snoops' why did you decide to visit Little Jimmy Deng? What did you think he had that could help us? I noticed you seemed nervous there, and why did that thug Benny push me and search me so roughly? I think you owe me some explanations. If you can't then I will go ask Paddy O'Regan, as I'm sure he knows plenty about Little Jimmy and his dealings. You know more than you are telling me, and I have no patience for that."

"Little Jimmy was a kingpin with the gangs here. No one would dare touch Jimmy. His word stood. Even amongst the warring gangs he had influence and could stop disputes. His reach is far beyond San Francisco and California. The Deng family goes back a long way in time. The family was amongst the first who settled and formed Chinatown. They ran many rackets and continue to be a force. The younger generation has tried to establish gangs and challenge them. This has led to some real bloodshed."

'Snoops' immediately fell silent. Barry remembered the comment that Paddy had made about his suspicions of 'Snoops'.

"I think you know a lot more than you are telling me. I intend to find out more."

"You will find yourself in trouble and possibly dead. Leave it alone. I will try to learn why Claude has been targeted. I am sure it is some mistake and can be dealt with. Please do not go digging around."

"I don't understand. You say that Jimmy was the 'kingpin' of the gangs and no one would touch him, yet he has been snatched."

"The only ones who would do that are the ruthless gangs in Hong Kong. They do inhumane things. They have been trying to usurp power from Little Jimmy and selling his territory and deals to the junior gangs. They know no fear."

Barry ordered yet another round of drinks. He was satisfied that 'Snoops' was starting to talk.

As Barry was about to ask more questions, he saw Claude crossing the courtyard heading towards them. Even though Claude had been driving for hours, he looked remarkably fresh in a crisp blue pinstripe shirt and navy khakis with Gucci loafers on his feet. Not a single one of his hairs was ruffled.

"Good evening, gents. I hope you have had a pleasant evening. The drive up to the Mansion and back was very relaxing at this time of day. I am starved. I'm going to order some bar food. Do you wish to join me?"

"We ate earlier but I could handle something light. 'Snoops' took me to Tony's Pizzeria. A great place. We should go sometime, Claude."

"I think an order of calamari, crab stuffed mushroom caps, oyster Rockefeller, and fried polenta in spicy tomato sauce. That should get me through to the morning. Now, tell me all you have found out."

The effect of the five Jamesons on 'Snoops' was evident. They had loosened up his tongue and his speech was slightly slurred. He stood and excused himself and wandered across the courtyard in the direction of the men's washroom. Barry seized to opportunity to quickly tell Claude of the events of the evening

Claude sat back in the chair and stretched his arms up behind his head. Unbeknownst to 'Snoops', Barry had been disposing of his own Jamesons and was in full control.

"Claude, I don't trust that son of a bitch one inch. He knows something and is concealing it from me. I also had a warning from Paddy O'Regan about him. I suggest you ask Al Pine a little more about why he recommended him. He is meant to be the best, but I think he is devious."

"Barry, I will speak with Al Pine in the morning."

'Snoops' returned and declared he was leaving for the evening.

"Good night. I'm going to stay with Claude and have a snack. We will see you in the morning."

Barry looked at Claude and shrugged.

"I think we are on our own to solve what is happening. I suspect that our 'Snoops' has been bought. I won't be sharing anything I find with him. I have no trust in him at all."

They continued to sit in silence until a waiter arrived with a large tray containing their food. He set it down on the little glass table, along with individual plates and cutlery. Barry and Claude ate in silence. Finally, Barry stood.

"I am tired and we have a lot to do tomorrow. I wish you goodnight and will call you early to have breakfast."

Barry sauntered off to the elevators, leaving Claude alone to reflect and think of what he had learned of Barry's earlier adventures that night.

His thoughts were interrupted by another waiter. He tapped Claude on the shoulder.

"Sir, that lady over there would like to join you. She said she had dealings with you in the past."

In the dim light, Claude looked across to where the waiter pointed. A dark-haired brunette sat alone. Her long hair hung over her shoulder and down her chest. She was dressed in a low-cut expensive black dress and a gold Fope necklace adorned her neck.

"By all means, ask her to join me."

Claude watched as the waiter relayed the invitation and she gracefully arose from the chair. He was trying to place where he had seen her before, but could not. This frustrated him, as he had an excellent memory of all the women he had known or loved.

As she approached, Claude stood to welcome her.

"Good evening and who do I have the pleasure of meeting?"

"Good evening, Claude. Do you not remember me?"

Claude stared at her but his mind drew a blank.

"Give me a minute. I never forget a beautiful face or figure."

Claude's natural flirtatious character was surfacing.

"I think this will be fun. We had a moment. I am going to enjoy teasing you until you remember."

She signaled the waiter and ordered a Dubonnet, all the time glancing at Claude and smiling.

"Poor Claude. Maybe you weren't focused on my face as much as other aspects of my body."

"We certainly had some fun."

The Dubonnet was delivered and she sat enjoying the encounter while enjoying her drink. She had no intention of reminding him of when she had been a nurse in France and enticed him while he was in the hospital there.

Claude squirmed, wondering how he could not recall this woman.

"It was nice to see you again, Claude but I must now leave. Others are waiting for me."

Chapter 16

'The Descenders Skydiving and Flight School' airfield, Napa, California.

Buzz had watched the interaction between Cynthia Honeysucker and Marie-France with some amusement. He was well aware of Cynthia's unabashed romantic interest in him., but the feeling was not mutual.

"Buzz, what is she doing here? You have never brought any trollop here before. Is she going to be a student? I'm not sure the plane will get off the ground due to the weight of all that makeup."

"Cynthia, just behave. She is part owner of de Passioné Estates. She is a client of the business. We have worked for her son, Claude de Passioné. Maybe you remember him. We did an aerial survey when he was negotiating the takeover of an adjacent vineyard."

Cynthia certainly remembered Claude. She had fantasized about him for weeks after he had visited their offices.

"That old wreck has a beautiful son like him? You men have no taste in a fine woman such as me."

"I am not going to stand here to argue with you. I'm going to call the State Police. See what they want."

Buzz disappeared into his office. Cynthia tried to overhear the mumbled conversation. Buzz reappeared a few minutes later.

"They are asking for our help. Seems that a kid has gone missing in some farmland. The police helicopter is assisting the coast guard chopper with a maritime rescue out from Bodega Bay and is unavailable. This is the ideal circumstance for me to test out our new Bell helicopter."

"I'll have the flight techs check the chopper immediately. Are you taking dragon lady with you?"

"Yes, I think I will, and remember she and her son are customers of ours. Be respectful, as hard as that may be for you."

Buzz walked out to his old pickup truck and advised Marie-France of the decision to take up the new helicopter. She was thrilled.

A young engineer approached Buzz.

"Good morning. We took the chopper up for a series of test flights yesterday. Everything checked out. It is a beautiful machine to fly. Very responsive."

Buzz looked around. The sky was bright blue without any clouds. A gentle wind was blowing in from the west. All around the little airfield were farms with cattle grazing contently.

"Marie-France we have a perfect morning for our flight. I have been requested to assist with a rescue operation of a missing child. Before we get involved in the search, I'll stop at a little fly-in restaurant east of here. It's an airport used strictly by recreational flyers. We can get a quick bite and then continue."

The new helicopter sat shining in the early sun. The white and gold paint sparkled. Marie-France was excited.

Buzz opened the door and assisted her up into the right-hand seat. He then climbed into the pilot seat and when settled gave his engineer the thumbs up. Buzz activated the cockpit radio and dialed in the frequency of the local air traffic control. He announced his location and intended flight information. The headset crackled as he received the response. He then reached down and activated the switches to start the chopper. There was an initial low whine that increased as the rotors spun faster. The helicopter swayed slightly as the rotors turned and found speed. Buzz looked at Marie-France and reached for the controls and within seconds they were airborne. The noise from the engine was loud. Buzz handed Marie-France a headset, which she pulled on.

They skimmed across the farms and continued east. The day was clear. There was no mist or pollution and they were able to see for miles ahead.

Buzz provided a commentary regarding the landmarks as they rapidly flew overhead them. Marie-France was entranced and listened intently to each word he spoke through her headset. She was curious about certain of the equipment in the helicopter and asked Buzz what the function it served.

Buzz pointed to the large flat panel display and flipped a switch Immediately a picture of the land below and in front of them filled the screen. Buzz reached and used a joystick. The picture on the screen zoomed larger.

"The chopper is equipped with a high-power camera and video recorder. It is used during aerial surveys. There is also a high-power searchlight for the night or low light conditions.

Marie-France moved to the right to look out at the land below. She was surprised how by shifting her weight the chopper lurched slightly. She instantly decided to stop eating chocolate doughnuts with her coffee and silently hoped that Buzz hadn't realized the lurch of the chopper was due to her moving.

Buzz pointed ahead to a small grass runway that was flanked with aircraft hangars. He spoke into his mike and announced his arrival and awaited the response to proceed with landing.

The response came quickly and Buzz flew to a location adjacent to a long flat white building. He moved the controls and the chopper descended until there was a gentle bump and pitch forward. He reached forward and cut the engine, after which he opened his door and jumped out. He walked around and opened the door for Marie-France and assisted her down.

"Buzz, that was amazing. I enjoyed that. Maybe I should learn to fly."

"Maybe you should. Let's go in and get some of the food. They make amazing ham and cheese croissants. Never had any like them before. The coffee is special and the blueberry muffins."

Marie-France breathed in the rich aroma of the little restaurant. Men were sitting and eating. Some recognized Buzz and waved.

Marie-France and Buzz ordered the croissants and coffee and sat at the window overlooking the runway and parked planes.

"Buzz, do you think I could learn to fly a plane?"

"Why don't we try a lesson or two, then I will know. I hope I can take you up skydiving. There is no sensation like it."

"I am not sure. Would I be scared?"

"No. I would be in a harness parachute with you and control the jump."

Marie-France fell silent as she thought of Buzz's body pressed up against hers as they hurtled toward earth.

"Yes Buzz. When can we try that?"

"I can take you up this weekend. Now, we should go. I need to go and assist the search team who are looking for that little boy. Can I drop you at your home? I know exactly where it is."

"Oh, the maids and servants will be in awe. I go out with a stranger and come home in a helicopter. What a thrill."

Buzz threw down some money and rose from the table.

"It's time for us to leave."

They walked back to the chopper. Marie-France felt like a queen as Buzz opened the door and assisted her back into the machine.

Within minutes they were airborne and headed back to the Valley. Buzz spoke occasionally into his headset with local air traffic control and then with the police command post coordinating the search for the little boy.

They flew over a small hill and Buzz started the descent to drop Marie-France at the Mansion. He banked the chopper and followed the long driveway from the house up to the main entrance to the house.

Marie-France tugged at his arm and started speaking. Buzz pointed to the microphone Attachéd to the headset and lifted it to her mouth.

"Buzz, there is a strange car parked off our driveway. I was not expecting anyone. It worries me. There are too many strange things happening."

Buzz sharply turned the chopper and dropped altitude. He reached up to the controls and activated the Flat screen. He zoomed in until the license plate was clear and then snapped a couple of high-resolution pictures.

"This will allow us to find out who your mysterious visitor is."

He continued to skim over the treetops and landed the chopper on the grassy patch in the center of the circular drive entrance to the Mansion.

After assisting Marie-France out of the chopper, Buzz flew to join in the search for the missing child.

Chapter 17

Downtown, San Francisco.

Claude had not slept well and his mood reflected it. He had lain awake wondering about the woman in the bar. How did she know him? He wondered if she was in any way linked to the strange events of recent.

He stood at the mirror of the hotel bathroom shaving. The phone in the bathroom jangled. It startled Claude and he turned to answer it. As he did the razor slipped in his hand cutting a long line down his face. Claude cursed. The day was starting badly. Blood from the cut spilled down onto his crisp white Egyptian cotton shirt.

Claude snarled into the phone. His mood was worsening.

"Good morning to you to Claude. I take it that the night at the bar did not go well. Crikey mate. You should be like us Aussies. Have a beer or two and forget the skirt."

"Barry, I am in no mood for any of this nonsense. Call Al Pine's office. Make sure he knows we are coming. I don't want to sit there waiting for him. I think you should tell him not to have 'Snoops' there either. I've been thinking. You are right. Something isn't right with the whole scene, and I agree that he has some knowledge of things he isn't sharing."

"Right then. I'll meet you at the restaurant off the lobby in ten minutes. Try and find a better mood."

Barry was in the lobby before Claude. He picked up a copy of The San Francisco Chronicle from the front desk counter and sat scanning the local section looking to see if there was anything on the shooting in Chinatown and the missing Little Jimmy Deng.

There was no mention. Barry folded the paper and watched people as they hurried about starting their day.

"Good morning, Barry. I hope you slept well because I didn't. I think today will be long and difficult. Let's get this meeting with Al Pine over with, then our business meeting at the French Consulate. I am anxious to get home to the Mansion."

"Claude, please sit down for a minute. I am concerned. I have never seen you this upset. We need to be careful, but we also have to have some trust in those who are looking after us. What is our security company doing? I am aware that they are sending some people to the Mansion to bolster security."

"They want me to keep a low profile. I cannot. I have a business to operate and a life to live. They have given me a special car to drive and it's a tank. We need to find out why this is happening and end it. I cannot, and will not, live like this."

"Claude, I am not convinced the problem is here in San Francisco. These local thugs could get to you easily. I think the problem lies beyond here."

Barry stood and walked with Claude toward the restaurant. They passed the front desk and there was the woman who had teased Claude the previous evening.

Barry watched as Claude approached her. Claude started laughing.

"I remember now. You were the nurse who made my stay in that hospital in Paris bearable after I had been attacked in that prison. I won't forget that. I hope you are well and happy. What are you doing in San Francisco? You are a long way from France. Are you here for a while? I would like to invite you to visit my vineyard and winery."

She turned and smiled as she spoke to him.

"Claude, I have never forgotten you. I had hoped that one day we would be together. I am now married. It was a nice dream of mine for several years, but now it is too late. I wish you all the best. Goodbye Claude."

"Please come and join us. We are having a quick breakfast before we leave for meetings."

"I am sorry, but I cannot. My group is leaving shortly for the airport. I am returning to Paris today."

Claude reached into his jacket and removed his wallet. He withdrew his business card and handed it to her. The card contained both his French and California address and phone numbers.

"Please call me sometime. Bring your husband, I would like to meet him."

She leaned forward and kissed Claude on both cheeks, and then handed a card to him. Barry stood in silence and observed the whole exchange.

As they continued onto the restaurant, Barry turned to Claude.

"Jesus mate, you bloody well like to play with fire. She's married now. I can see she's still interested in you. Stupid woman, don't know what she sees in you. You better learn to keep it zipped up with her. I can only see trouble there."

Their talk over breakfast was mainly related to business. Since Claude had taken over the vineyard adjacent to his, they had been able to increase the volume of wine. Barry was insisting on a more aggressive marketing and sales program. Eventually, the talk drifted to Claude's problems.

"Barry, I have been doing some serious thinking. I am convinced that my troubles are tied to Wendy Wong or as she calls herself, Misty Moon. I had no idea of her involvement in crime until Al Pine's PI exposed her. I had no idea she was married or a gang leader. She had me fooled. After the accidental death of my fiancée, Claire, I was convinced I had found a new love. I was ready to do almost anything for her. I would never have met her if it wasn't for the physiotherapy treatment recommended by that crooked Dr. Stubbs at the hospital. I think now that they had done their homework very carefully. They knew who I was and the wealth associated with the de Passioné wine business. In retrospect, I believe it was a plan for them to kill me off and take over the business. They probably intended to operate it as a legitimate front for their drug smuggling and other criminal activities. How could I have been so stupid to be sucked in by Wendy Wong and her mob?"

"Claude they haven't given up. You are in danger. You either have something or know something they desperately want. I think our friend 'Snoops' knows a lot more. There was something between him and Little Jimmy Deng. He didn't seem that surprised by the attack at The Hung Lo Culture Club."

"I think we will have an interesting meeting with Al Pine. I think he owes us a little bit of an explanation about 'Snoops'.

They finished their breakfasts in silence, each thinking of Wendy Wong (a.k.a Misty Moon) and what evil plans she had.

"Claude, I think we will just take taxis today. I suggest we don't drive anywhere. After the meetings, we must return to the Mansion as quickly as possible."

Barry flagged a taxi as they exited the Hyatt Hotel. He and Claude climbed into the rear seat and gave the driver directions to Al Pine's office.

The downtown traffic was heavy and they slowly wound their way to the high-rise building in which Al Pine's offices were located.

As they left the taxi, Barry scanned around to see if anyone had followed them before entering the high-rise building where Al Pine had his offices.

They rode up to the 12th floor where the law offices of Mattar and Mattar were located. Claude did not need to identify himself as the receptionist immediately called through to Al Pine's office upon recognizing him.

Al Pine arrived within seconds.

"Good morning. I hope all is well with you. This has been a bit of a difficult time for you. Come to my office. Can I get you some coffee and pastries?"

Barry responded.

"That would be appreciated. You don't have any Aussie meat pies here by chance?'

Al laughed at the joke.

Claude and Barry followed Al down a long corridor framed with artwork from noticeable international artists. Al held open the door to his office and ushered them in. Claude and Barry took a seat on an oversize couch. Al drew up a rich red leather chair and sat beside them. A young girl entered with a trolley containing a large jug of coffee and trays of pastries.

Claude served himself a coffee and then turned to Al.

"I'm not going to pull any punches here. Both Barry and I have concerns about 'Snoops'. How long have you worked with him? Has he ever been able to provide you with information of any value? You claim he is one of the best in San Francisco, but I am wondering why you feel that way. We have both observed strange behavior when we have been with him. Furthermore, Paddy O'Regan at the San Francisco police has strong reservations about him."

Al's face reddened and he sputtered an inaudible reply.

"What checks did you personally do on him? How did he end up working for you?"

Barry sat quietly watching the interaction and responses from Al Pine.

"Claude, Barry, he was working here for another partner. He has worked on many cases and so far he has been able to obtain pertinent information that has helped us during trials. I will ask the partner who first retained him to join us."

"No, not so fast. We don't want to get any others involved in case they too may be involved in something with 'Snoops'."

Barry took over and described the strange interaction at the Chop Chings restaurant between Little Jimmy Deng and 'Snoops', and then the visit to the opium den that claimed to be the Hung Lo Culture Club and the shooting."

Al Pine listened and thought for a while before answering.

"You are right. The fewer people who know of this and what has happened to Claude, the better. I will arrange to have a casual chat with the partner who brought 'Snoops' into our firm."

The phone on Al's desk rang. He was surprised and annoyed.

"I left instructions that I was not to be disturbed."

He pressed the handsfree button and barked his name.

"Sir, I am most sorry to interrupt you but Mr. 'Snoops' Dugan is here in the lobby. He says it's most urgent and must see you immediately."

"Tell him to wait. I am in a conference."

Al turned to Claude with a look of desperation.

"Shall I ask him to join us?"

"Absolutely not. Arrange to meet him in another office or the boardroom. Tell him you have clients in your office. See what he wants."

Al slipped on his suit jacket and left to meet 'Snoops' and find out what was so important that he would just show up at the law firm unannounced.

In the reception foyer, 'Snoops' was pacing back and forth. A look of anxiety and nervousness etched his face. Al had never seen him like this before.

"Good morning. I am busy with a conference now but can take a few minutes out to chat with you. Come we will use the conference room. My office is occupied."

As they made their way to the conference room, Al noticed that 'Snoops' was sweating profusely. Large wet areas of sweat had marked the underarms of his crumpled shirt. He was obviously under some stress.

"Tell me what is so important that you have come here this early in the day to speak to me."

"You have caused me some serious problems. I would never have accepted the job if I had known who Claude de Passioné and his partner Barry Jones were. I was seen with them and now the Triads in China have sought retribution. They have snatched Little Jimmy Deng and last night at home I received this."

He reached into the brown bag, he was carrying and removed a severed hand with a note Attachéd.

Al's stomach turned.

"What the hell 'Snoops'? What's your involvement with the Triads and Little Jimmy Deng and why did they send you this?"

"When I was in the police I did some favors for money. They know my weak points and will use them against me or worse, if they think I am interfering in their business they will kill me. Claude de Passioné and Barry Jones are their business. I took Barry Jones into Little Jimmy Deng's office. They know and think I have sold out for money."

"I will advise Claude and his partner that you are no longer under contract to help them with the investigation. Now I must return to business. I cannot and will not help you further."

Chapter 18

Al Pine returned to his office and immediately poured himself a strong coffee.

He sat and relayed the discussion to Claude and Barry. Barry was happy to hear that 'Snoops' was off the investigation.

"I knew it. He is trouble and would sell his mother for a dime. We are better off solving this alone. Will he go to the police?"

"I doubt it. I think he is too heavily involved with those gangs. No, he will stay quiet now and lay low."

"Claude, we had other business to discuss. Shall we proceed with that?"

"No. We have another meeting to attend. I suggest you come up to the estates and we will chat there. The business we need to discuss is more about procedures and law. Boring stuff so I should be somewhere that interests me. I would probably fall asleep here in your office."

"Claude, I realize that you must continue to live your life, but please, take extreme caution until these events are solved and cease."

They stood and thanked Al Pine and asked to be shown out.

The French Consulate for their meeting was fortunately in the same building and they took the elevator down to the sixth floor.

Barry walked ahead and pressed the buzzer. Behind the armored glass doors, he watched as a security guard pressed a button for the intercom.

"We have an appointment with the Cultural Attaché, Dennis Richards."

The security guard asked their names and then entered information into the computer on his desk. The electronic lock clicked open and he waved them in.

"Please go to the reception desk, there you will be assisted."

Claude looked across the reception area to a large ornate antique desk. A middle-aged woman sat behind it. Her Gallic features were evident. Her skin was very white and her hair was tightly tied back in a bun. Severe tortoiseshell-rimmed glasses framed her face. Claude surmised she was all business.

« Bonjour Comment puis-je vous aider ? »

Before he could announce their appointment, Barry spoke to the woman.

"Morning, dearie. We are here to see Mister Dennis Richards."

avec quel invité (e)?

"With Mister Dennis Richards."

"Monsieur Ricard?"

"No. I said, Mister Richards. Don't know any Monsieur Ricard."

Claude was embarrassed and spoke to the receptionist.

Pardonner mon collègue, il est d' origine autralienne

In return, he received an icy stare and a look of scorn.

The receptionist stood and left her desk muttering

« Il ne vient pas des alentours…celui-la »

Claude immediately intervened in his native impeccable French.

Minutes passed after she announced their presence, and then Denis Ricard briskly walked into the reception area.

Claude looked at the bespectacled Denis with his shiny silver hair, pearl drey suit, pale blue shirt, and silver tie.

"Bonjour. I am Denis."

"Bonjour Denis, I am Claude and this is my business partner Barry."

"Welcome, I am pleased to meet you. Come with me to my office."

In Denis' office, they made small talk, and again, more pastries and coffee were offered. Barry was considering the possibility of making it a habit. The pastries were good and the girls were pretty.

"I see you made a 'good impression' on Celine our receptionist. Don't worry. She is a little stiff. My name is pronounced like 'duh knee' in French. She will get over it. I invited you here to discuss an upcoming event at the Consulate. As Cultural Attaché I am responsible for the management and organization of events. We will be hosting an event for executives of companies here in San Francisco that are doing business in France and those looking to establish contacts to do business in France. The guests are exporters and importers and range from High Technology executives, fashion and food importers, travel companies, and more. A very mixed group. There will be over three hundred guests. We are looking to have some fine wines available. There will be some French businesspeople invited who will be looking for product representation in California. For the event, I would like to source some of your great California wines from the de Passioné Estates as well as some from your French wineries. We will work with you to arrange the shipping from France using the Consular system. Is this something that de Passioné Estates is interested in providing"

Claude was ecstatic.

"Indeed Denis. I suggest you visit our winery as my guest. In fact please visit and plan on staying a weekend. We have guest facilities. I will give you a tour and arrange a wine sampling for you. When is the event taking place?"

"The invitations are being sent out this week. It will be held in six weeks. I would very much like to visit and stay. When do you consider it would be convenient?"

"I know it's short notice, but I suggest this weekend if it works for you. We will need a little time to assemble an order of the wines for your event."

"I am available and look forward to visiting."

During his conversation with Denis, Claude had glanced across at Barry who had engaged a particularly attractive young French girl in conversation. She was intrigued by the yarns of his fictitious adventures in the outback of Australia.

Claude watched as Barry handed her his business card and watched as he wrote down the girl's contact information. It seemed there was no stopping Barry when an attractive woman seemed available. He watched as she looked at a gold watch on her wrist and spoke to Barry. She leaned up on her toes and kissed Barry on both cheeks. Barry looked over at Claude and gave him a huge smile.

Chapter 19

The Mansion, de Passioné Estate, Napa.

Claude and Barry returned to find a very excited Marie-France. They had barely parked the armored Chrysler and entered the house when she bounded down the stairs to greet them.

"Claude, I have had so much fun with Buzz. Yesterday he took me for a ride in his new helicopter. It was unlike any plane trip I have taken. I have decided to enroll in his flying school and learn to fly. First I will need to go to the city and buy the appropriate aviator suits."

Barry looked at her as if she was becoming even more insane. The thought of Marie-France alone and flying a plane terrified him.

"That's nice, Mother but surely there is a lot of study for the use of the controls and navigation that will need to be done first."

"I am sure my dear Buzz will help me."

Claude considered the news and thought back on some of her past ventures. In comparison, taking up flying lessons seemed the sanest of them all.

"When will you start these lessons?"

"Buzz and I have a weekend planned. I think we will start this weekend."

Claude thought the timing was perfect, as it was the weekend he was going to host Denis Ricard, and with Marie-France gone he would be spared the possibility of any embarrassment.

Marie-France was about to leave them when she remembered the car that had been parked off the driveway into the estate.

"Claude, were you or Barry expecting any visitors here this morning? There was a strange car parked on our property not far from the gates."

Claude looked over to Barry, who shook his head.

"No, we had no one scheduled to visit. What was the type and color of the car?"

"Let me think. It was a dark color. Yes, it was black I think. I do not remember what sort of car it was."

"Mother, please try and remember. With the strange things that have been happening it is important."

"Claude nothing is important as my new love for Buzz."

Barry lost control. He half laughed and sneezed. The glass of beer he had poured himself flew out of his hand and that in his mouth sprayed out.

"Young man, you should have more respect for me. I was the wife of a Marquis, God bless his philandering departed soul. He would be happy that I am carrying on a normal life."

It was too much for Barry. He bent over howling with laughter. The thought that Marie-France was living a normal life was just too much.

Claude had gone pensive.

"Please try and remember more about that car."

"Why should I try and remember? Buzz took a picture of it from the helicopter."

"Where is Buzz now? I need to see that picture if he still has it."

"He had gone to assist the police in a search for a missing child. He would need to return to his office and leave the helicopter. Maybe you should call and leave a message with the bitch Cynthia Honeysucker at his office. A nasty little piece. A real hussy. She dresses like a hooker."

It was just too much for Barry. His laughter was infectious and soon Claude was laughing with tears running down his cheeks. The thought of Marie-France calling anyone a bad dresser was beyond belief.

Marie-France stood looking at them as if they were deranged.

"Men. They just don't know how to differentiate between natural beauty and a tramp."

After she stormed off, Claude picked up the phone and called the flying school. He was advised that Buzz was in the process of returning and she would pass him the message on his return.

Barry composed himself and sat himself down on the large overstuffed sofa.

"Claude, I am concerned you are taking this whole thing too lightly. What I saw in Chinatown at Jimmy Deng's was not pretty. He was scared when 'Snoops' confronted him, then he disappears. Now we find out that 'Snoops' is crooked. We are no closer to finding out anything. Where does the girl who shot you fit in? Is Misty Moon, or should I call her by her real name, Wendy Wong, involved? Who is that tall Chinese who was at the hospital and calls himself We Hoe? There are so many people involved. Why did Crystal Moon come here to warn you of something so serious that she refused to leave the note or package? I think it's time to sit and talk with Paddy O'Regan. I don't think he is as stupid as that Irish act he puts on. I sat and talked to him and I am sure he knows a lot more than he shared."

"Barry, I have made arrangements with our security firm to increase our protection"

"Claude you walk around as if nothing has happened. These are sinister people."

"I am not scared of them or their threats. I have nothing to hide."

"Then why are they making such a huge effort? It doesn't make any sense. Please stop worrying. Let me call Paddy O'Regan and arrange another meeting. Just you, me, and Paddy. No 'Snoops'. I think we will make some progress without 'Snoops' there."

"Go ahead. Where should we meet him?"

"I'll let him decide, but not in Chinatown. It seems the walls have eyes and ears there."

Together they sat in silence thinking of the bizarre events that had occurred. Finally, Claude stood and announced he was retiring for the night. Barry was surprised and glanced at his watch. He decided Claude had other matters he wished to handle privately.

"I think I too will have an early night. That San Francisco trip has me a little worn out. I will see you tomorrow."

Claude watched as Barry gathered up his jacket and walked towards the front door to leave, knowing Barry had other plans for the night. As he was walking out, the phone rang. Claude snatched it up and was pleased to hear the gravelly voice of Buzz calling back.

"Buzz, I understand when you were flying back to the house with Marie-France, you took some pictures of a car in the entrance to the vineyards and Mansion. Do you have those pictures? There have been some strange things happening here and I want to know who that car belonged to."

"Well, if Marie-France agrees to have dinner with me tonight I'll print them off and drop them by a bit later. Is she there?"

Claude called his mother to take the phone call. After Marie-France picked up and was talking with Buzz, Claude left her to the conversation and went to his office. He sat reflecting on the earlier comments that Barry had made. It was only then that Claude started to understand the seriousness of the situation. He considered his options and wondered aloud whether he should stay in California or return to the family vineyards in France. He pondered this and it dawned upon him that the safest was neither. He recalled his days in the South Pacific and his romance on the island of Rarotonga with Atarangi. He closed his eyes and sat back recalling the evenings on the beaches and the smell of frangipani carried on the warm island breezes. It seemed so far away from the life he was living in California and farther from his early life in France. He realized he was missing Atarangi. He remembered her soft features and enchanting smile.

Sleep came easily to Claude and he drifted into a dream of the nights he had spent with Atarangi.

Chapter 20

Claude sat alone in his office examining the color photos that Buzz had delivered. He tried to identify the car but was unable to place the Crown Victoria parked in their driveway near the entrance. Claude was appreciative of the fact that Buzz had been able to capture both the front and rear of the car, yet could not determine whether the car was black or a dark navy blue.

He bent over his desk and using an eyepiece magnified the image. Two figures were sitting in the front seat, yet the image was not clear. Claude could not make out any useful details.

As he continued to examine the pictures, Barry Jones arrived at the door to his office.

"Gidday, Mate. Was up for today?"

"I'm trying to get some details on that car Marie-France saw parked on our property. The images are a little blurred but there is enough detail for me to make out the numbers on the license plates. I'm going to call Paddy O'Regan to help identify who was here."

Barry took the photos and examined them before commenting.

"That looks like a government car. Look at those oversize donut-shaped tires and wheels. Like a cop car."

Claude glanced at his watch. It was still too early to call Paddy O'Regan. He decided to join Marie-France, along with Barry while he waited and enjoy breakfast before starting into the day.

In the dining room, Marie-France was already seated drinking a coffee.

"Good morning mother. Are you having anything else for breakfast besides coffee?"

"Yes Claude, I am. I'm waiting for Buzz to arrive and join me. He and I have plans for the day. I have never been to Catalina Island and Buzz has business there today. He is going to take me along for the trip."

"That should be nice. It's a beautiful morning to fly."

Claude couldn't but help noticing the particular clothing she had chosen to wear for the trip. She was dressed in a festive yellow jumpsuit, purple sneakers, and a thick gold rope belt. A large gold and enameled iguana brooch adorned her right shoulder. She had certainly dressed for the trip.

Claude and Barry had hardly poured their coffees when they heard the drone of the approaching helicopter. Within minutes the loud blade slap drowned out any attempt at conversation as the helicopter dropped and settled in the front garden.

Barry went to the window and watched as Buzz jumped down from the cockpit and ran toward the Mansion. The helicopter sparkled in the early morning sun. It was a beautiful-looking machine.

Marie-France quickly walked to the door and hugged Buzz as he entered. Claude shook his head in wonderment.

When they were all seated, one of the kitchen staff arrived to take their orders.

Marie-France ordered Hueveros Ranchero. Buzz decided that was the ideal breakfast and ordered. Barry, remembering his breakfasts in Australia ordered a porterhouse steak with three fried eggs. Claude ordered warm croissants and a bowl of fresh blueberries.

The group sat talking and was interrupted by the ringing of the phone in the foyer area. A member of the staff answered and excused himself as he entered the dining room.

"Mister Claude, It is the police. He asked for you."

Barry looked at Claude with an expression of concern. Claude left the table and crossed to the foyer and took the phone. He announced himself.

"Claude, sorry to bother you, it's Paddy in San Francisco. I need to speak with you urgently."

"Now this is a coincidence. I was going to call you this morning. I need help with a small matter."

"Claude, this is important. Have you seen Barry Jones?"

"Yes, he is here having breakfast with me."

"Can you two come to see me now? It is best that you do or some of the other precincts will put out a notice to apprehend Barry for questioning."

"What is this all about?"

"I do not wish to discuss this by phone. I suggest you bring an attorney with you."

"I will call Al Pine's office and we should be there in the next two hours."

Upon returning to the table, the others all watched Claude as he sat. It was Barry who spoke first.

"What the hell was that all about?"

"Well, Barry it seems the police want to interview you for some Unknown reason. It must be pretty serious as they advised bringing an Attorney. That was Paddy O'Regan."

Barry stuttered and looked bewildered. Buzz and Marie-France stared at him.

"I have done nothing. It must be something to do with my visit to Chinatown the other night."

"I suggest we don't keep them waiting. I'll call Al Pine to meet us at the precinct. Let me gather up those photos and some papers and we will take that Chrysler I have come to love and be on our way."

Claude rose and noticed that Barry seemed flustered.

"Barry is there anything you want to discuss before we get to Paddy O'Regan's office?"

"I have no idea what this is all about."

"I guess we will soon know."

Part 4

The investigation deepens

Chapter 21

San Francisco, Chinatown Precinct

Throughout the drive, Barry had been quiet which made Claude nervous. He was sure that had there been any trouble, Barry would have told him.

They parked in an area supposedly for visitors. There were cop cars parked haphazardly in all directions. Claude pulled the Chrysler up against the bordering wall away from the other vehicles.

As they climbed the grimy grey concrete steps to the entrance, Al Pine called up to them. They turned to see Al Pine hurrying across the street to join them.

"What is this all about? You both know I am not a criminal lawyer. I do corporate matters. What sort of trouble have you two gotten into now?"

"Relax, Al. As far as I know, they simply wish to interview Barry and asked me to come along."

"That doesn't sound like a simple request, especially if you were advised to bring a lawyer."

As the trio climbed up the steps, they noticed the looks from some of the cops as they glared at them.

"Nice warm reception we are getting. Barry, are you sure there is nothing I need to know? What about you Claude?"

"I told you in our meeting of the things that have happened. This must be related."

As they walked to the reception, a young cop very quietly whispered under his breath 'Cop killer' as he passed them. It was barely audible.

Al Pine spun and confronted Barry.

"Did your temper get the better of you? Did you attack a cop?"

"Just relax, Al. I did no such thing."

At the reception desk, the cop on duty picked up the phone and called Paddy. Within minutes several cops arrived to escort them to an interrogation room.

"Paddy, what the hell is this about? Are you arresting my client? This is very irregular. I demand an explanation. These men have come here voluntarily. Are you charging them with anything? If not, tell those other goons to leave."

"Gentlemen, you are not under arrest. Based on what Barry has told me of the problems you have recently experienced I think the matter we wish to discuss is somehow linked."

Al Pine placed his briefcase on the steel desktop and removed a yellow legal pad. He sat waiting for Paddy to speak.

"I'm going to ask Sgt. James of the Marine Unit to give you details."

Sgt. James was an extremely fit slim, wiry individual.

"Good morning and thank you for coming here so quickly. I won't waste time but will cut right to the chase. Overnight, one of our patrols was called to the shores of Alcatraz. Upon arriving they discovered a grisly scene. The bodies of two men were bound together. Both had been mutilated. The coroner is currently investigating whether these men were alive when dumped into San Francisco Bay, or had died prior. They are Little Jimmy Deng, a Triad boss, and one of our former officers 'Snoops' Dugan.' We suspect their bodies were taken out in a boat and dumped. The perps probably expected the current to carry them down past the Golden Gate Bridge and into the Pacific where the fish and sharks would eliminate any trace of them. They had been in the water a while as fish had already eaten parts of their exposed flesh."

Claude and Barry gasped at the names.

"The bodies show all the signs of a Chinese gang murder. Little Jimmy's hands had been cut off and his tongue cut out. What remains of it was Attachéd to a wire and hung like a necklace around his neck. It is a method of execution used by the Mah Tong gang if they believe you have stolen or betrayed the gang. In the case of 'Snoops', he must have suffered before they shot him between his eyes. His back has almost no skin left from where he was flogged and burned. They must have been trying to get information from him through torture. Our interest in speaking to Barry is clear. He was probably one of the last people to see 'Snoops' and Little Jimmy alive when he visited the Hung Lo Culture Club with 'Snoops'. I should mention that we have Little Jimmy's partner, Benny from the club in custody. I am sure that Little Jimmy was not aware of the dealings Benny had with the other gangs. For them to have gone to this length there must be a huge deal planned or in operation. Our guess is drugs, weapons, terrorism, and human trafficking, but it must be major and involve gangs in China and Europe. Our informants in the gangs have indicated there has been a lot of activity involving unknown men from China and Russia over the past month. Our intelligence has not uncovered too much. A lot of these men are unknown to us or the other forces."

Paddy took over the conversation.

"It's not pretty. We need to know everything that happened that night at the Hung Lo Club. Barry, you were there. You were the last to see them together."

Barry told the group of the meeting between Little Jimmy Deng and of the shots and the kidnapping. He explained he left after with 'Snoops' but had no more to add. He then remembered and pointed at Al Pine.

"Claude and I had a meeting with Al Pine the next day and Al was called out as 'Snoops' had shown up unexpectedly at his office."

All the eyes turned and focused on Al Pine. Al spoke.

"He was in trouble. The gangs suspected something between him and Little Jimmy. He had a severed hand in a bag. He said it belonged to Jimmy. I asked him to leave."

"At this point, I think you are both in extreme danger. Claude, you must try and remember anything that happened when you were with the girl, Misty Moon. She is involved in many illegal activities. So far she has avoided arrest here and in China. She has information on some very powerful and influential people here and in China and has been able to evade authorities because of this. We suspect you have in your possession something of great importance to these gangs."

"There is nothing I can recall. It was only a brief relationship."

"Did she give you anything? Maybe a book, a gift?"

"No, there is nothing that I can remember."

"This has escalated beyond San Francisco and now the FBI and the Feds are involved. You can expect a visit soon."

"Paddy, can you look at these? This car was parked on the driveway leading into the Mansion. It is one more of the strange things that have happened."

Paddy took the photos and scanned them. He frowned and passed them over to another detective.

"Take these to intel. See if they can make the plates."

The detective snatched up the pictures and left. Ten minutes later he returned and handed a printout to Paddy.

"Well, gentlemen, that car is from the government pool and is assigned to the FBI. I think you will have your visit sooner than later. Now, how do we keep you out of sight of those gangs? I urge you to convince your mother to leave at once. It would not be unusual for them to kidnap and try to extort information if they believe you have something they want."

"Paddy, if you can arrange it, Barry, Marie-France, and I can leave California and reside at one of our vineyards in France. We could leave unannounced to the staff at the Mansion and on a private plane. I will explain we are taking a Caribbean vacation. Is it possible to request that assistance from the Feds?"

"It is possible, but it will take a few days. So far the news of finding the bodies has been kept from the press. We can only do that for so long. We need to get you into hiding before that is released."

Claude reflected on the situation. He was puzzled and spoke directly to Paddy.

"Paddy, as we were entering the building, a young cop muttered 'Cop Killer' to us. How many here know of this development?"

"Only the Marine Unit officers, homicide the gang unit here."

'Then I suspect you have a leak in your organization, and that is a problem. Who else is aware of this situation?"

Paddy thought for a while before responding.

"Only my assistant, Jenny Chin. She had tailed Barry and 'Snoops' that night and saw them enter the Hung Lo club. She has had access to the reports."

"I suggest you assign her to another case. It is too coincidental for a leak to happen so quickly and be known by a low-ranking cop. Who is she romantically involved with? How long has she been on the force? How did you choose her as your assistant? I think you need to take a long hard look at those around you. Trust no one."

Paddy was furious at Claude's comments.

"How dare you question my judgment. I have a good mind to arrest Barry Jones as a key witness and for his protection. Maybe I should do the same to you as you must have key evidence that these gangs are after. I'd put you in isolation for your safety,"

Al Pine interrupted.

"You have no evidence. You would be violating their rights. As legal counsel and an officer of the court, I strongly advise you against taking any action against my clients. This meeting is over."

"Paddy, Al, please be calm. I'm sure Paddy will agree after he thinks this through. In the meanwhile, I need to arrange for a private plane to take Barry, Marie-France, and me to France. We will be safer at our Chateau there."

"Before you take any action, I suggest you allow me to contact the FBI and the Feds to interview you. I am sure they will assist in helping you with secret travel arrangements."

"I will need to change several business appointments before leaving. I had made an invitation to the French Cultural Attaché to visit the winery this weekend. I will need to contact him and postpone that invite."

That comment got Paddy thinking. He sat silently in thought.

"Claude, did you ever have Misty Moon to the Chateau in France or spend time with her there?"

"Yes, she did visit and stayed with me there."

"I will ask the Feds to contact their counterparts in France and advise them of the situation here. You need not worry as it will be done at the highest level."

Chapter 22

The Mansion, Napa Valley, California.

It was late afternoon when Barry and Claude returned to the Mansion and told Marie-France the plan.

The news of a trip to France thrilled Marie-France, yet she was concerned that her plans with Buzz Kutz would be disrupted.

She was still excited about the trip she had with Buzz to the island of Catalina and was enthused at the enjoyment she had with the trip.

"Mother, I have business in France for which I must be present. Barry will accompany us. While there we will take a vacation, so it is not all business."

Claude was careful not to disclose the real reason for the trip.

"When will we leave? I need to pack my best formal and casual clothing."

Claude could only imagine what fashion statements she would unleash on France. He thought of his desire to visit Paris and of the nurse he had met again at the Hyatt since the time he had lived in Paris. He intended to finish his amorous business with her, whether she was married or not. He thought of the brief affair they had enjoyed while he was a patient in the hospital. He recalled how willing she had been to satisfy his young lust and felt his arousal starting. He smiled.

Barry had gone out into the vineyards to speak with the team managers regarding picking grapes and tending to the vines. He explained that he and Claude needed to be away for a few days and reviewed the work plans for the men. He was satisfied with the plans and pleased with the foremen who he had convinced to join de Passioné estates from their former jobs at vineyards in Australia. He had also been able to hire one of the best vintners from Australia as the de Passioné head vintner.

In his office, Claude called Denis Ricard at the French Consulate in San Francisco.

Denis was quick to take the call.

"Bonjour, Claude. I am looking forward to my visit this weekend. Is there anything I should bring?"

"Denis, unfortunately, something has come up. I need to fly to our winery in France to attend to some urgent business. I apologize but cannot change this situation. When I return to California, we can reschedule."

"I understand these situations and how things can happen unexpectedly. How long will you be in France?"

"It was unexpected and I am not sure. I may be there for a couple of weeks."

"If that is the case, I will be there too. It would be my pleasure to invite you to dine with me at The Epicure at The Bristol Hotel."

"I would enjoy that. Let me provide you with a telephone number at the Chateau. Maybe you will have time to visit while in France."

"I will have some flexibility. There are friends I need to visit. I look forward to seeing you in Paris."

Claude and Denis continued to chat for several minutes. Claude assured Denis there would still be time to provide the wines for the social event the Consulate was hosting. Denis responded that he was looking forward to the drive through the wine country in his 1965 British Racing Green Aston Martin DB5. Claude responded how he too enjoyed driving his Ferrari 250LM around the vineyards. They had found a common interest in classic cars.

After Claude hung up the phone he reflected on a feeling that he had met Denis previously. It was a strange feeling yet it seemed real…like a Déjà vu.

Claude was about to leave his office when he saw a glint of light from the windscreen of a car approaching the Mansion. He stood and watched as the car drove slowly down the long driveway. As it got closer, Claude recognized it was a black Mercedes. He was both curious and apprehensive. He slid open his desk drawer and removed the Glock pistol he kept for protection. He wondered if the gang had become emboldened and decided to confront him at his home.

The car swept into the rounded path and stopped beneath the portico. Claude continued to watch as the driver's door opened and a man stepped out, It was a tall Chinese man, As he watched, Marie-France raced around the front of the car with her arms outstretched, and upon reaching the man gave him a huge hug. Claude was confused.

Maire-France escorted the man into the house and called Claude.

"Claude, this is the man who came to visit you before. He is so charming. I am so happy he has returned for a visit."

The man approached Claude with his hand extended.

"Claude, I am pleased to meet you. My name is Wee Hoe, I am with the United States Department of Homeland Security. There is a matter we need to discuss with you."

"I believe it would be best to discuss this privately in my office, but first can I offer you a coffee or beverage."

"See, Claude. I told you he was a nice man. He is very polite. Wee let me get you something to drink. What would you like?"

"A glass of ice-cold water would be appreciated."

Marie-France almost broke into a run to get Wee his drink from the kitchen.

"She is such a delightful person. You are lucky to have her as your mother."

"I understand you spent time speaking with her on an earlier visit. I also understand you had a package for me that you refused to leave with her. What was that all about?"

"It was a letter requesting you contact us and some other material requesting some business information. We have reason to believe your business has been compromised by an international crime ring. I am aware you had a meeting this morning at the Chinatown precinct in San Francisco. What you learned there is only a small fraction of the overall scope of the operation. It is huge. I am the liaison with other Federal departments who are actively involved in this investigation and the plan to shut them down. Several of their key communication locations are under our surveillance in different countries. Your name and the of your business have been in some discussions. We need to know why."

Claude remained silent as Marie-France returned with Wee's water'

"Wee, it is best if we go to my office and talk. Let's not bother Marie-France with all this boring business."

Wee picked up on the cue and immediately agreed. He thanked Marie-France for the water and followed Claude into his office.

"My mother isn't well, and I don't wish to burden her with all the things that have been going on. I wish to be frank with you. There is nothing I have done that explains any of this. I have never been involved with any criminal activity, other than what happened in my student days in France when I unwittingly took that job with an art dealer and it turned out to be an international art smuggling operation. I was a poor student at the Sorbonne and looking to make some money independent from the wealth of my family. I have never had any contact with those people since. My brief affair with Wendy Wong, or as I first knew her, Misty Moon, was over within months. I am perplexed however as to why her sister, Crystal Moon came here to warn me of danger. You must know more and I ask you to tell me what is going on."

"We have been able to verify that the wine exports you send to the Russians are part of an elaborate scheme. The wine is removed from the shipping containers and sold here in the United States at heavily discounted prices. The containers are then loaded with arms and shipped to the intended locations in Russia. After they leave the United States the shipments are redirected to Mid-East arms dealers. Part of the profits from these deals is then sent to China to pay for large shipments of synthetic drugs, heroin, and cocaine. The drugs are exported by the Russians to Holland, Germany, France, and other European countries. The Russians have sophisticated distribution networks established, often using motorbike gangs. Through our intelligence gathering, we have discovered your name has been mentioned as someone who has damaging information and you must be 'neutralized'."

Claude listened in disbelief.

"I do not know of any of this. I have had very few interactions with the Russian buyers here. They order and we fill and ship the orders as requested. The containers are loaded here and shipped to the addresses provided after we receive funds. It is a simple business transaction."

"In the intercepts, we have made, it seems the Chinese do not believe the Russians. They are convinced you are working with them and have in your possession information on the whole operation. There is a powerful Triad called the 14-K They operate in many countries and wield power over many of the other gangs. They are the most brutal of all the Triads. Someone has advised the 14-K that you are a threat to the operation. We are attempting to learn more. I suggest you take extreme care. I understand that Paddy O'Regan is arranging for you to disappear for a while. That would be prudent. I suggest you tell no one of this."

"I am starting to regret returning to operate our family business after the murder of my father, the Marquis. It has been nothing but trouble."

"You have had contact with someone who has put you in this position. I suggest you review who you have had contact with, and who could gain from your demise."

"I only have one business partner, and that is Barry Jones. We are equal partners now. I don't suspect his involvement in any of this."

"My advice is to trust no one at this point. Now I must leave. We will be in contact very soon."

Chapter 23

The de Passioné Chateau, France

Things had moved quickly after Wee Hoe's visit to the Mansion in California. Marie-France had been difficult as she was insisting on having Buzz Kutz join them. Claude had been aggressive and adamant in refusing her demand. This had resulted in her sulking and acting childishly. Claude had ignored her tantrums and issued her an ultimatum. She reluctantly accepted his terms.

They had been taken to the airport in Oakland, California where they were put on a private plane destined for France. Other than some basic refreshments, the flight was long and boring. Upon arrival in France, they were hustled into a van and driven at speed to the Chateau.

As the van turned into the grounds, Claude felt a tinge of nostalgia. Although he loved the Mansion in California, his early life had been at the Chateau.

After he and Barry were settled in, they met with the various managers of the vineyard operations and also the head vintner. All of the business operations were functioning well. Claude and Barry were pleased.

Later in the day, he decided it was time for him to act on his desires, and called Barry to join him for a discussion.

"Barry, there is a personal matter I will be attending to in Paris. I am asking you to look after things here until I return. Please watch Marie-France. Do not let her leave the Chateau or have anyone visit. We need to be extremely careful until things get resolved."

"Where are you going? When will you return? How can I reach you?"

"I am going alone. I have a thought and wish to check some things out. I suspect all this situation may be tied to an old acquaintance. I intend to check."

"You are taking a huge risk. I suggest you leave this up to the professionals who are trained in these matters. Already the French RAID (Recherche, Assistance, Intervention, Dissuasion) are involved. They have already visited here and checked the backgrounds of the workers and others with whom we deal. They have replaced the men our security company provided."

"Barry, this is personal and something I must do. Be assured I will be very careful."

At this point, Barry knew it was pointless to continue to argue or try to convince Claude otherwise. As a sign their meeting was over, Claude stood and left for his room.

In his private room, Claude took the crisp white business card from his wallet. He lay on his bed considering whether to make the phone call or just arrive at her address. Minutes passed before he reached for the phone and punched in the numbers. He listened as the tones of the phone indicated the call was ringing at the other end. After several rings, the phone was answered. Her voice was unmistakable.

"Good evening, Martine. It is Claude de Passioné. I am in France and will be visiting Paris tomorrow. Would you please join me for lunch?"

There was silence.

"Martine. Are you still there?"

"Yes, Claude. I don't know that I should. I am very busy. Maybe another time."

"Martine, I do want to see you. Please let me see you."

"As I told you in San Francisco, my life is very different now."

"Please have lunch with me. Just for a couple of hours. I promise that after you will never hear from me again, but I must see you."

"Oh, Claude. Do you think that for one minute I would fall for that line? I am reluctant to see you because I still have strong emotions for you. It is not you that I fear, it is me. I may not be able to stand the pain of seeing you and then knowing we will never be together. I have thought of you so many times since those days at the hospital when I was a nurse. I wished we had been together many times. My life has changed so much. We would have had so much fun and enjoyed each other. How can you torment me now by calling like this? You knew I loved you, yet you abandoned me when you left that hospital. You decided to leave your family and travel the world. Claude, you have interfered and destroyed the lives of other people. And now you want me to have lunch and see you?"

"Martine, I had no idea you felt that way. In those days I was crazy and trying to find myself. Please meet me and we can talk all this out."

Again there was a long silent pause before she responded.

"Claude, you must promise it will be the last time and we meet only for lunch."

Claude was ecstatic. He jumped up from his bed.

"Where shall we meet?"

Martine thought for a while before responding.

"We shall meet at noon at Les Petits Plats in the 14th arrondissement."

Claude was thrilled. He knew the bistro from his student days. He looked forward to walking through the district with its artists and galleries. Memories of his student days flooded into his mind.

"I am so happy we will meet and spend some time together. I will see you then at noon tomorrow."

"Remember Claude, We have an agreement. This will be the last time I will see you."

After he hung up, Claude decided to invite Barry and Marie-France to join him for a drink in the Chateau's spacious drawing-room. He was in high spirits.

Barry was curious at the way Claude was behaving. He had known Claude for years and had never seen him so happy.

"Bloody hell, mate. What's got your dickie? You win the lottery?"

"I am feeling safer and more relaxed since we arrived back in France. I have decided to stay here until certain issues back in America are solved. You are free to return if you wish. I am going to remain and oversee the winery. I think it is time for us to introduce some new wines and I will work with Georges, our new vintner on developing these. I feel invigorated again. It seems I have wine in my blood now. I never thought I would want to be involved in the family business."

Marie-France had been listening and finally spoke.

"I wish to return soon. I want to take those flying lessons with Buzz. I still don't know why you would not allow Buzz to join us here. It would be a nice vacation for him."

"Mother, you hardly know the man. You met him at a dance and he has taken you for a couple of flights and made you promises I suspect he cannot keep."

"Claude, he brings me happiness and love in my life. Who are you to question that?"

"Mother, since the Marquis died you have associated with several questionable men and organizations. I know. I had to rescue you from them and get rid of them."

"Don't you question my choice of men and lovers. I have chosen wisely. Look at the Marquis and the wealth he shared with us."

"Mother, the Marquis was a morally bankrupt womanizer. You know that. Look at what happened at his funeral and the eighteen mistresses showing up. Consider how he died. He was shot in his lover's bed by the jealous husband. I don't think he was such a great testament to your ability to select men wisely. For all you know, Buzz may have a dark and shady past."

"How dare you. I am your mother. Never forget that."

Barry was thoroughly enjoying himself. He had never seen Marie-France speak so forcibly or with such clarity. He wondered what she must have been like in her younger days before drugs and free love destroyed her during her hippie days.

"All right then, Mother. I will contact Buzz and arrange for him to join us. I just hope you are right about him. I am taking a huge risk by inviting him here."

"Thank you, Claude. You will soon see what a fine man he is."

Barry was amazed and wondered if Claude had gone a little soft in his head since arriving back in France.

"Claude, you are ignoring the advice we were given. We are meant to maintain a low profile."

"I intend to contact certain people who are connected in those criminal circles. I remember some from when I worked in Paris at the Antique and Arts shop. I still remember where some of them lived. I am sure they will be aware of the gangs involved. I will try and get a message to them. We cannot expect the legal authorities to establish credible contact. I need to have someone who is on the other side contact them. I'm sure there will be a cost to have this done. Tomorrow I will leave in an attempt to find one person in particular. He is probably the only one with the contacts. I will go alone."

Marie-France was confused, as nothing was not making sense.

"What are you two talking about? Is this about making a new wine?

Part 5

Legal treachery

Chapter 24

San Francisco, Offices of Al Pine, Attorney

Review of the developments that had occurred, and the disclosure of the involvement of the Mah Tong gang by Paddy O" Regan and the Marine Unit's Sgt James, troubled Al Pine. He was upset that he had lost his partner who had been involved in the sophisticated rackets they had been running. His involvement in crooked dealings with 'Snoop' Dugan had been deeply hidden for years. Al Pine had been able to use confidential information entrusted to him by his clients and disclose it to 'Snoops'. It was all over now, but he would need to destroy information in case his offices were searched. He was especially worried that the scams he and 'Snoops' had pulled on the de Passioné family and their business would be discovered. He sat back and thought about the situation. He needed to take action. He decided it was time to retire from his law practice, and would announce it at today's annual partners' lunch. He was certain it would be a surprise to his other partners and raise the curiosity of some.

Al sat thinking about recent events. He was aware of some of them, but he did not know about the murder of Little Jimmy Deng or 'Snoops'. The Mah Tong gang had not kept him informed.

He was troubled and wondered why he had been requested to attend the meeting with Paddy O'Regan and the other officers. There were no charges to be laid. It was just a routine informational meeting to update Claude and Barry Jones. It seemed an irregular request for Claude and Barry to take an attorney to such a meeting.

The rest of the morning he spent sifting through his files and removing any in which 'Snoops' had been involved. He filled banker's boxes with anything that could incriminate him. He was particularly careful with the de Passioné files. He wanted no trace of his crooked dealings and profiteering on the family or their businesses.

As he was about to leave for the monthly partners' lunch, his desk phone rang. He was tempted not to answer it but then thought of the events that had happened and decided it was best to give an appearance that all was normal.

The receptionist announced the name of a person who he did not know, but he took the call.

"Al Pine speaking. How may I assist you?"

A gravelly voice responded. Al froze.

"This is Agent Wayne Steel with the FBI. We need to meet with you regarding any dealings you had with a 'Snoops' Dugan. When are you available? We need to meet soon."

"Today is out of the question. I have client meetings all day that are back to back."

That was Al's first of many lies, that would eventually trip him up.

"How about I be at your office first thing in the morning. Let's say seven-thirty."

"That will be fine."

Al cursed as he hung up. He decided he would return that evening after the office closed to continue laundering his files. He wanted no proof of any irregularities in the files.

There was a gentle knock at the door and Sally Masters, his secretary, and assistant of the past ten years entered.

"Al, are you alright? You look pale and tired. Is everything OK? Who was that gruff man who just called?"

"It was an FBI agent. They wish to interview me about that PI we used, 'Snoops' Dugan. I always knew he was trouble."

"I warned you many times about him. Friends of mine in the San Francisco Police warned me and spoke of the suspicions they had."

"You are right. I should have listened to you. It is too late now."

"Why? What has happened?"

Al quickly recalled that the police were not releasing the information.

"I'm not sure. Seems he's got into some sort of trouble."

"He certainly looked disheveled and worried when he came here the other day."

"I suggest you forget that. As far as I'm concerned that never happened."

Sally looked at him quizzically. She knew better than to argue with Al. She had witnessed and experienced his fiery temper. She looked at her watch.

"Al it's time for you to leave for the partners' lunch. It will take you time to walk to the club."

"Sally, I want you to join me as my guest at the lunch. I have something important to announce."

"I have never been to a partner's lunch. Is it allowed?"

"I don't give a damn. You are my guest and will be joining us."

Sally looked around at all the boxes on the floor of the office.

"Al, what are you doing with all those files?"

"I have so many inactive and dead files they need to be sent to central storage. I am sorting through them as I am probably the only one who can decide whether a file is closed, dead, or just inactive."

"Do you want me to help?"

"No, I am almost finished. Now let us leave for lunch."

Together they left the office and rode down in the elevator. Neither recognized the grey-haired man behind them until they reached the ground floor. As they were exiting the elevator Al remembered he was the new Cultural Attaché at the French Consulate, Denis Ricard. He stopped and exchanged pleasantries and recalled he had suggested that Denis visit him at his Pacific Heights home. He had hoped to get new business from the Consulate for the firm.

During the ten-minute walk to the San Francisco Advocates Club, Al was quiet and barely spoke. He was busy preparing his retirement announcement and strategizing a way that would not arouse too much curiosity amongst the partners. He had intended to work for another five years.

They entered the club and made their way into the dining room. The partners were standing in small groups and enjoying pre-lunch drinks. Al was ordering a drink for Sally and himself, when Bob Pritchard-Jones, the senior partner approached.

"Al, it is not acceptable for a woman to be in here. Why did you think to bring Sally?

"I think you will understand in a few minutes. Please relax. Those are old principles you are holding onto Bob. The world is changing."

Al watched Bob Pritchard-Jones' strawberry-shaped nose redden and the purple veins in his cheeks pulse as his blood pressure increased. Bob Pritchard-Jones was known in the firm for his volatility.

"Al Pine, you better have a very good reason."

Two of the firm's junior partners joined Al and Sally, but Al was in no mood for small talk. He gulped down his scotch and ordered another. He left Sally and the two junior partners and made his way to the washroom. He was perspiring and struggled to maintain his composure. He freshened his appearance and prepared for the speech he needed to give.

When he returned everyone was seated. Sally waved to him and pointed to an empty seat at the table. He smiled and sat with the others. Bob Pritchard-Jones was at the head table and stood to address the group.

"Good afternoon everyone and welcome to the firm's fifty-first-year annual partners lunch. We, as a firm have a lot to be proud of. Our achievements have resulted in landmark cases, legislative changes, and the progression of California law. I am proud of you all. I know that many of you do not like long speeches as you hear enough of them in court. So, please enjoy the fine lunch that has been prepared for us today."

Before Bob Pritchard-Jones could sit down, Al Pine was on his feet.

"Bob, if you would indulge me, I have an announcement to make. After long consideration, I have decided that this will be my last week at the firm. Effective immediately I am retiring from the firm and the practice of law. It has been a long, profitable, and satisfying career. It is time for me to move on and make way for the younger bright minds with their new ideas and concepts. I wish to thank you Bob and all the other partners with whom I have worked over the years, and especially my assistant Sally Masters."

There was a subdued round of applause.

He sat down. The room fell into a hushed silence. No one was expecting the firm's top-producing attorney to retire.

Al looked around the room at the other partners. Some were staring at him while others were staring down at their plates. He thought of vultures circling for their prey and wondering who would get the revenue rich files when he left, and most of all, the file for the de Passioné family and their businesses.

Bob Pritchard-Jones stood. His nose was crimson and the veins on his face had swollen enormously.

"Well, Al. You have always had a way of surprising us and the judges you appeared in front of. I thank you for the years of service and help in growing the firm. You will be missed."

Al stood and beckoned to Sally to join him. He walked to the front of the room and gave a small bow and then walked with Sally out of a side door. He was done with all the nonsense that went on at the firm. Now he had his own interests to protect.

They walked away from the club and Al noticed that Sally was sobbing. He reached and put his arm around her.

"Don't worry. I will be fine and I am sure the firm will look after you. My life will be tending to my garden, fishing, and doing some traveling. It is time for me now."

"Why now, Al? You have never mentioned retirement. Did something happen that has made you want to retire? Is it something to do with 'Snoops'?"

"Sally, I have been working at the firm seven days a week for many years. I am tired and feel that I have sacrificed many things in life. I want to enjoy life with the time I have left and while in good health."

Part 6

French Moments

Chapter 25

Paris, Les Petits Plats in the 14th arrondissement

The little café was filled up quickly with customers for lunch. Claude arrived early for his rendezvous with Martine. He watched as a mix of artists, businessmen and others arrived. It was an eclectic mix.

Small groups walked together along the boulevard chattering and laughing. He watched them and wondered what jobs they did and what their conversations were about. Suddenly, he saw her. She was walking briskly, but alone. Her long auburn hair flowed effortlessly behind her. She was dressed in designer blue jeans that were tucked into fashionable black leather boots which matched her shoulder bag, and a billowing pure white blouse. Claude marveled at her beauty.

As she entered the café, men made comments and called to her. She just smiled at them. Claude rose and went to escort her back to his table. She leaned forward and kissed him on both cheeks. This elicited a loud cheer from the men in the café. She laughed. They sat at the small table and Claude signaled the waiter.

"Bonjour, Claude. I am pleased we have this chance to relax and talk. Many years have passed since I last saw you. Tell me what has happened in your life. I hope you have stayed out of troubles like those you were involved in when I first met you at the hospital."

"Martine, many things have happened. Some good and some not so good."

Claude continued and told her of his travels, the death of the Marquis, and his return to the family's vineyard and winery. He did not discuss the current situation, or how he had been shot.

Martine listened intently and hung on to each word. Her intended plan to remain aloof and not get enraptured by Claude was quickly crumbling.

They were interrupted by a brash waiter who impatiently inquired what they wished to order. Claude smiled and remembered how curt the waiters in French restaurants could be.

Martine ordered the French Country Salad with Lemon Dijon Vinaigrette.

"That sounds interesting. What is in that salad?"

"Goat cheese, asparagus, Balsamic vinegar, arugula, and lemon."

"That sounds interesting I will order that as well, plus a bottle of de Passioné Estates Chardonnay."

The waiter looked at them in disgust and pointedly asked if that was going to be their total order for lunch. Claude waited for him to leave.

"I intend to have a little fun with him. What will you like after the salad? I know their lobster creations are amazing."

"Claude, I shouldn't. I have my figure to watch."

"There is nothing wrong with that figure. Let me order for you. I used to come here as a student. I promise the food will be excellent."

The waiter returned with the salads and presented them with a great flourish. Claude was aware the waiter was exhibiting his sarcasm.

They sat and slowly ate their salads and when finished, Claude signaled the waiter.

"Now we wish to order lunch. I remember the lobster prepared in a champagne sauce. We would like two orders of that."

The waiter was becoming exasperated with Claude, who pretended not to notice. Martine saw the humor and was trying hard not to laugh.

"Claude, you have not lost the devilment in you that I remember and loved."

They finished their lobster meals and relaxed for a while, then Claude decided to have some fun.

"Now we will make him crazy. Would you like crepes prepared at the table? Maybe Crepes Suzette?"

Martine laughed at the thought of the arrogant waiter preparing the flambeed crepes.

"Claude. You are being bad. I love it."

As he thought, the waiter was more than annoyed at the request for the crepes, however, he persevered and Martine and Claude enjoyed a fine dessert. Claude had one final surprise for the waiter.

The waiter appeared with the expensive check for the meal. He smirked at Claude who was pretending to be shocked at the price. The waiter thought it justice that Claude would be embarrassed by the amount of the bill in front of his fine lady. Claude had other ideas. He reached into his jacket and took out his wallet and produced a black American Express card which he handed to the waiter. The waiter looked at it and gasped at the name on the card, it read

Claude de Passioné,

de Passioné Wine Estates.

Paris, France and Napa Valley, California

The waiter's face reddened and he hurried away. In minutes the owner arrived at their table with apologies while offering a future complimentary evening at the restaurant. Claude declined.

"I have had a most enjoyable time. Thank you for inviting me today."

"What are your plans for the rest of the day?"

"I was going to spend time looking in the stores. I had taken today off."

"I would like your company in joining me for a walk through the park and maybe later we can stop for a coffee."

Martine paused. She was tempted. Claude was everything she remembered.

"That would be nice. I haven't visited the park in a long while."

"Then we will visit Parc Montsouris. I remember it well. I spent many hours there when I was a student at Sorbonne."

Together they walked in silence to the park. Claude wondered why he had never pursued a relationship with Martine and she wondered why he had ignored her those years ago.

The park was beautiful and added to the peace that both Martine and Claude felt. Martine pointed out some of the exotic plants and trees as they walked through the sprawling grounds. As they approached the lake at the center of the park, Claude pointed to an old park bench. They sat and gazed at the view. Couples were sitting or lying on the lawns, while some sat reading books or finishing their picnics. It was an idyllic scene.

They sat and engaged in small talk. Time flew by quickly. Claude stood and asked Martine if she would enjoy a café latte from the little bistro in the park. She nodded and Claude left only to return with two delicious café lattes. Martine was relaxed and happy. Claude decided to ask her a question that had been bothering him.

"Martine, you came to lunch with me alone. I was hoping you would have brought your husband. You told me in San Francisco at the hotel, that your life has changed. That you were married with children."

Martine stayed quiet and stared down at the ground.

"Claude, it was one of the poorest decisions I have made in my life. I am divorced now. I met my former husband and initially it seemed like a marriage made in heaven, but after several months turned into a marriage from hell. He abused me both mentally and physically."

She paused. Claude looked at her and noticed the formation of tears that soon splashed down her cheeks.

"What about the children? I am confused."

"They were his children from a previous marriage. He treated those children so badly as if they were animals. I understand why his first wife left him. He is a monster. He took all of my money and left me with nothing. I have had to build my life again."

Martine sobbed. Claude was shocked and felt a pang of regret and sorrow that he had not established an earlier relationship. He reached for her hand to comfort her. She responded by resting her head on his shoulder. He wiped away a tear and went to kiss her cheek but she turned to him and locked her lips on his. Claude experienced electricity and instant arousal. The kiss lingered and finally, she withdrew. She looked directly into his eyes and smiled.

"Martine, what you have told me is terrible. What can I do to help? Where are you living? Do you have everything you need? Surely I can help you."

"Thank you Claude, but no. I have returned to nursing at a local hospital. It pays my rent."

"Where are you living?"

"I rented a small apartment in Montmarte. It is close to the hospital. The other renters are an interesting mix of people. I have friends there who are artists and others who work in factories. I love it there. You must come and visit."

"I would like that. When can I visit? I do not know how long I will be in Paris before I am required to return to the United States."

"I am not working tomorrow. Why don't you join me tonight? I will prepare a meal. We can stop at the local market and buy some fresh food."

"Tonight I will join you. I will need to call the Chateau and advise my partner Barry, as he will be concerned for my safety. There has been a series of strange events after I was shot."

"I had no idea you had been shot. What happened? Who did it?"

Claude told her of all that had happened in California and why he was taking refuge in Paris.

Martine was horrified.

"Claude, now you have me worried. Will you be safe here? What do those gangs want from you?"

"I have no idea what they want. It is not money The police and the Feds think I have something in my possession that is of great importance to the Triad gangs. I cannot think of anything."

Martine slipped her arm through his and hugged him. Claude relaxed and for the first time in weeks felt at peace.

They continued talking throughout the afternoon until the sun started to set and the trees cast long shadows across the park grounds.

Martine stood and pulled Claude up.

"I think we should leave now. We need to visit the markets while they are still open."

Reluctantly, Claude stood. He did not wish to end the serenity of the afternoon.

Chapter 26

The markets in Montmarte were busy, as office workers ending their day shopped for fresh produce. Displays of art by local artists were intermixed with the fruit and vegetable stalls. The markets were cheery and noisy. Certain of the produce sellers called out their offerings hoping to sell off their remaining goods before their stalls closed.

Claude enjoyed being amongst the chaotic sound of the action. He helped Martine select items. The stalls were filled with cheeses, figs, grapes, apples, and many other fruits and bread. Next to the stalls of the market, there was a Boucherie with fresh cuts of meat on display in the large glass window. The store was crowded.

Martine chose a beef tenderloin. They left the store and stopped at the boulangerie for a baguette, some cheeses, and pastries. Before leaving the market, Martine visited a gourmet store for some escargot.

They left the market to walk to Martine's apartment. It was located on the second floor of an old building. The building was architecturally interesting. Martine's apartment was huge and had floor-to-ceiling leaded windows that opened onto a Romeo and Juliette balcony that overlooked the boulevard and part of the market. Claude approved of the apartment. It fitted with his vision of Martine.

"Claude, please excuse me while I go and freshen up. After we can sit out on my balcony and enjoy an aperitif before our dinner."

Martine left Claude in the living area of the apartment and went to refresh. Claude examined the bookshelves which were packed with the classics and many medical texts. He was looking at one of the texts when Martine returned, looking even more beautiful. Claude put the book down.

"Martine, why do you have so many medical books?"

"I had originally wanted to study and become a doctor. Until I married and divorced, I was studying and had been accepted at university. It is now a dream that has been shattered. I do not have the financial means to complete medical school."

"I am sorry to hear that. You probably would have been a good doctor."

He looked at Martine and even though she smiled, it was a sad smile.

They sat outside on her balcony with their drinks and watched as dusk developed and the twinkling lights of Paris in the early evening came to life.

"I am going inside to start and prepare our dinner."

"Let me join you. I do have some skills in the kitchen. They have progressed a long way since just cooking up the cans of baked beans I prepared as a student."

Martine opened a bottle of wine, turned on some soft music, and they set about preparing their meal. Martine was humming to the music and Claude lost himself in the preparation. It was a peaceful and happy scene.

With the food preparation done, they returned to the balcony.

"Claude, I am curious. Why did you never marry? Surely many girls would have been happy to have married you?"

"There were many girls but only one was so special I wanted to marry her. On the day I was to propose, there was a terrible accident. I had taken her to The Tides Restaurant in Bodega Bay, California. As we were leaving the restaurant, a young student in an old Volkswagon accidentally hit and killed her. Since then I have not met anyone else. She will never be replaced in my mind. I loved her dearly."

Martine sensed his deep loss and reached over to take his arm and comfort him. She watched awkwardly as tears ran down his cheek.

"I am sorry Claude. I did not mean to pry. If you loved her I am sure she was a very special person."

"I cannot change what happened. I must go on in life. Maybe one day I will find new love."

Martine regretted asking the question and steered the conversation to another topic.

"Claude is it hard to learn the wine business. There are so many different species of grape and processes."

"I am still learning. Through Barry's Australian connections we have been able to hire an excellent vintner for our bold reds. Barry worked in the business in Australia. For our white wines and some reds, we hired a French vintner with years of experience. We are always concerned with the quality of our product."

She listened to Claude but didn't hear him. Her emotions were racing. He was everything she had wanted in a man…attractive, educated, funny, caring, and rich. She wondered what it would take to win his heart.

"Claude, I believe it is time for us to start our dinner. Everything is ready. I will let you choose the wine."

She laid down the appetizer of garlic escargot. Claude selected a white burgundy. They sat and enjoyed the escargot and wine.

When they were finished, Claude rose to bring his Chateau Briand to the table. He set it down and returned to bring the Parisian potatoes and fresh asparagus. He carefully carved the meat onto their plates and poured a rich Bernaise sauce over the meat, before pouring them each a full-bodied Cabernet.

"Claude that looks wonderful. You are an accomplished chef."

The meal was exquisite. Claude was pleased with his efforts to impress. After they had finished, they sat sipping their wine and talking. Claude looked at his watch. Hours had passed.

"Martine, can I use your phone? I need to call the Chateau and advise Barry I will be staying in Paris tonight. It is too late to return now and I have had a little too much wine today."

"Certainly. It is over there by that couch on the shelf of the side table."

He called the Chateau and asked to be connected with Barry. The servant who answered advised Claude it would be a few minutes before he could get Barry to the phone. Claude waited until Barry's raspy voice came on the line.

Claude explained he had run into an old friend and was staying the night in Paris. Barry wasn't fully convinced.

"I reckon it's that Sheila you met at the Hyatt in San Francisco. You are such a dumb bastard at times. You can't see straight for that pecker of yours blocking the view."

"Thanks, Barry. I will see you in the morning."

Upon returning to the table, he found his dessert had been served. A custard-filled millefeuille, A cheese plate was at the center of the table containing Camembert, Brie, Reblochon, and Vieux Boulogne, and a bunch of fresh green grapes.

After dinner, they retired to the oversized couch in her living room. Martine dimmed the lights and selected more soft music. After an hour Claude wanted to leave.

"It is late and I must find a hotel room for the night. This afternoon and evening were fun. We should plan to do it again. Maybe you would like to visit the estate. We have guest rooms."

"Claude, don't be silly, I have another room here. You are welcome to spend the night here."

"Thank you but I will need to leave early in the morning and I do not feel it is right."

Martine moved toward him on the couch and rested her head on his chest.

"Claude, please do not go. Please stay the night."

She reached up and draped her hand around the back of his neck and drew him toward her. She lifted her face to his and kissed his lips. It was a long simmering kiss that left no doubt of her intentions. Claude attempted to pull back but found his emotions and lust had taken over.

"Martine, I cannot. You have been another man's wife."

"Claude, I told you he was a manipulating monster. We never consummated the marriage. I never had a sexual affair with him."

Martine reached up to his shirt collar and slid her hand inside his shirt and flicked open the buttons. She rose on her knees and drove her hands over his chest, and finally dropped them down to his belt. She reached below his belt and felt his firmness. She threw her head back and looked directly into his eyes as she smiled. Claude had a look of passion in his eyes. Martine dropped her hand further and squeezed his erection. Claude reacted. He stood and lifted her from the couch and proceeded to her bedroom. He gently lowered her onto the bed. Martine smiled and put her finger to her lips.

"Claude, There is something I must do."

Martine left the bed and entered the small bathroom. Minutes later she returned. Claude was dumbstruck. Martine stood in front of him wearing the finest French undergarments. Her bra was pink silk lined with black lace and her panties were brief and matched the bra. Claude reached out to her and she responded by lowering herself onto him.

Martine sat on his chest and stripped away his clothing. She recalled his physique from the hospital when she had bathed him and later exerted herself on him. She admired every inch of his body. Claude rolled her onto her back and immediately commenced kissing he neck and dropped his head down to her breasts. He reached her shoulder and flicked off the strap supporting her bra. He kissed and gently caressed her erect nipples with his soft lips before sliding his hand down to her panties and pushing them down her long slender legs. Martine smiled and quietly moaned in delight. Claude moved further down her body kissing her stomach until he reached her golden zone. Martine shuddered with pleasure and called out his name. Claude mounted her body and the unbridled passion began.

There was little sleep as they coupled and shared the passion of the night.

Claude awoke late. He looked at his watch and was surprised at the late hour. He swung himself out of bed and pulled on some clothes before leaving the bedroom. He found Martine on the balcony dressed in a long white robe and drinking a coffee.

"Good morning, my lover. I didn't wake you as you looked so rested and comfortable. Let me get a coffee for you and you can join me."

As Martine stood and turned her robe opened. Claude stepped forward and hugged her. His arousal was fast and within a minute they were back in the bedroom, naked and embroiled in continued passion. Martine wiped small beads of perspiration from Claude's forehead as they both lay expended.

They lay quietly until Martine suggested they take a shower together. Claude wondered whether he would be able to perform in the shower and decided against the proposal.

"Martine, I must call the Chateau. I had expected to have returned there by now. There will be a concern."

"Alright. I will take a shower. You know where the phone is. Please be here when I have showered."

Claude stood alone thinking. Even though he enjoyed Martine's company, he was experiencing a feeling of being in a sensual trap. He did not wish to be caught up in a serious affair and commit. He needed to find a way to leave Martine gently and extract himself.

Part 7

Digging Deeper

Chapter 27

de Passioné Chateau

Barry watched as the taxi pulled up at the entrance of the Chateau and Claude climbed out. He observed Claude's unshaven face, haggard look, and crumpled clothes. There was no guessing as to what Claude had done the previous evening. Barry shook his head. Even with the danger of the Triads looking for Claude, he continued to live a reckless lifestyle. Barry wondered who the woman was that Claude had 'entertained' for the night.

Claude dragged himself up the steps and into the Chateau and joined Barry in the living room.

"Good morning, Barry"

Barry made a marked point by holding his watch up in front of his face and looking at it in an exaggerated way.

"I guess it's still morning. Just. Crikey boy, you look like shit. I hope she was worth it. I guess at your age, those nocturnal adventures are getting beyond you. Do us all a favor mate. Go wash and clean up before the staff sees you. When you come back you might want to call that guy from the French Consulate in San Francisco. He's called here twice looking for you."

Claude left to go to his room, shower, and change into new clothes. While he looked haggard, the night had invigorated him. Ten minutes later he rejoined Barry.

"Barry, have you made a final decision on returning to California? I think you are more valuable here, plus the authorities recommended you would be safer here."

"I'm a big boy. I can look after myself. I'm thinking that this might be the ideal time for me to nip off to Australia and visit my old mates and family. I doubt those Chinese pansies will come looking for me there. I don't even know why they are interested in me, seems you are the one that they want."

"I have been thinking about everything that has happened. I am convinced that this has something to do with Misty Moon. I am going to contact her and try to end all this. The more I thought about the smuggling of arms and drug trafficking, she is the one person I know involved with those gangs in China. I need to ask her why all this is happening. It may be naive on my part, but it's worth trying."

"You got to be stark raving bloody mad to do that. She will lie and mislead you. Look, these guys aren't playing around. Consider what they did to Little Jimmy Deng and 'Snoops'. You would just be setting yourself up. These are major players. We have Russians, Chinese and other mobs here in Europe who she could enlist to find you. Claude, are you sure there is nothing you have that they so desperately want?"

"There is nothing. I have gone over things. In my mind, I have even gone back to those days as a student when I took that job at the Art and Antique shop in Paris. I cannot recall any gifts or items I have been given."

"OK. I'm heading out with the guy we hired from Oz. Seems we grew up in the same area. He wanted to discuss some ideas for a varietal wine. Sounds interesting. Of course, nothing will get decided until we talk and discuss it with our distributors. We may be able to provide samples as he wishes to produce a test run. We are going off for a lunch and I expect we will be back in the late afternoon. Don't forget to call that guy at the French Consulate. I left a number by the phone in your office."

"Enjoy your lunch. I will be here. I have some family business to attend to this afternoon."

Barry stomped off out of the room. Claude found the Chateau quiet. Normally there were sounds of the staff moving about doing their jobs and Marie-France pursuing one of her new interests. He shrugged and went to his office to phone the Cultural Attaché of the French Consulate in San Francisco.

In his office, he punched in the numbers Barry had scribbled on a piece of toilet paper. He listened as the phone rang at the Consulate. It rang continuously until Claude remembered the nine-hour time difference. He hung up and wondered why the Attaché had been calling at an hour that would have been late at night. Claude decided that before working on the legal and administrative matters for the family, he would take a nap after his strenuous night.

He went to his bedroom and fell onto the bed and within minutes was in a deep sleep. Claude was awoken by voices coming up from the rooms below. He heard Barry's thundering voice. He looked at his watch and was shocked to find that it was seven in the evening. He got up from his bed and took a quick shower before changing into some casual clothes for the evening.

Dressed and refreshed, Claude went down to the living room where he found Marie-France sitting with Barry.

"Oh Claude, I have some great news. Buzz is going to visit us. He is going to fly over on Friday. I am so anxious to see him."

Claude looked at Barry and raised his eyebrows.

"Don't blame me Claudy boy. I just spent the last half hour telling her that it is not a good move on her part. We have enough problems."

"Claude, he was rude to me. He raised his voice and at one point was shouting. I'm surprised he didn't wake you up."

"He did."

"Buzz is my friend and I will look after him. I will take him to Paris and visit the places he told me he wants to see. I will ask one of the drivers to take us."

"Mother, I just want to be sure you will be safe and that Buzz is who you think he is. Do not object, but I am going to have him checked out."

"If that is going to make you happy and stop your doubting, then go ahead. I'm tired of the way you and Barry have been behaving recently."

Claude looked at Barry who nodded.

"Mother, we need to have a long talk. There are a lot of things happening that you should be aware of."

Claude sat and took Marie-France's hand and told her everything that had transpired since the shooting. When he had finished, Marie-France looked at him and frowned.

"So tell me, Claude, what's the problem?"

"The problem, Mother is that someone is trying to kill me and possibly you and Barry. They are in pursuit of something. I have no idea what it is. You must be extra cautious. These are really bad people."

"I'm not worried. My Buzz will protect me."

Claude was exasperated.

"Let's all go and have dinner. I have work to do tonight."

Claude summoned a staff member and advised him that they would soon wish to have their dinners in the dining room. The man acknowledged the request and asked them for their desired meals.

When they had finished their dinner, Claude returned to his office. He looked at the time and calculated that he should be able to contact the people in California with whom he needed to speak. He took the paper with the number the Attaché had given Barry and punched in the number. The phone rang twice before it was answered by the same humorless receptionist. Claude identified himself and requested the call be put through to Denis Ricard.

Denis answered the call and was happy to hear Claude's voice.

"Claude, I hope you will be in France next week. I am going to be visiting on official business. I also have some private matters to look after. Would it be possible for me to visit and we can discuss the order for the wines that we will serve at our upcoming event?"

"Of course. Please remember I extended an invitation to you to come and stay at the Chateau with us. How long will you be in France?"

"The official business will only take a few days. I arrive in Paris this Sunday, so by Wednesday I should be free."

"I will inform our house staff to prepare for you. Will you need transport to the Chateau?"

"No, I will have a staff member drive me. I will call you after my arrival and update you."

Claude hung up, pleased that he would have a guest that would detract from the ongoing tensions that were building. He picked up the phone again and punched in another number. The phone was answered on the first ring.

"Good morning, Mattar and Mattar Law Partners."

"Good morning, It is Claude de Passioné. Please connect me with Al Pine."

"One moment please."

Claude waited on the line for what seemed an eternity. Finally, a voice boomed through the phone.

"Good morning, Claude. It's Bob Pritchard-Jones. Can I assist you?"

"Sorry to disturb you. I had asked to speak with Al Pine."

"Claude, unexpectedly, Al Pine announced his retirement from the firm and the practice of law. He has not been in the office this morning and attempts to reach him have been unsuccessful. I would like to arrange a meeting with you to discuss our ongoing business relationship. If you wish we can come to you or alternately you can visit here. We value your patronage and will be here to assist you in all matters."

"I am in France at our vineyard. I am not sure when I will return but will contact you. In the meanwhile, I have an urgent need. My mother is involved with a man with the given name of Buzz Kutz. He operates a company that is a flying school, a sky diving operation, and provides aerial services. The name of the business is 'The Descenders Skydiving and Flying School'. He must be licensed in the State. It should be easy to find him. I need a complete background check. Credit info, criminal, personal, divorce…the whole profile, and I need it fast."

"I will personally oversee this request. You can be assured of complete discretion. I have a question for you. I understand you and Barry Jones were here at the office and working with Al Pine on some matter. It seems as if the files in his office are missing. Can you tell me what the matter was that you were working on?"

Claude sensed a problem. For the senior partner to not know work that was being performed for the firm's largest client did not seem correct. He decided to keep the matter private. Something was not right. Surely Al Pine would have told Claude of any plans he had for retirement, and why did it happen so quickly and unannounced?

"It was nothing of significance. Just some regular state filings and export issues. Nothing too exciting. I will await the results of your investigation into Buzz Kutz."

"Please provide me with a number to contact you."

Claude provided his number in France. After he hung up he sat and reflected on the conversation. It was unlike Al Pine to just disappear. He had known Al for years and shared some of their most confidential information with him. It seemed too coincidental for him to retire without warning and then disappear. Claude wondered about Al's relationship with 'Snoops'. He wondered if there was more to the relationship than he knew. He decided to take another approach to find out about Buzz Kutz. He picked up his phone and called Paddy O'Regan.

Paddy listened to Claude's request and the information about Al Pine.

"Paddy, something is not right. Too many strange things are happening. Can you assist?"

"If I find anything that is of importance to you I will let you know."

Claude realized he had just been stonewalled by Paddy.

"Thank you, Paddy. I appreciate your assistance."

Chapter 28

Paddy O'Regan sat back in his chair and thought of all the recent incidents that somehow seemed linked. He had long had his doubts about 'Snoops' and had gone as far as starting an internal investigation of him. He rose and went to an old grey filing cabinet at the rear of his office. In it were the files he had started but were incomplete. These were not the normal files associated with most crimes such as break and enters, murders, theft, and other offenses in that category. The files contained information on politicians, high-ranking government members, and the San Francisco area's crime bosses.

Paddy removed his wallet from his jacket and extracted the key to the cabinet. He withdrew three folders…Little Jimmy Deng, 'Snoops' Dugan and Al Pine.

He returned to his desk and spent the next several hours poring over the files. He was sure there was a common factor that had been overlooked. He could find nothing that linked the three to any crime, but an interesting observation had been made by the Surveillance Team. They had observed Al Pine in several meetings with the leaders of the Mah Tong gang. When confronted and asked about the meetings, Al Pine had begged off stating it was privileged information and they had retained him for some legal matter.

Paddy returned to the file on Little Jimmy Deng. There were pages and pages of gang perpetrated events and photos of opposing gang members who had been killed, but not a shred of evidence that tied him to the crimes. Paddy started writing a list of the dates of the murders. He had an idea.

He turned his attention to the file that Internal Affairs had started on 'Snoops' Duggan it bothered Paddy. No one had investigated or explained the fortune that 'Snoops' had amassed. Paddy had asked him and was informed it was from land and real estate holdings his family held and after their death, it passed to him and he sold off most of it. Paddy had maintained a false friendship with 'Snoops' hoping that one day he would make a mistake or say something to give his game away.

Paddy looked at the limited financial data that the Internal Revenue Service had provided to the police. It was scant. Paddy decided he needed more, but his authority as a San Francisco cop was limited. He picked up the phone and called the State Attorney's Office only to be advised that he had left for his fishing lodge for the weekend, and if the matter was urgent he could be reached.

Paddy decided the matter could wait until Monday. As he replaced the files, another thought hit him. Who was Barry Jones? Claude had met him at a bar and the friendship had developed over the years, but Paddy knew little of him. He decided it was time to check Barry Jones out. Was Barry involved in any shady dealings?

Paddy logged his dying computer into the Central Police Network. After entering his police authorization credentials he was able to access the multi-state database of felons. He entered Barry Jones. Immediately pages of data lit up his screen. Paddy realized he needed to refine the search, but he did not have any further information on Barry Jones. He remembered that Claude had made him a partner in some of the businesses. The corporate records would contain more information.

Paddy accessed the corporate records database and searched under Barry Jones and also added de Passioné Wineries. There was an immediate hit. The information Paddy was looking for was displayed on the screen. **Barry Alan Jones, Born 1968, Sydney,**

Australia. More on file. Paddy scanned the record and then returned to the Central Police Network where he entered the information. Minutes passed before he received a response, then it came:

Subject:

Barry Alan Jones, Born December 1, 1968. to Henry Trevor Jones (carpenter) and Philomena Silva (housewife) Wollongong, Australia.

Arrest record:

June 5th, 2015

Stopped in New York City by Traffic Officer, Charles Rolston. Offense: running a red light. Jones resisted and argued with the officer.

Arrested for disorderly conduct, resisting arrest, and threatening an officer.

Paddy read on and roared with laughter when he read the details of the offense. Barry had advised the officer 'that he would never develop hemorrhoids as he was a perfect arsehole.'

The description fitted. Paddy thought back to the times he had met Barry. He clicked off the computer satisfied Barry was not involved.

There was only one other person to check and Paddy intended to visit Al Pine at his Pacific Heights home in the morning. He checked his watch and was startled to see it was past seven in the evening. Paddy's week had been frustrating and tiring. He decided he needed relief and a Jamesons at O'Malley's would relax him. He reached for the phone and called his Irish Colleen. She was his one true love and mentor. He had been with her for fifteen years and proposed to her at least thirty times, and each time she refused him.

"Colleen, I'm beat. I have been here working on an old file. I would love it if you could join me at O'Malley's and after we can go for dinner."

She agreed to meet him. Paddy went across his office to a small dresser and removed his civilian clothes. He stripped off his police uniform and quickly dressed to go and meet with his love.

Paddy opened his office door and exited into the main administrative area of the precinct. He was surprised to find his assistant, Jenny Chin still working at her desk.

"Jenny, what are you still doing here? Everyone has left for the day. Why are you still here?"

"I stayed because you were working and I thought you may need help."

"No, Jenny. I am just reviewing some old files. Now it is time for you to leave."

As Paddy walked away from the precinct, he recalled the words Claude had used when he thought there was a leak in the department, and when the young cop had muttered the words 'cop killer' after the bodies of Jimmy Deng and 'Snoops' were discovered bound together.

Paddy's mind was still processing the situation of 'Snoops' and Little Jimmy Deng when the nagging thought hit him. He wondered whether Jenny Chin could be the leak. He quickly dismissed the thought.

Paddy arrived at O'Malley's to find Colleen already there and waiting for him. She was radiant. Her red hair highlighted her peaches and cream complexion. Paddy considered himself a lucky man.

He had met Colleen on a trip to Dublin, Ireland and she had followed him to the states after a short and intense relationship. Neither had ever wanted anyone else. It was true and unconditional love.

"Paddy, you look tired and worried. Why are you working those crazy hours? Surely there must be younger detectives who can take over."

"Colleen, it's the experience. I have been following the deeds of many of these criminals for years. The new guys know nothing of the criminals and the past horrors they have caused."

"I ordered you your favorite drinks..a Jamesons and a Harp Ale. After we have our drinks, I'm taking you for dinner at one of the touristy restaurants on Fisherman's wharf. We can dine on fresh crab and other seafood. After that, we will go back to my apartment. You look too tired to be driving the long distance to your home."

"That I won't argue about."

"Will you consider retiring when this case is over?"

"Yes. I have already been thinking about what is next for me, and possibly us."

Colleen blushed and reached to kiss him.

After they finished their drinks, they sauntered off to the Randy Crab on the wharf and acted like tourists for the rest of the evening. Paddy felt the pressure lifting from him like a veil being removed.

Chapter 29

Colleen did not wake Paddy. After the long and passionate night, she decided to let him sleep. She gently left the bed and went to her little kitchen to make a coffee and prepare breakfast for them.

While the coffee was brewing, Colleen went and showered. She dressed in casual jeans and a shirt for her Saturday shopping trip in the market and went downstairs to her front door to pick up her Saturday copy of 'The San Francisco Star and Chronicle'. As she climbed the stairs back up to the kitchen she flipped open the paper and read the large bold headlines.

Prominent San Francisco Attorney found dead in his Pacific Heights residence.

Colleen paused to read the opening paragraphs of the report. There was little detail. The article stated that the news was breaking as the paper went to print and details were yet to be released by the police.

Aware that Paddy was working on several recent homicides, she decided to wake Paddy and show him the news.

Groggily, Paddy awoke. Colleen handed him a coffee and then the paper. The reaction was immediate. Some of Paddy's best Irish curses filled the air. Colleen watched him.

"Jesus, Mary, and Joseph. It must be Al Pine. I was planning on interviewing him at his home this morning. I need to dress and go back to the station immediately. No, let me call for a duty officer to pick me up and drive me to Pacific Heights."

Paddy dressed and gulped down his coffee. A young plainclothes detective arrived within fifteen minutes. Paddy kissed Colleen and promised to call later in the morning.

"Morning, Paddy. It's a great way to start Saturday. The guy's name is Al Pine. The station received an anonymous call around midnight. It looks like a suicide. Found in his swimming pool with his wrists slashed. There is a farewell note."

"Is the coroner there? Has he indicated whether he believes it is suicide?"

"It's too soon to draw any conclusions. There are some detectives on site going through the house. They called about an hour ago and requested the forensics team. Seems they may have found something."

"Tell me what you know about the person who called in the report of his death."

"The desk sarge took the call. It was over before he could get it recorded. He said it was a young-sounding female voice."

"Get me a meeting with the senior partner of Mattar and Mattar, Mr. Bob Pritchard-Jones. We are going to need more on the cases that Al Pine was working on and also the cases where the firm used 'Snoops' Duggan. If he refuses, then we will go to court and get an order compelling him and the firm to disclose the information."

The mention of a young female voice triggered a reaction in Paddy. Again, he thought of Jenny Chin.

They drove on to Pacific Heights and Al Pine's large home. They stopped outside the front. It was magnificent. Located on a rise that afforded a full view of the bay. Lush gardens surrounded the home and stands of tall Eucalyptus trees bordering the property. Several police cars were parked on the street in front of the home and the black coroner's van had been reversed into the driveway.

Paddy left the car and was surrounded by reporters calling questions.

"It is too early to comment on the situation here. We are not releasing any information at this time. There will be an official statement released later at the precinct."

He headed to the front door. Before he reached the door, one of the cops from the patrol car directed him to a side gate and a path that lead back to the pool.

Al Pine's inert naked body lay exposed on the pool deck. Paddy recognized the coroner as Dr. Janus, a humorless and dour person.

"Good morning, Doctor. What do we have here? Is it suicide?"

"It's too damned early in the investigation to say either way. All I will say at this point is there are enough things to make me suspicious but until there is an autopsy, we won't know for sure. I need the forensics people here fast. I need them to document and photograph some items of concern. Time will diminish certain evidence on the body. I hope they get here soon."

"How long has he been dead? Can you estimate?"

"From the rigor mortis and gelling of the blood, I would say he died at least as early as yesterday evening."

"Have you been inside the house?"

"No. I am waiting for the forensic team. I didn't want to disturb any evidence if there was foul play."

Minutes passed and the team arrived. Dressed in disposable white barrier clothing, masks, and gloves with blue boot covers. Paddy knew the leader of the team and was pleased to see it was him. The man was fastidious.

A member of the team walked to the pool and spoke with Dr. Janus. Photos were taken and the body moved into different positions. Close-up pictures of Al Pine's wrists were taken. Another member lowered a sterilized bottle into the pool for water samples.

"Why are you taking samples from the pool?"

"We will do a chemical analysis to determine whether the water in his lungs is the same. If not there is a chance he may have been murdered elsewhere and the body dumped into the pool."

Paddy watched as two assistants to Dr. Janus picked up the body and lowered it into a black body bag. They stood and proceeded to the black van with their grim cargo.

Paddy was tempted to enter the house, but the thought of contaminating a crime scene dissuaded him. As he stood alone considering what actions to take, one of the younger patrol cops approached him.

"Lieutenant, can we leave. We have been on this shift for over fourteen hours and we have another shift tonight."

"I see nothing can be achieved by your being here, so yes leave. Thanks for your work here,"

Paddy was about to leave the scene when a member of the forensic team called to him.

"Lieutenant, there are some things here we have discovered that may be related to all this. There are boxes of legal files. I think you need to view them. Let me get you some protective clothing to wear. We don't want to introduce any foreign matter onto the scene."

Dressed in the standard white coveralls and boots, Paddy entered the house. He walked through the house, slowly observing the state of each room. In the living room, he was astonished at the number of bankers' boxes stuffed with legal files. Each box had an alphabetical letter identifying the clients' names for the files in each box. Paddy proceeded to pull out the boxes labeled with a 'D'. There were several. He casually flipped over the file folders in each box. The only folders were for Duggan and Deng. Paddy realized he had hit pay dirt. He assumed the boxes would contain the evidence he had been searching for over the years. He asked for the head of the team to have the boxes photographed as they were found and to carefully seal each box for delivery to the station.

While inside the home, Paddy decided to do a little of his own investigating. He walked into every room on the ground floor and then the rooms on the second floor. The house was filled with trophies for sailing, golf, and motor racing. There were also awards for philanthropy. Paddy was saddened but not surprised at the hypocrisy of the wealthy benefactor, whose real activities were disguised by the elaborate front he had established. He wondered how the de Passioné family would react to the situation. He then remembered Claude's urgent request for a complete check on Buzz Kutz and decided to return to the police station to initiate the investigation.

Chapter 30

de Passioné Estate, France

Claude and Barry were in Claude's office when a servant arrived with the news that there was an important call for Claude in the living room. He explained it was a police officer from the States. Claude naturally assumed the call was regarding Buzz Kutz.

He signaled Barry to join him and quickly ran down the stairs to the living room.

"Claude, here. How are you, Paddy? I hope you have news for me."

Claude went quiet as Paddy told him of the death of Al Pine under suspicious circumstances. Claude asked Paddy to wait while he filled in Barry on the latest development. Barry held his finger to his lips.

"Claude, tell him we will call him back. We need to see how this will affect our business in the States."

Claude arranged to call Paddy back after an hour.

"Let us discuss this development. This may impact our operations in the United States if confidential business information has been leaked from Al Pine to some of these parties. We need to know if we are vulnerable. It seems we are unwitting participants in some deadly schemes. What we thought were normal business relationships have turned out to be otherwise. Our wine exports have been used as fronts by the Russians and Chinese for international criminal activities. We need to know if the US government will attempt to implicate us. I suggest we use our high-level political contacts to assist us. We will need attorneys with political connections to help us. With all this happening, I am going to cancel my trip home to Australia."

"Barry, it's not necessary for you to cancel. I can handle things here. I will keep in contact."

"Bloody hell, mate. Do you think I'm going to walk away at a time like this? No way."

"Barry, I insist you go. We must go about our business and lives as if things are normal. I am sure our actions are being watched. I intend to find out who has used us to this extent."

"Claude we had no issues until you got yourself involved with that Misty Moon sheila. I just don't understand why she has created all these problems. Why is Al Pine dead? Where did 'Snoops' Dugan fit into the game? It is obvious to me that there was huge money involved within that international crime syndicate. I am concerned that the FBI may decide to investigate us and seize bank records for the companies and our own personal accounts. No, mate. I'm not going back to Australia until all this calms down and we get answers, so accept you are stuck with me."

Claude knew that Barry was right. The extent of the discovery of the activities of the crime syndicate that had been uncovered would likely draw the FBI, Interpol, and other International police to investigate. Barry was correct in suggesting they needed to hire some powerful and politically connected help.

"I may not agree, but maybe you should stay until we know what actions are going to be taken. I don't want you getting detained in Australia or elsewhere. I suggest we immediately plan a return to California and take action to protect ourselves and the company. I am going to track down Crystal Moon and get her real story. She's the one with access to Misty Moon and she seems to be involved in all the gang-related activities. I need to know more about her and those she is involved with."

Claude sat back and stared absentmindedly into space as he thought of the time he had spent with Misty Moon and what he had discussed and done with her. He could not recall anything that had led to the attempt on his life. He tried to recall any conversation with her in which she mentioned her younger sister Crystal Moon. He drew a blank.

"Barry, I think we need to contact Paddy and request his help. Although this expands beyond just San Francisco now, I am sure he can arrange to put us in contact with the right people."

For the next hour, Claude and Barry sat and turned over past situations to understand what had transpired and their plan.

"Barry, I need to stay and look after some business here. I suggest you return. I will be fine here with Marie-France, plus I have a guest arriving after the weekend. It is Denis Ricard from the Consulate in San Francisco. He will be selecting wines for some events they are planning."

"This is damned annoying. I had arranged a weekend of fun with that young French girl I had met at the French Consulate in San Francisco. She is coming here in advance of Denis Ricard to arrange logistics for him. I'm quite taken with her."

"Barry, it's nice to see you are appreciating our French culture and beauty."

Claude laughed but ceased as Marie-France appeared in the room. He gasped. He had seen her wear strange clothes in the past, but this was beyond bizarre. She swirled and the bright orange and green toga spun up into the air revealing black fishnet stockings and gold boots. Her somewhat plump legs and lily-white abdomen momentarily flashed.

Barry's mouth hung open.

"Do you like it? I bought this today for when Buzz arrives and we go for dinner and dancing."

"Mother, I don't think that would be an appropriate dress to wear to dinner. I'm sure Buzz would like a smart sophisticated style. That outfit is more for a hippie festival. It's very nice but wrong for your date."

Marie-France pouted and started to sulk.

"Why not sit down and join us in one of our award-winning wines. Which would you enjoy?"

"Claude, you have become the expert. I will let you decide."

"I suggest our 5-year-old Sauterne. I will have a bottle served with a cheese plate and fresh grapes."

Claude was pleased with the distraction and left to find help in the kitchen. As he left, Barry gave him a look of desperation.

Chapter 31

Claude and Barry sat in Claude's office and placed the call to Paddy O'Regan. The call was answered by a receptionist who wasted no time in getting them connected to Paddy, whose booming voice came onto the line.

"Top of the morning to you. I hope you haven't eaten too many of those snails over there."

"Paddy, there's a nine-hour difference between California and here. While you are eating your doughnut and slurping coffee we have put a full day's work behind us. It's seven at night here now."

"Well good to hear from you too, Claude. You sound nice and moody today. What's up that's ruffled your feathers?"

"Paddy, we have been discussing the situation with all that has happened. We are most concerned as Al Pine had confidential materials relating to the de Passioné businesses. Those papers mustn't get into the hands of the gangs. It will open us to extortion and blackmail. Can you get the files and seal them? Will a court order be required? I do not want them ending up in the hands of the FBI or any other authority. I also ask you to seize all records at the law firm of Mattar and Mattar that Al Pine had. Can you do that?"

"It will not be easy. I will attempt to obtain them as critical to the investigation, but you will need to proceed to court to get them sealed. Who will be representing you now that Al Pine is dead?"

"Pritchard-Jones, the senior counsel at Mattar and Mattar has been in contact. I have lost confidence in that firm and we will be investigating a new firm to handle the affairs of the de Passioné businesses. I will advise you who we select."

"You may want to speak to me before you make a final decision."

"I will do that. Where do things stand in the investigation?"

"We have determined that Al Pine was murdered and someone attempted to make it look like a suicide. Coincidentally, there has been a marked increase in warfare between the gangs we know are involved with drug trafficking and other illegal activities. Seems we have some new players here who are not known to us. There is one that will be of interest to you. A young woman who goes by the name of Crystal Moon. I believe you had some interaction with her. Expect to be asked about that. She has a partner we are especially interested in. His name is Vu Mai. He is known on the street as 'Blood Eyes' due to the way he kills or maims his enemies, by gouging out their eyes. He is vicious and active with Crystal Moon in local gang activities. He is a dangerous criminal. Very few in either the Vietnamese gangs or the Chinese will mess with him. We are arranging detailed surveillance of Crystal Moon. The heavyweights from Washington are moving in and taking an active interest. I suspect they will be knocking on your door very soon. We have been dealing with the local police in your county regarding the attempt on your life. They have no real information. We are convinced that there is some item or information that is in your possession, Claude. It must be very incriminating for them to seek you out."

"Paddy, I have thought about this. There is nothing I can recall. I was shocked when the information on Wendy Wong, who calls herself Misty Moon, was disclosed to me. Do you know what Crystal Moon's real name is?"

"No, she was unknown to us up until these recent events."

Claude looked across at Barry, who had been fidgeting since the mention of Crystal Moon surfaced. Barry was angry that he had been manipulated by her into believing her story.

"Paddy, this is Barry. Is it possible to get records from Immigration on her travels and anything else?"

"I can request that, but we are moving out of my jurisdiction. I will need to get the Feds involved."

Claude stayed quiet and considered this news. Finally, he spoke.

"Paddy, I am going to stay here in France to attend to some business matters. Barry is intending to return to California and I ask that you provide him with the necessary protection. I expect to return with Marie-France in the next couple of weeks. Of course, I am available to assist and cooperate with the authorities. I ask you to keep the de Passioné family business out of press releases for the time being. We do not yet know what we are dealing with."

"Claude, that will be difficult. The press has already linked Al Pine's high-profile clients to his death and the mystique surrounding it. I will try, but I cannot promise that."

"Paddy, we are sharing all we know with you, but I sense there are things you are not sharing with us that are important. What is it you are concealing?"

There was silence for minutes until Barry intervened.

"Christ mate, we're sort of all in this bloody mess together. Seems to me this could either make or break your retirement. If you want me to assist, then play it straight."

"Barry, this is a developing situation. During the early investigative stages, we get lots of tips. Most are dead-end or guys taking us for fools. I've told you all we know at present."

"I don't think you have. Seems to my Aussie intelligence that you are a bit too evasive about old Al Pine there. So, what's the real story?"

Again the phone fell silent. Paddy's confident voice faltered when he answered.

"Yes, there is more. Other than the business relationship he had with 'Snoops', we discovered he was involved in a sex cult that is controlled by the gangs we are now investigating. It seems that Crystal Moon was the boss. We have evidence that the girls were trafficked here from Asia. We are still investigating Al Pine's role. We are unsure if he was just one of the high-priced clientele, or if he played a role in the money laundering and subversive crimes."

Claude groaned and dropped his head into his hands.

"Oh, how could we have been so stupid to miss all of that? He came to the estate as our guest. Never once did we suspect he was involved in anything other than events of San Francisco's wealthy society. He always seemed so proper and law-abiding.

This makes it all that more important to get our company information from the firm and sealed by the court."

"Claude, I will speak with our legal counsel and contact you. We must be careful how we proceed."

"I will advise you when Barry will return to California. At the moment, he is giving me a look as he has a date with a pretty young thing tonight."

"Claude, before we disconnect, I must tell you the check on Buzz Kutz is complete. It makes for good reading. His father was an industrialist with many factories in the Hudson Valley area in New York. He made components and products for companies such as IBM, General Motors, Boeing, and other large companies. When he died he was still the sole shareholder of the companies and left everything to his son, Buzz. His inheritance was huge. He has no criminal record, his military record reads like that of a paperback hero. Your mother has nothing to worry about with him. He may appear rough, but he is a solid guy."

"Thank you. That will make it easier when he arrives to stay this weekend."

"I must hang up this call as there is a briefing on the latest in the Al Pine investigation. If there is anything important, I will contact you. Goodbye."

Claude turned to Barry and observed his partner and friend before he spoke.

"Barry, we have a lot of work to do if we are to survive this."

"Yes, I agree. Now I must leave to meet Yvette. Don't wait up for me as I'll probably be late. See you in the morning."

Laughing, Barry reached for his jacket and headed to the door. On the way he encountered Marie-France.

"Barry, I expect you to be nice to Buzz when he arrives this weekend. He's more of a man than you will ever be."

He was about to respond when Claude called out for Marie-France. She scowled at Barry and turned to join Claude who was descending the stairs from his office.

Part 8

The Gangs react

Chapter 32

Oakland, California.

In the empty warehouse next to the shipping docks, Vu Mai sat at the head of a long table with several members of the Mah Tong gang, along with members of his own private gang. Vu's bodyguards stood blocking the exit as well as two standing behind him. Each had an M4 carbine hanging loosely in their hands. The M4s were prizes from a military shipment the gang had hijacked a year earlier.

The warehouse was dark and swirls of cigarette smoke drifted upward to the overhead bare incandescent overhead lights. The place was dank and smelled of death. Many of Vu's opponents and enemies had met their fate in the warehouse.

Vu looked around the table at each gang member. He had memorized what each one of them had been involved with. Each had been responsible for multiple murders. Vu was under no illusion that if he showed any weakness in leadership, one of these gangsters would take him out in a bid for leadership. As head of the gangs, he enjoyed immense riches from the crimes. He decided that he would soon retire and disappear into populous Viet Nam and live in anonymity. First, he had a mission to complete. He needed to find the item in the possession of Claude de Passioné. He would not rest until he had it. If the gang members around the table knew it was missing, his hold over the gangs in San Francisco would be greatly diminished. Only his most trusted lieutenants were aware that he was looking for a personal item. None knew its real significance.

Vu addressed the gathering.

"We are meeting here today as things are getting out of control on the streets. Too many of those who are linked to us have been killed. The cops are getting too close to our operations. I am ordering all of you to cease the killing and fighting between the gangs. If it continues I will command my men to kill anyone who disobeys me. We have some shipments coming in the next weeks that must not be interrupted. The containers from China will arrive here and be loaded into this warehouse. The contents will be removed and the arms for the mid-East loaded into the containers to be shipped. None of you get any ideas as the warehouse will be armed like a fortress by my men. You will each get your allocation of the drugs based on your payment."

Around the table, there was a murmur as the gangsters exchanged questions. Vu and his bodyguards spun and looked to the door as it banged open. He was relieved to see it was Crystal Moon. He had feared the news of the meeting may have been leaked. Crystal walked briskly to the table. Her eyes took in each person sitting at the table. She stopped walking and fixed her eyes on one particular person. As she stared at him he lowered his head to break the gaze. In an instant, she drew a semi-automatic pistol from her jacket and fired. Bullets ripped into the man. Blood and parts of his head splattered the others at the table who had ducked for fear of being shot. She kept firing into his torso. Satisfied she walked to Vu and kissed him on his forehead.

"In case any of you forget I am the boss. What just happened will remind you not to play games with me. Vu, get your boys to remove that garbage from the table."

Two heavily armed bodyguards proceeded to heft the remains from the chair at the table. As they lifted him his body fell apart where the bullets had cut him in pieces. One of the bodyguards retrieved a shovel leaning against the wall and scraped body parts off the floor.

The stench of escaping gas from the dismembered body and intestines caused several of the gangsters to choke back vomit.

Crystal took a seat next to Vu and assumed control of the meeting.

"OK, now to resume the meeting and discuss our business. I need to make plans. There is a container arriving here next week from the Philipines. It is a special container that was modified to ensure its cargo was not spoiled during shipment. There are twenty-four Asian beauties available. Who wants to start the bidding?"

The meeting took on the feel of a regular auction. Bidders were outbid by others. Obvious resentments between different gang members became obvious. When the exchanges became too heated, Crystal laid her gun in front of her on the table.

The auction was over in minutes and Crystal took each suitcase presented by the buyer and had the cash removed by the bodyguards and checked to ensure it was not counterfeit and placed into a metal case. With the counting completed, she ordered Vu to accompany the guards and move the cash to a safe in a secure office in the warehouse.

She waited for Vu to return before continuing the meeting.

"Our shipment of cocaine is confirmed. We have set the price. There is no bargaining. The demand is high. Place your order and payment and you will be given a time and location to pick up."

Several gang members pushed back from the table and left a small group to conduct their business. Vu watched each of them and noted who was not buying. He was convinced there was a leak in the group and had decided to trace it. He leaned over and whispered his concern to Crystal.

Crystal looked at each of the members not participating and recalled each one's gang activities. There was one that worried her. He was the uncrowned boss of a run-down drug-infested district in Los Angeles and she had expected a high level of interest from him. Something did not appear right.

Within minutes the shipment was sold. The details of each purchase were recorded. Contact information was provided to advise the buyers of the pickup location.

Crystal stood to leave. As she did so, she leaned and whispered into Vu's ear. He looked at the gangster from Los Angeles, then summoned his bodyguards.

The meeting was over. The gang members left the warehouse and walked to the collection of high-end vehicles parked on the pier. None stopped to speak to each other. It was strictly business amongst the untrusted.

Vu walked out and watched as the cars pulled away. He smiled as he saw his two trusted lieutenants follow and knew the car and its occupant would never make it to the airport for the trip to Los Angeles. Vu smiled as he contemplated how he could move into the Los Angeles gang scene after the kingpin was removed. He had always fancied Los Angeles and the addicted Hollywood stars. He considered them better customers than the rich young engineers of Silicon Valley. He thought of the Hollywood actors as idle and vacuous targets for the drug and sex business. Vu thought of the unlikely patrons for the girls. He laughed at the absurdity of it. The customers for the girls were powerful business executives, members of society, and the extremely rich. Vu assumed they could probably buy their way into anything, but instead chose the cheap little whores from Asia.

With the Los Angeles gang leader eliminated, he resolved he would have Crystal recruit some local gang members and establish a powerful presence in Los Angeles. He would not bend to the Latinos or Blacks. He intended to dominate.

Vu stayed and watched until the last car pulled away. He noticed a black Mercedes parked off in the distance. He had never noticed the car parked at the docks previously. He stood and observed the car. After several minutes it slowly made a U-turn and left.

Vu returned to his small armed and secure office in the warehouse. His 'accountant' was at a desk totaling the money the various gangsters had deposited for their drug allotments and the girls imported as sex slaves. The 'accountant' placed each gang member's payment in envelopes and labeled them. He was thorough, but sadistically cruel and delighted in enforcing punishment on anyone who omitted to pay their dues to Vu and Crystal.

As Vu reclined on a luxurious leather chair, Crystal returned and entered his office. She seemed agitated.

"Vu, my source in the police informs me that there is a special task force assembled to investigate us and the deaths of Al Pine, Dugan, and Jimmy Deng. She tells me we are under surveillance and observation. I am concerned that we have not retrieved our property from that Claude de Passioné. If the authorities get that information, not only will we be exposed but also all of our international networks. We must get Claude de Passioné before it is too late. He knows too much."

"Crystal, if they had that information, we would know. They would have taken action. They have not. I do not think it wise to kill de Passioné as it will result in them intensifying their investigation. I suspect de Passioné is unaware of what he has in his possession. For the time being, we will continue without making any changes. They will assume that we are just a local gang."

Vu sat with Crystal and told her of his plan to take over the operations in Los Angeles after the demise of its leader who he assumed had turned and was cooperating with the authorities. Fortunately, the LA gangster was unaware of the full extent that Vu and Crystal's activities encompassed. Crystal listened intently and was excited to have the opportunity to establish a group to wage street warfare to establish gang leadership. It had been a while since she had seen action on the streets.

Chapter 33

de Passioné Estate, France

The week passed without any incidents. Claude tended to the administrative business with the winery, while Barry oversaw issues with the operation of the vineyards.

After the turmoil of California, the relative calm seemed surreal. Claude wondered when the next crisis would arise. Barry continued to date Yvette from the French Consulate and Marie-France bubbled with excitement at the pending arrival of Buzz. She had planned some special events to surprise him and had kept them secret from Claude and Barry.

Claude glanced up at the antique wall clock. It was approaching six in the evening. The time Buzz's arrival was expected after his ten-hour flight from San Francisco. Claude tidied up the papers on his desk and went to freshen up and sit with Marie-France until Buzz arrived.

He sat in the salon with Marie-France enjoying a bottle of their latest Chardonnay. He was pleasantly surprised to see that Marie-France had dressed in clothes that were somewhat conservative for her, yet flamboyant to everyone else. The pink ruffled chiffon blouse revealed her sagging breasts and the skin-tight shiny white leggings and yellow high heels accentuated her well-rounded thighs.

Dusk was setting in when the taxi pulled up at the entrance. Marie-France accelerated her portly frame at astonishing speed to greet Buzz. Claude followed at a saunter. He did not want to see Buzz smothered in the unbridled passion of Marie-France who would surely throw herself at him.

Buzz jumped from the taxi with energy that surprised Claude. Even after the ten-hour trip and the hours spent at the airports for security, customs, and boarding processes, Buzz seemed fresh and alert, dressed in designer blue jeans, Gucci loafers, an Egyptian cotton pale blue shirt and, a tan suede jacket. He rushed across to Marie-France and lifted her into the air in a strong embrace. Claude looked on in amusement. He was pleased to see Marie-France with a stable character.

"Welcome to the estate, Buzz. Marie-France has been looking forward to having you join us. Let me get a servant to take your luggage in and up to your room."

Buzz, Marie-France, and Claude climbed the stairs at the entrance to the mansion and went and sat in the living room.

"Buzz, I am sure after that trip you would like to take a shower and freshen up. We are having a special dinner tonight to welcome you. Barry and his latest paramour, Yvette will be joining us."

The small group stood talking for a while until a maid arrived to assist Buzz to his room and provide him with toiletries for his shower. She handed him a thick terry cloth bathrobe and left.

Buzz relaxed as he showered and looked forward to the week ahead. He strategized on how to tell Claude and Marie-France of the plans he had. It was to be a surprise.

Dressed, Buzz joined the others in the drawing-room where pre-dinner drinks were being served. Barry crossed the room and slapped Buzz on the shoulder.

"Gd'day mate. Bloody good to see you even if you are a Yank. I guess you're going to go off and see the sites."

"Well, I do have some plans and there are some people I need to see here. Possible business opportunities."

Yvette sidled up beside Barry and nudged him.

"Buzz, this is my sweet little Sheila. A French girl from around these parts. You can ask her about what things to do or see."

Yvette gave Buzz a flirtatious look and smile. Her interests seemed to be changing.

"Monsieur Buzz, it will be my pleasure to spend some time with you and assist you in planning some trips."

Barry was too busy squashing a fly that had landed on the camembert cheese to notice the flirtation, however, Marie-France was preparing to sabotage the little coquetry. She launched herself toward them.

"Why Yvette, you look....I need to search for the word. I am sure that Barry could tell us as he's from Australia and they have all those nasty bugs and snakes there. Yes, you look like a piece of nature."

Barry turned from picking the dead fly out of the camembert and spoke.

"Marie-France, I think you mean she looks like a Cockatoo. Damned pretty birds but they squark a lot."

Yvette's face reddened and her temperature rose.

"Barry, take me home immediately. If you won't I will call for a taxi. I did not come here to be insulted by that bitch, who herself looks like Dorothy from The Wizard of Oz in that ridiculous outfit she is wearing."

That comment was enough for Marie-France. She reached to the table and decorated Yvette's pretty face and hair with the fly-infested camembert.

Not to be outdone, Yvette grabbed the plate of crudities and dressings and decorated Marie-France.

Claude stood with his mouth open watching the spat, while Barry attempted to push himself between the women. Yvette broke away and ran to the door weeping. Barry followed her in hot pursuit.

Claude walked up to Buzz and rested his hand on his shoulder.

"Welcome to Crazyville, Buzz. That was unplanned. Not quite the entertainment we had planned for this evening."

"After that trip from San Francisco and bored on the plane, that was very refreshing."

Marie-France approached them. She was dripping dressing from her forehead. Carrot sticks and asparagus spears protruded from her cleavage, while broccoli flowers bobbed around in her hair as she moved.

"Claude, you will instruct Barry to never bring that little whore to my house again."

Marie-France spun on her heel and left to shower and change into clothing suitable for dinner.

"I guess it will just be Marie-France and us for dinner. Barry is smitten with Yvette. I doubt he will return soon."

Thirty minutes passed before Marie-France returned. She had dressed in a silver sequined dress. She had washed and styled her hair and applied new makeup. No sign of her spat with Yvette remained.

No one spoke of Yvette or the confrontation. A servant entered the room and announced dinner was to be served in the main dining room. Claude was relieved. He wished for dinner to be over so he could retreat and leave Buzz and Marie-France to each other's company.

It was late when the dinner concluded. Claude excused himself and left. As he climbed the stairs up to his bedroom, he heard the phone in his office ringing. He turned and walked down a couple of steps and into his office.

"Hello. Claude here."

The voice of Paddy O'Regan crackled through.

"Good evening, Claude. We may have more information on the case. As I told you, the Feds are all over it now. There is only so much I can do now. They have set up sophisticated surveillance systems. This is far more than just local gangs settling scores. It turns out that the Feds had turned the leader of an LA gang and he attended a recent meeting here. Unfortunately, he has been found executed to demonstrate to other gang members not to betray Vu Mai or Crystal Moon. You will be pleased to know we have been able to secure your company records and files from the law firm Mattar and Mattar, along with records from Al Pine's home. We were lucky to have a sympathetic judge grant the order to seal everything for the de Passioné businesses. There is, however, some worrying news. This afternoon the Feds tracked two of Vu Mai's trusted men. They boarded a plane for France. I urge you to be very careful and maintain a low profile. The French security force and Interpol have been alerted. We suspect they are coming after you."

"I expect to return to California in about a week or so. I have completed my work here and there are things at the vineyards in Napa that need my attention. I will probably not be in contact with you until it is time to leave, or if something major happens. I expect you to do the same if anything develops."

Chapter 34

Breakfast at the Chateau was a casual affair. Claude found Marie-France and Buzz already sitting on the garden patio.

Marie-France was dressed in a Safari outfit with heavy black hiking boots and Buzz wore casual, but expensive shorts and a shirt. A sweater was hung around his neck.

Breakfast was a relatively simple affair with fresh fruits, toast, and eggs benedict. Champagne from the neighboring district was served with the meal.

"Claude, Marie-France, I have a special announcement I wish to make."

Immediately Claude became concerned. He wondered what Marie-France had trapped Buzz into.

Marie-France dropped her napkin and stared at Buzz in anticipation.

"I have a surprise for you both. I have hired a canal barge and for the next week, Marie-France and I will be cruising through the wine districts."

Marie-France squeaked in delight and jumped to kiss Buzz.

"We will start our cruise in Paris and then travel through Champagne to Burgundy and the Loire. We may be gone for more than a week. I have hired a private barge so Marie-France and I can be alone and enjoy each other's company. I am looking forward to sampling great wines and food at the locations we will visit."

"Buzz, that is great. I am sure it will be most enjoyable. I do have a diplomatic guest visiting soon. My time will be taken up with his visit, so this is good news. His visit is business. When will you leave for the cruise?"

"We will drive to Paris later this morning."

"No, I will drive you into Paris. I need to do some business there, plus I want to get away from here for a while. Let me know when you wish to leave. I will change clothes and pack an overnight bag as I may stay with a friend."

Marie-France looked across at Claude and scowled.

"Don't let Barry bring that little tramp into my house while we are gone. She is no good. I know the sort of woman she is. He would be better off without her."

"Mother, I don't think you can talk. I recall some rather questionable situations you were involved in while father, the Marquis, was still alive."

Buzz observed the interchange and decided it was time to change the subject. He was determined to calm Marie-France before their trip.

"I have done a lot of research to plan a memorable trip. I have a list of wineries and restaurants we will try. This should be an adventure. The barge I have reserved for us is 'Le petit oiseau bleu'. It is meant to be one of the most luxurious. I will be the captain for the week and sail the barge. I am looking forward to sailing through the locks and different canals."

Marie-France was relaxed. She stood and kissed Buzz on his cheek.

"I am going to go and pack some of my best clothes for those events, but also casual outfits for the cruising."

Claude wondered what she would possibly wear. The other boaters would be exposed to her distinct fashion statement.

Buzz was pleased to have some time alone with Claude. He wanted to ask questions.

"Claude, what is happening with the police investigation? Has there been any new development?"

Claude briefly updated Buzz. He wondered why Buzz was so interested and if Buzz was in any way involved with the events of recent. He recalled how Marie-France had met Buzz. None of their relationship made sense. Buzz was extremely wealthy and could have attracted many cultured women of standing in society. There was the possibility in Claude's mind that Buzz had ulterior motives. It was the first time that Claude had any suspicions of Buzz but quickly dismissed the thought as he recalled Paddy O'Regan's report on Buzz.

"Buzz, you had mentioned some possible business interest here in France. Is it something I may be interested in participating in?"

"Until I meet with some folks I do not know. I will certainly inform you."

Claude knew not to question Buzz any further, plus his mind was wandering to the evening date he had planned in Paris that evening. He recalled the passion he had shared with Martine, yet was worried about her possessiveness. He enjoyed her company but did not like to feel trapped. He was conflicted about whether to call her for a date or prowl for a new friend.

The shrill ring of the phone snapped Claude out of his pensive mood. He grabbed up the phone and after answering listened to hear Barry's voice.

"Good morning Claude. I am still angry with the performance that Marie-France created last evening. Her behavior was unforgivable. I am not sure I will be able to be civil when I next see her."

"Barry, you know how she is, besides today, she is leaving for a week to cruise the canals of France with Buzz. Where are you now?"

"I am at Yvette's hotel in Paris. I will return this afternoon."

"I am driving Marie-France and Buzz into Paris. Which hotel are you at? I will meet you. We can have a late lunch. I am planning on spending the night in Paris."

" I am at Hôtel de Fleurie."

"I do not know that hotel. Where is it located?"

"It is located on Saint-German-des-Prés, in the 6th Arrondissement."

"Ok, I will find it. I should be there in about two hours."

Claude gathered up some clothes and packed them into a small case. He called to Buzz and Marie-France to hurry as he now had an appointment in Paris.

Claude waited at the foot of the stairs and was amazed at the amount of luggage Marie-France had the servants carry down. Claude thought to himself that most people would take less on a world trip. This was a casual one week trip on a barge.

Buzz appeared minutes later with several shirts and trousers hung from coat hangers. When he saw Marie-France's luggage he was in disbelief.

"Marie-France, we are only going for a week. Do you need all that?"

"Buzz, as you know I take great pride in my clothes and appearance. There will be no one dressed as exquisite as me at any restaurant or location we visit. It is important to me to maintain my image and of course my beauty for you, my love."

Rather than argue, Buzz shrugged and Claude instructed the servants to load the luggage into the Peugeot he had rented.

He watched as Buzz escorted her to the car and assisted her to the rear seat. Unfortunately, there was too much luggage to fit in the trunk and several bags were placed on the seat beside her. She was indignant.

Buzz smiled. There was no alternative for him other than to sit in the front beside Claude for the trip.

Claude cranked the engine over and finally, the little car sputtered to life. He dropped it into gear and the car lurched away, the tires emitting a yelp as they spun on the sealed driveway.

Chapter 35

Chinatown Police Precinct, San Francisco.

Paddy O'Regan paced in his office. Federal law enforcement had assumed control over his investigation and he felt cast aside. He watched as the DEA, CIA, FBI, agents from the Treasury, and the Alcohol Tobacco and Firearms agency sat in a meeting in the conference room. Paddy was furious he has been excluded.

Paddy decided he would leave and find a 'greasy spoon' for a quick lunch when the phone on his desk rang. In his dark mood, Paddy contemplated not answering, however, curiosity got the better of him. He snatched up the phone and barked into it.

"O'Regan."

He listened without comment to the caller. Without uttering a word, he hung up and grabbed his jacket before continuing on his way out to lunch. As he walked the litter-strewn streets of Chinatown, Paddy calculated the number of days until his retirement and his move to San Diego, where he intended to buy a fishing boat and take tourists on day trips.

His thoughts were shattered by several nearby gunshots and the splintering of the glass windows of the store he was passing. Instinctively, he drew his Glock and rolled to the ground. There was no doubt in his mind that he was the intended target. Crowds ran screaming in all directions. Paddy scanned the chaos but failed to identify who may have fired the shots.

Paddy recalled the phone call he had received before leaving the office and the death threat delivered in that call. He had become a target.

As he climbed to his knees, two uniformed cops rushed toward him, with their guns drawn. They assisted him to his feet. Rotting cabbage and other remnants from the bags of garbage outside the Chinese restaurant hung on his clothing. Paddy's mood worsened and he vowed revenge, starting with an all-out assault on the gangs no matter how small their infractions were. He shook off the hands of the cops helping him and spun around to hurry back to the precinct.

He stormed into the station and ignored the comments others shouted at him about his appearance. First, he went to his office and removed his coat, then to the locker room where he stripped and showered. He dressed in just his coat and bundled up his clothes to take to the one-hour laundry. He decided against venturing out onto the streets dressed in just a coat. He summoned Jenny Chin and asked her whether she would help him by taking the clothes to the laundry. Jenny sensed his mood, and rather than argue agreed to help.

Paddy sat back at his desk and again watched the men and women in the conference room. Several large whiteboards had been provided. There were charts and arrows drawn on them. He decided that because of the shooting, he was going into the room. Before he would take action against the gangs he needed to inform the Feds.

With unkempt wet hair and dressed in a trench coat he opened the conference room door and pushed his way in. Silence fell as the occupants stared at him. A senior FBI agent stood and queried Paddy.

"What the hell happened to you? You can't just barge in here. We are strategizing a coordinated plan to deal with the mess you and your officers have uncovered. We will provide a full briefing to you and the other senior officers."

" There was an attempt to kill me minutes ago. I think you need to know that and include me. I am planning an aggressive clampdown on the gangs. What just happened is in my jurisdiction."

"That would not be wise. We do not want to disrupt them at this time. We need them to continue with their activities and not suspect anything. We are establishing a surveillance center here. Technicians from Intelligence in the CIA will be arriving here. We will need space to establish the operation. We will be monitoring phones, access to banking, offshore communication, and all shipping activity and documents. We are going to need your assistance. Until we had a plan there was no point in including you in the meeting. Now it is different. We are going to break for lunch now. After lunch, we will meet again and your participation is invited. Hopefully, by then you will have some clothes."

The assembled men and women laughed as he exited. Paddy's mood worsened as he realized he had been belittled. He decided that tonight would be a night at the Anchor Steam Bar with Colleen. He was tired of the police work and dealing with the underbelly of society. Tonight at the bar he would ask Colleen to marry and move to San Diego with him. The thought of San Diego and running his fishing business with her improved his mood.

His thoughts were interrupted by the buzzing of his desk intercom. He pressed the button to answer.

"Paddy, there is a detective here from San Jose. He's asking to speak with you."

"OK. Escort him up."

Paddy was surprised when a tall, willowy blonde was shown into his office.

"Good afternoon. I'm Ingrid Johansen. I am the lead detective in San Jose for the investigation of gang-related crime. There has been an incident involving a well-known gangster from here. I understand you have an active investigation underway concerning this person and the gang he controls here in Chinatown. He is dead. The victim is Skinny Lam. There was a shot out near the private aircraft hangars at San Jose Municipal airport. There is another victim as well. It is Benecio Fernandez, the leader and unofficial 'king' of the eastside Los Angeles gang. He had been cooperating with LA police and had become an informant. His cover in LA had been blown, but we don't understand why the gang in your district is involved. We fear a gang war has started and it is to take control of other locations. With Fernandez gone, there is no leader in LA. We have been watching Vu Mai and his mob. They have been very active in San Jose but we have not been able to apprehend them in the process of any crime. We have placed undercover men in maintenance positions at the airport as there has been a marked increase in private jet flights that are being used by the gangs. We wish to cooperate and share information."

Paddy sat back and swiveled in his chair. With his hands folded on his lips.

"I'm sorry, but our investigation has exposed some significant information. I am no longer in control. If you look through that glass window into the conference room, you will see Federal agents from all the agencies. They are taking over the investigation. You will need to address them."

Ingrid stared through the glass window and observed the meeting.

"Please get me introduced."

Paddy stood and escorted Ingrid to the conference room door. He knocked loudly before entering. The assembled group of agents turned and stared at Ingrid.

" I would like to introduce Lead Detective Ingrid Johansen from San Jose. She has come here with information that I believe you should be aware of."

The group listened and made notes as Ingrid told them of the investigation that was ongoing in San Jose. When she had finished, a senior agent spoke.

"Later we will be providing a briefing on our joint agency project. Until then, we request that you do not take any actions that may tip off the gangs. This investigation is huge and not only does it involve us here in the States, but many other countries. We will be working closely with Interpol. Please leave your contact information, and when appropriate we will ensure you are invited to the presentation."

Ingrid too, realized she had been dismissed.

Paddy and Ingrid left the room and stood awkwardly wondering how they could proceed.

"Ingrid, let's go someplace away from here and have a coffee. I have a lot to share with you. It will help you understand why that Federal task force has been assembled. First I need to see if my clothes have been returned after an incident that occurred here a few hours ago."

Ten minutes later, Paddy returned attired in his freshly laundered clothes and escorted Ingrid out of the precinct and to a local coffee shop.

For the next hour, Paddy told her of the investigation he was running and the deaths that had occurred. He told her of the puzzling situation with Claude de Passioné. Ingrid sat and absorbed the information like a sponge.

When he had finished she told him of the investigation in San Jose. It was obvious that there was involvement by the same gangs in both areas.

" I will be most interested when those Feds provide the briefing."

She handed a card to Paddy and stood to leave.

The numbers on this card are direct secure cell numbers. They ring directly to me. Goodbye, and thanks for sharing the information. I hope to see you soon."

Part 9

Romances

Chapter 36

de Passonié Estate, France

The week had been quiet for Claude with Marie-France gone from the Mansion. Barry had spent time working with the vintner and on some administrative and marketing issues. There had been no discussion of the troubles that Claude was facing. It seemed that things had almost returned to normal.

Claude was relaxing in the living room and reading the news when the glint of sun reflecting off a car flashed through the windows. Claude stood and looked down the long driveway as a classic vintage limousine drove up toward the Mansion. Claude frowned. He was not expecting any visitors. He called out to Barry who was working in the office upstairs.

"Barry, we have visitors. Are you expecting anyone?"

"No, but I'll be down in a minute."

Claude continued to watch the slow approach of the beautiful vintage white 1956 Excalibur limousine. The car turned and stopped at the entrance stairs. A uniformed chauffeur quickly walked back and opened the rear door. Claude was surprised to see it was Buzz, who exited the vehicle and turned to and extend his hand to assist Marie-France from the car. He was smiling and Marie-France was beaming with joy.

Barry joined Claude and whistled in appreciation when he saw the limousine.

"That is an elegant ride. I wonder what that is all about. Let's go out and meet them."

Claude did not need much convincing, as he wished for a closer look at the limousine and its interior.

As they started down the stairs Marie-France ran across to embrace Claude.

"We had such a great time cruising the canals and stopping for visits to different wineries and restaurants. I want to do it again."

Claude looked over to the limousine to see Buzz handing the chauffeur money. Marie-France and Buzz's luggage had been carefully placed at the base of the stairs and one of the servants of the house was already taking the cases up and into the house.

Claude joined Barry and they engaged the driver in a discussion about the Excalibur. The driver was proud and only too eager to show off the vehicle. He lifted the cover to the engine compartment and then allowed Claude and Barry to sit in the rear. They were as excited as schoolboys.

The driver started the vehicle and was about to drive away, but stopped. He told Barry and Claude to sit in the rear and he would drive them out to the main road and back to the Mansion.

Upon their return, They found Buzz and Marie-France in the living room laughing. Claude frowned when he saw the ice buckets of champagne and the best crystal champagne flutes arrange on the table. He looked at Marie-France.

"What is this all about? What is the occasion?"

Buzz roared laughing before walking up to Claude with an extended hand.

"Claude, I am here to ask for your mother's hand in marriage. Meet your stepfather. You are will be my stepson. Marie-France and I are getting married."

Barry stood looking on in disbelief. He was still annoyed at Marie-France and how she had treated his friend Yvette. He turned to Claude and then turned to Buzz.

"You must be bloody nuts. I guess too much wine along with the sun has fried your noggin. I'm not sure that old girl's got many miles left in her. She's pulled the wool over your eyes, mate."

Barry spun and stormed out of the room, as Buzz glared at him.

Claude was dumbfounded and unsure how to react to the situation.

"I guess congratulations are in order. When and where will the happy event take place?"

"We haven't decided on a date yet, but we are thinking of a beach wedding, probably on a Caribbean island. Buzz has some ideas and we will be checking out the islands. I am going to need time to plan the event and of course to design a magnificent wedding gown."

Claude could only imagine the wedding gown she would design.

"Mother, I am very happy for you. Of course by your getting married this will have an impact on the business concerning ownership and other legal issues. We will need to discuss this in detail. As well, I am concerned about you and Barry. You were wrong to criticize his friend Yvette the way you did. Please find some way to apologize for your behavior. I need Barry to assist more than ever, given the recent troubles we have had."

Before Marie-France could respond, Buzz interrupted.

"Claude, we will prepare a legal document that will exclude my involvement or ownership interests in the Wineries or Vineyards.

Similarly, you and Marie-France will be excluded from any interest in my businesses. Of course, we can review that arrangement at a future date. My only interest is the friendship and love I have for this incredible and beautiful woman."

Marie-France sat beaming from ear to ear. She had truly caught her man.

Buzz opened and poured the champagne. Claude was not happy.

"Mother, I am going to get Barry to join us. Please find some way to apologize. We do not need dissension between us."

Marie-France slowly nodded and Claude left to find Barry. As he was walking past the phone, it rang. He picked up the receiver and within minutes smiled.

"Bonjour, Claude. It is me, Denis Ricard. I am here in Paris and have completed the work that required my attention. If it is convenient I would like to come to stay from this afternoon. Is that convenient?"

Claude welcomed this development as it would provide an alternative to the wedding and the interpersonal issues that had developed recently.

"Yes, certainly. How will you get here? Do you know what time you will arrive?"

"I will have a driver from the office take me. I expect it will be around six this evening."

"I look forward to your visit."

Claude hung up the phone and turned to Marie-France and Buzz.

"I have a special guest coming this evening. He will be staying with us for the next few days. Now I am going to get Barry and get the matter between you and him resolved."

Marie-France started to speak, but Buzz placed his hand on her arm and interjected.

"I think that is a good idea. Let's get Barry to join us and get this matter solved."

From the look on Marie-France's face, she was not happy with having been manipulated.

Claude returned minutes later with Barry. It was apparent Barry's mood had not improved. He glared at Marie-France. Buzz broke the silence.

"Let's be civil and calm. Marie-France has issues with Yvette. Maybe you should tell Barry why. I am sure that once he understands, this matter will get fixed. Once we get this over with, we can celebrate our upcoming marriage and welcome Claude's friend. Claude, who is this friend?"

"Barry, I am sorry for that outburst and my reaction to that Yvette. I was watching her. I know women like that. She is no good for you. She will take every possible advantage of you. It is unfortunate that men are so stupid and cannot see when they are being used. Barry, I watched her making subtle moves on Buzz. You are just a convenient moment in time for her. I apologize to you, but I did not want to see you get used and hurt by her."

"Marie-France, I appreciate your concern, but I am old enough, big enough, and ugly enough to look after myself. We Aussies aren't stupid when it comes to sheilas."

Recognizing the conversation with Barry was over, she turned and directed questions to Claude. She, like Buzz, was curious.

"Claude, who is this Denis Ricard? You have not spoken much about him. Is he a nice man?"

"Denis is the Cultural Attaché for the Consulate in San Francisco. We have met on a few occasions. He happens to be in France and is coming here for the weekend partly for pleasure and partly for work. He has requested assistance in selecting wines for an event the French Consulate is hosting in San Francisco for business leaders. Barry and I will assist him in selecting wines. I have asked our vintner to be present this weekend to provide information to Denis."

They continued talking for a while, waiting for the arrival of Denis. Buzz and Marie-France told Claude and Barry of the adventures they had experienced on their canal cruise through the wine districts.

Chapter 37

The last light of the day cast long shadows across the front gardens of the Mansion. Denis looked from the car window at the magnificent setting and how the Mansion was situated amongst the sloping vineyards. It was a picture-perfect scene.

The driver slowly drove down the long tree-lined driveway to the house. Denis noticed Claude waiting on the bottom stair. While Denis was pleased to be visiting, he had a concern. He needed to diplomatically find a solution to the conflict between Marie-France and Yvette. He needed her with him, as she was responsible for handling the logistics of the supply contract, ordering, shipping, and transferring funds for the purchase of the wines.

Yvette had told Denis of the nasty exchange that had taken place, during the drive from Paris. Until he could discuss the matter with Claude, he had arranged for her to stay at a nearby small hotel. He was sure the issue could be dealt with quickly and she could join them during the weekend.

Claude walked forward and opened the car door and reached inside to shake Denis' hand.

"Welcome to Chateau de Passioné. You have arrived at an excellent time. This evening we are having a small celebration. Come. Let me get you settled. I will have someone bring your luggage to the room."

Denis climbed from the car and stretched. He cursed to himself that age was creeping up on him. A few years earlier he would not have stiffened up during such a trip.

"Claude, it is my pleasure to be here. Last week at the Ministry was hectic. I am looking forward to this break from the insanity of overseeing France's cultural affairs in the States. It seems everybody has something to comment on or recommend. Too many involved."

"You needn't worry. This weekend we will sample some of our best wines and the chef has arranged some fine meals and brought in the best local cheeses for you to sample. There won't be any politics for you to worry about here."

"Claude, I do have a political matter to solve here. Please assist me. I have been informed of the nasty argument between your mother and my assistant, Yvette. I would like to get the damage repaired. Yvette is an important part of assisting with the purchase of the wines and planning the event in San Francisco. She was to accompany me here to take details and handle the subsequent relationship between the French Government and de Passioné Estate. I have left her at a small local hotel for this evening. Can you assist?"

"It may be possible. The timing is good. My mother has just been proposed to by her partner. She is in a great mood and very happy. Tonight we are having a special dinner to celebrate. I suggest you wait until she gets to know you and when appropriate I will mention it. I will try to control the discussion. Don't worry as I'm sure we can solve everything. The one I am concerned about is Barry. He is treating it as a personal insult. He will be thrilled, however, to know that Yvette is here."

Together they ascended to stairs and entered the Mansion. Claude led Denis to the living room where Marie-France and Buzz were sitting and talking excitedly about the wedding plans. Claude introduced Denis. Marie-France was ecstatic to have a diplomat staying at the Estate and selecting their wines.

She fell silent and gazed at Denis. She sensed a familiarity with him, but could not place where or when she had met him previously. It perplexed her.

After the introductions were made, Claude assisted Denis to his suite on the second floor. Denis was amazed by the décor in the expansive room.

"Please take your time to settle in, then come down and join us. I will let Barry know you are here."

Claude found Barry in the office, hunched over a pile of papers.

"Barry, I have some news for you. Denis has arrived for the weekend. He is freshening up and will join us downstairs in the living room. I request that you join us. Marie-France and Buzz are excited and happy. They have not stopped talking about the upcoming wedding. It has given my mother something to focus on."

"Claude, with all due respect, mate, I am not feeling particularly fond of Marie-France at the moment. I reckon she destroyed any possible relationship I could have had with Yvette. She was a perfect bitch."

"Yvette is here. Denis has put her at a nearby villa and intends to clear up the matter with Marie-France. Yvette has an important role in selecting the wines and planning the events in the States. I think when Marie-France realizes that she will soften. Furthermore, it will probably be of less importance now she is preoccupied with planning for her wedding. I am asking you to come and join us. You are too clever a man to allow that spat to destroy a relationship or allow it to work to the detriment of the business relationship we will have with the French government. Come and help make things right."

Barry stood and leaned against the wall while staring at Claude.

"And if things get worked out, then what?"

"Denis has requested she stay here over the weekend to assist him. I am sure she will have time for you. If we can solve this immediately, I will ensure she joins in the celebratory dinner tonight."

"Alright then. I will come down in a few minutes. Just need to finish a few things with these accounts and I'm done for the weekend. I must warn you that if Marie-France continues or does not apologize, I will not be staying around for any dinner. I find the whole thing very bizarre. I reckon that Buzz guy should go and get his marbles checked. I'm not sure what he sees in her."

"Barry, she is my mother and no she is not perfect. There are times when I wonder how her eccentricities allowed her to get this far in life. I often wonder what she was like when she met my father, the Marquis. He was always pursuing beautiful women. What was Marie-France like as a young woman? What did he see in her?"

"Claude, don't tempt me, mate. You may not like my comments. Let's drop the conversation."

Claude left Barry to his work. He returned to his private room and placed a call to Paddy O'Regan.

The phone rang for a long time before Paddy answered. He did not sound happy.

"Paddy, have there been any developments?"

"Claude, I am no longer at liberty to discuss the case and the FBI has assumed total control. I do not get informed of the latest. All I can tell you is that there is something huge at play. They have installed a surveillance set up here in the basement. The equipment is the latest and most sophisticated. The security at the precinct has been increased. We have security guards at the entrances and no one can just walk in. They built a completely secure area for that equipment. There are technicians wearing headsets, computers set up, and a bank of video screens. There are special eavesdropping systems. It's like a movie set. In addition to our people, we have international guests here. Several Interpol and more from Asia. The center operates all day and night. None of our detectives or regular cops are allowed down to that floor. Armed FBI agents guard and control who enters the basement."

"I wanted to advise you that Barry will be returning to California soon. He is planning a trip to see friends and relatives in Australia. I will probably take a vacation then. My mother has decided to marry Buzz Kutz in a moment of weakness. He seems a good guy. I hope for her sake it all works out. She has been much calmer since he entered her life."

"Claude, have there been any more strange things happen there in France?"

"No, it has been quiet. No more unexplained things happening."

"Should anything of significance happen here, I will inform you. Keep well. I must go as I have a meeting to attend."

Claude left his room and went down to join the others in the living room. He was pleased to see Barry sitting and talking to Buzz. Marie-France was standing next to the large white marble fireplace chatting to Denis, who had dressed appropriately for the special dinner, in a midnight blue velvet suit accented by a hot pink ascot tucked into a brilliant white dress shirt. On his feet were Giorgio Brutini loafers with an intricate design matching his suit.

Claude stood at the door and quietly observed the conversations. After a few minutes, Denis waved Barry to join him and Marie-France. The conversation between the three of them was animated with the gesticulating of hands and the placing of hands on each other's arms. As he watched, Marie-France went forward and hugged Barry. It seemed the storm had passed. Barry looked over at Claude and raised his thumbs.

Minutes passed and Barry broke away from the group and approached Claude. He was beaming.

"Hold the dinner, mate. I'm off to get Yvette."

As Claude walked over to speak with Buzz, he heard the roar of Barry's old truck race up the driveway as Barry left for Yvette.

Chapter 38

Yvette was nervous and apprehensive to enter the Mansion and face Marie-France. Barry assured her all would be fine. They entered the house and joined the others in the living room.

Marie-France came forward and hugged Yvette and offered an apology for the scene she had created. She inhaled the sweet scent of the Anais Anais perfume that Yvette was wearing. Little did Yvette know of the revenge Marie-France was planning.

The atmosphere was calm. Conversation flowed freely. There was no hint of any adversity. It was a perfect evening for the dinner to celebrate the announcement of Buzz and Marie-France's upcoming wedding. A server entered the room and announced dinner was ready to be served in the formal dining room.

Over dinner, Denis spoke of his career as French Cultural Attaché in San Francisco. Everyone was intrigued by his stories. Again Marie-France sensed a familiarity with Denis but was unable to remember why she should feel this.

As dinner progressed, Buzz commandeered the conversation and told of their trip by barge through the canals of the wine district. Denis was intrigued and expressed a desire to do the same.

With the dinner finished, the group returned to the living room.

Barry had consumed a little too much wine and his bravado surfaced.

"Where are you and Buzz going to tie the knot? Here in France or somewhere exotic?"

"It was going to be a surprise for everyone and Marie-France, but since you asked I will share it. I have made inquiries and have a plan for the happy occasion. We are going to be married and honeymoon in Aruba."

Barry looked puzzled.

"Where the hell is Aruba? Do they still wear grass skirts and the men hunt?"

"No Barry. It is a small but sophisticated island in the Caribbean not far from Venezuela. It's part of the Dutch Kingdom. I have been there on vacation and assisted a small aviation company to start its business. I enjoyed my time there and the people. The climate is great. It's only 12 degrees from the equator, beautiful white sand beaches, and turquoise ocean."

"Sounds like an ideal place. Maybe I will visit there one day."

"You certainly will, as you are one of my guests at the wedding. I am hoping that Claude will agree to be my best man."

Claude was stunned. He had not expected to be asked to participate.

"It will be my pleasure. Do you know when this event will take place? I will have to return to California very soon."

"There are several business matters I need to attend to before we marry. I am thinking it will be at least two months from now. There are people to invite and I need to make arrangements to accommodate my guests on the island. I have contacted the Hyatt Hotel to discuss arrangements."

Marie-France had watched and listened to Buzz's conversation with Barry. She walked over to Yvette and took her wrist and spoke.

"Yvette, to show how sincere my apology to you is, I would like you to be my maid of honor. I will be delighted if you accept."

Claude was finding it difficult to accept the bizarre events of the evening. He looked at Barry, then at Yvette. It was obvious she was in shock.

Denis Ricard had watched quietly. He sensed the undercurrent that flowed between different people and was equally confused by Marie-France's invitation for Yvette to be maid of honor. He felt awkward and as if he was intruding in a family affair.

"Everyone, I would like to excuse myself and retire. I need to spend some time speaking with Yvette regarding some consular matters. I wish to thank my kind hosts for a memorable evening."

He turned to Yvette and addressed her in French. Before they could leave the room, Barry spoke, his wine-fuelled bravado still evident.

"Not bloody likely, mate. She's with me tonight and I have some important things to talk to her about. I'm taking her away from this zoo to spend some private time. There is a little wine bar that is nearby. Come, Yvette. Let's leave this asylum and enjoy a little time together."

Yvette was torn. She looked at Denis then at Claude, unsure what she should do. Claude spoke.

"Yvette, it is alright for you to go with Barry. I understand you both need a little time together. Besides, I would like to spend time chatting with Denis."

Barry gathered up her jacket and assisted her to put it on.

"Good night everyone. We will return later. See you all in the morning."

Buzz stood, stretched, and yawned.

"I am going to finish the evening and must leave now. I am tired after our trip and need to sleep. I have a long drive back to Paris. I will return later tomorrow."

"No Buzz. We have a guest room that you can use. I will not allow you to drive back to Paris at this hour and in your tired condition. Marie-France can show you the room. If you need anything, Denis and I will be sitting here talking."

"That is very kind. Yes, I am extremely tired and appreciate this."

While Marie-France assisted Buzz to the guest room, Claude went to the antique sideboard and removed a bottle of cognac and two glasses. He returned to the couch and sat across from Denis. He poured the cognac and both toasted.

"Denis, I am sorry you had to witness that. Things can get a little strange around here at times."

"Hey, don't worry. I too have a family with wrinkles."

Claude was most interested in Denis' position as Cultural Attaché at the French Consulate. Denis described his role and the scope. Claude was surprised to learn that the San Francisco Consulate oversaw business for the French interests in the South Pacific.

"I will be traveling down the Noumea and Tahiti in a couple of months. We make regular visits annually. I am hoping to take some vacation time and enjoy a break from work while there."

"I spent time in the South Pacific when I was younger. I loved it there. I stayed for a while in the Cook Islands on the island of Rarotonga. I will never forget my time there or the beautiful young lady who spent time with me during my stay. Many times I have been tempted to return. One day I will."

Their chat was interrupted when Marie-France returned. She sat in the chair next to Denis. Strangely, she said very little. Instead, she continued to look at Denis and examine his features. Finally, she spoke to Denis.

"Denis, I don't know why, but I am experiencing déjà vu I feel we have met before. Your face and mannerisms remind me of someone. Please tell me more about your background if you will."

Claude was embarrassed by her direct approach and attempted to deflect the request.

"Mother, he is here to do important business and to relax this weekend. I do not think it is appropriate to ask those questions."

"No, Claude. It is alright. I do not mind. There is nothing to be ashamed of. My mother left France after meeting my father and moved to Quebec, Canada. She was very young and a beautiful woman. My father was a partner in a business. Our life and my childhood were happy and without any major upheaval. I studied and attended university. After university, I traveled through Europe and spent time here in France. It was then I became aware of the possibility of a position within the French government. Initially, I was rejected because I was born in Canada. It was only when I fought them and explained my mother was French that they conceded that I qualified. I started in a lowly position but quickly rose through the system with some of my thoughts and research, particularly in matters of culture. I returned to university here in France and studied historical culture and sociology. I became more involved with the Ministry and after several years I applied for a posting and Cultural Attaché. I have been in that position and have had several postings, including Canada where I was able to meet with relatives."

Marie-France stayed silent and continued to examine Denis' face.

"You look so familiar. What was your mother's name?"

"She was a fine lady. Her name was Terese. She often spoke of returning to France

"Do you recall her name before she married?"

"Yes, it was Larouche."

"Mon Dieu. She was my sister. You are my nephew. Claude is your cousin."

Chapter 39

Claude arose early. He sat in the kitchen with Jacques their chef who had visited the markets early in the morning for the fresh produce that would be used for the evening dinner. He sipped on a strong expresso as he thought of the previous night's revelation. He was both excited, yet annoyed, to find out so late in life, that he had cousins. Denis had told Marie-France of an older brother and that he had a twin sister.

The front door slammed gently shut as Barry and Yvette stumbled into the house. Yvette was laughing and Barry was attempting to quieten her. Claude left the kitchen and went to meet them. Both looked disheveled and had the look of having partied all night.

"Come into the kitchen. Let's get some coffee and food into you before Marie-France, Buzz, and Denis come down. I suggest you both go and freshen up before that happens."

Yvette laughed and steadied herself against the kitchen table. She decided to have some fun with Claude.

"Claude, do you have a spare bra or panties? I seem to have lost mine."

Barry roared with laughter and tears rolled down his cheeks.

"I think it's going to be a long day today. Please go and make yourselves presentable."

Jacques laughed as the couple left to try and put themselves together for the day.

"Monsieur Claude, it must be nice to be young and full of life and love. Don't be angry with them. Barry is your good friend."

"I am not angry. Sometimes I worry about Barry. People think he is rough, but I know him and underneath that façade is a good person. Jacques, I have a serious question for you. You may have heard from the other servants that Marie-France will marry Buzz. He is planning for them to marry on the Caribbean island of Aruba. I would like you to manage the reception. I will make all the arrangements for you to attend and work with the hotel's people. Are you willing to do that?"

"You need not ask. Of course. I will need to speak to the executive manager at the hotel to understand what we will have to work with. Do you know which hotel Buzz has selected?"

"Yes. It is the Hyatt in Aruba."

"I doubt we will have any problems then. I have worked other marriage receptions with Hyatt hotels in the past."

"The Estate will cover all your costs for the trip. You may take a friend or partner and after the wedding, I will give you a week's vacation at our expense. You have been a good and loyal chef for the de Passioné family."

Before Jacques could answer, Buzz arrived. He poured himself a coffee and sat at the table beside Claude.

"You got a big surprise last night. Sounds to me that it is good news. Marie-France will be joining us soon for breakfast. There is something I wanted to tell you first. There has been an issue back in California with the business. I will need to return within the next day. It is not a matter I can deal with from here. I received an urgent call a little while ago. I intend to ask Marie-France to go with me."

"I'm sure she will be happy to go with you."

"I need to ask you whether there have been any developments in the investigation in California. You have been very quiet about it. Have the investigators been in contact with you? Have you had any more threats or strange things happen? My office was visited by the FBI and with a court order, they searched for certain documents. My assistant, Cynthia Honeysucker called and told me some of the questions they asked. It seems that your mother's visit to my office has triggered something. Do you have any idea? Maybe she has whatever those Chinese gangs are looking for. I suspect the FBI visit was to determine if Marie-France had brought something to hide at the office."

"My only contact has been with the local police investigator in San Francisco. He tells me that the investigation has been taken over by the FBI and there are other international police forces involved."

"This is starting to sound very serious. Are you sure that there is nothing in your possession here or in California that is so important to those gangs? The fact that the FBI has taken control means that there is something of real significance. I suggest you be extremely careful. It may be possible that the gangs have backed off and are trying to let you lapse into thinking things are normal. My advice is to be on guard."

"Buzz, it is driving me crazy. These problems only started after I ceased my relationship with Misty Moon. That is the only thing I am sure about. She never gave me any gifts. On occasion, she would invite me and pay for dinner, but never did she ask for anything or discuss any of the crimes of which she is accused."

"There is something of great importance the gangs are fighting for. In my opinion, the police and FBI know what it is. I am sure they suspect you. Your phone is probably bugged and you can be sure some of the migrant workers are FBI plants. Be very careful what you say or do. Likely, Barry is also under surveillance as well."

Barry entered the room as Buzz finished speaking.

"I hear my name. What is that about?"

"Barry, we were discussing the investigation. Buzz believes that you may be under surveillance since you are my business partner."

"They can search me and watch me for all they want. I have nothing to be concerned about."

"You are wrong Barry. It isn't just the authorities who are watching you. You can be damned sure those criminal gangs are also watching you. Just be aware and be careful."

"Then it's going to get a little inconvenient for them. As I had discussed with Claude, I am going to be taking some time away from the business to visit family and friends in Australia. Been a while since I was back there. I invited Yvette to come with me to see the country and take a vacation."

"When are you planning to take this trip?"

"Yvette has to make arrangements to take time away from her job in San Francisco."

"Surely, with her boss here for the weekend, she should be able to arrange that easily."

Claude had watched the conversation between Buzz and Barry. He sensed Buzz had deeper concerns than he had expressed. He wondered why Buzz was so interested in Barry. Was it possible that Barry had somehow become involved with the gangs? He quickly dismissed that idea.

"Good morning everyone. Good morning my honey drop."

Marie-France burst into the room with her voluminous robe billowing behind her. She reached Buzz and locked him in an embrace before passionately kissing him. Claude was embarrassed.

"Today is a great day. I now know I have nephews and a niece. All of this extraordinarily good information and that I am getting married. I am so happy."

Minutes later, Yvette arrived dressed in jeans and a loose white blouse, ready for the day. Despite the all-night partying, she looked fresh and vibrant. She went and stood with Barry.

Chef Jacques hurried them from his kitchen into the dining room, to allow him to prepare their breakfasts. As they were chased out of the kitchen, Denis arrived dressed casually for a day of selecting wines and visiting the vineyards.

Breakfast was served with a flourish. Chef Jacques had prepared eggs benedict with a fresh hollandaise sauce, fresh croissants and for the American guests, he had prepared sausage, bacon, and home fries.

Silence fell around the table as they partook in the meal. Denis broke the silence.

"Claude, I am looking forward to the tastings and selecting those wines for our receptions in San Francisco."

"We will go after breakfast and start, but first I need to attend to some business. I will need an hour."

Denis nodded. He looked across the table at Yvette. She seemed to be in a trance. She had not touched her food.

"Yvette, do you feel well? Your thoughts seem to be elsewhere."

"I am happy to be back in France after spending so many months at the Consulate. I never realized how much I missed France until now."

Marie-France had listened to her comment and decided to speak.

"Yvette, I am sure that Denis will agree to allow me to take you shopping this morning. With my wedding happening soon we shall go and look at some bridal fashions. As my maid of honor, we will need to select a dress that compliments you. We will let the boys select the wines and when we return you can document and sample some. We will visit my favorite bistro for lunch. Today is ladies' day."

Yvette looked across at Denis, who nodded his approval.

"Go and enjoy yourself. You have earned it."

Part 10

Planned Revenge

Chapter 40

The chauffeur drove Marie-France and Yvette into the Faubourg Saint-Honoré district, the pulse of Paris design and fashion center. Yvette excitedly viewed the exquisite window displays as they drove by the expensive boutiques. Silently she wondered how she would be able to afford any of the magnificent clothes on display, given her meager government salary.

Marie-France ordered the chauffer to stop at **Boutique Lise Parisienne** . As they stopped, a doorman from the boutique walked to the curb to open the door of the car and escort them into the store.

In the boutique, a smartly dressed woman introduced herself and inquired how she could assist.

"I am going to marry again. I am looking for ideas for a dress as it will be a wedding on the tropical island of Aruba. This is Yvette, she will be my maid of honor."

The sales assistant frowned and considered the request.

"That is going to be a challenge, as most of our gowns are designed for weddings in cooler climates. Even those designed for weddings during the summer period may be too heavy. I suggest we consider making custom dresses for each of you. That way, you will get exactly what you desire. Let me have Henri come and join us. He is our senior designer."

She left them in the showroom and went behind a floral screen. Marie-France heard their voices discussing her request. Within minutes, a slim, tanned, bespectacled middle-aged man with jet black hair emerged from behind the screen

"I am Henri. I am here to assist you with the design of a dress for your marriage in the tropics. Not only will we need to make you a lightweight dress, but also one that can be transported easily and will not crush or wrinkle. Now, please tell me what you had in mind."

"I am thinking of a form-fitting sleeveless dress that will compliment my ageless beautiful figure and looks."

"I suggest a fitted bodice with an organza skirt which will billow in the wind. We will use a turquoise blue to match the Caribbean sea. I have been to Aruba and remember the time I went snorkeling. I will decorate the bodice with the colorful fish that are in the waters of Aruba. For the maid of honor, I suggest a bright orange organza dress that is off the shoulder and complimented with a large bow on the back in the same turquoise blue. Since it is a beach wedding you will be barefoot and wearing the same turquoise blue ankle bracelets. How will you be wearing your hair?"

"I will arrange to have our hair braided by a local stylist in Aruba after we arrive."

Yvette had wanted to object to the color of the dress but had remained quiet. The idea of braiding her long and stunning auburn hair displeased her greatly. Marie-France sensed Yvette's discomfort and felt some satisfaction at the revenge she was extracting after having been forced to apologize. This was just the first of several surprises she had planned for Yvette, whom she considered a little slut.

Henri could barely contain his glee. He had tried for years to dispose of the horrible blue organza fabric that the former designer had ordered. It was cause for celebration.

"Before we start the fittings, let's celebrate with some champagne."

Yvette was horrified. She had not expected to be exposed to a fitting that would require the removal of clothing as measurements were taken. She tried to object but was quickly silenced by Marie-France.

"Yvette dear, don't worry. We are here now and this will save us from returning later, and besides, it is my pleasure to pay for your dress."

Henri returned with a magnum of champagne and crystal flutes.

"Here is to a delightful wedding experience."

As he poured the champagne, Yvette felt a horrible sinking feeling. She hated the color orange and the thought of having her prized hair braided depressed her.

Henri sat back with his fingers pursed to his lips.

"I have an idea for the maid of honor dress. The bodice on the bride's dress will have those fish, so in keeping with the Caribbean theme, I will stitch shells on the maid of honor's dress. Yes, that is a brilliant idea. Now, let me get one of my assistants to come and take your measurements, then we can sketch some styles. Who will we measure first?"

"I suggest we start with Yvette."

The female assistant requested Yvette to remove her blouse and jeans. Yvette resisted.

"It is necessary to remove those clothes as we need to get exact measurements. Don't be embarrassed."

Marie-France was enjoying every minute. Finally, Yvette removed her clothing and stood in her bra and panties. It was then that Marie-France realized why she had been reluctant. On Yvette's lower neck and chest and the top of her breasts were purple love bites from her night of passion with Barry. Marie-France smirked and pointedly shook her head. A tear rolled from Yvette's eye.

Marie-France considered the first stage of humiliating Yvette a success. For a moment she considered canceling the other actions she had planned but remembered the night of their argument and Yvette's flirtation with Buzz. She decided to continue with her plans.

After Yvette's measurements were taken, Marie-France brazenly stripped for her session. The assistant suppressed a laugh when she saw the undergarments. It seemed Marie-France was wrapped in Spandex.

The fittings were finished and Marie-France decided she would proceed to the next level of humiliation.

"I think we should now have a leisurely lunch, then we can spend the afternoon browsing the stores."

"I would like to do that, however, I must return and assist Denis. Tomorrow afternoon we must return to Paris as we are on a flight back to San Francisco on Monday morning. I will have a lot of work to complete before we leave. Maybe we can have a nice lunch in Aruba."

Marie-France realized she had just been outsmarted.

"I agree. Let me ask our driver to take us home."

Throughout the drive, they remained silent. Yvette absently watched the scenery pass by while planning her escape from Marie-France.

It was early afternoon when they returned to the Mansion.

"Marie-France, I must thank you for an enjoyable outing. I must now go and assist Denis with the consular paperwork for the wines he has selected."

Yvette left the car and commenced walking to the wine tasting room. Upon entering, she was amazed to see at least forty bottles of different wines lining the long oak table at the center of the room. She found Denis with Claude sitting in a small anteroom off the main tasting area. From their happy moods, Yvette surmised that the wine had helped. Denis had a pad of paper on which he had noted the wines he wished to purchase for the Consulate.

"Yvette let's get the paperwork done this afternoon. Claude is going to drive us to visit some other vineyards tomorrow. We should pack this evening as we will be leaving Monday morning for our return flight to San Francisco. We will have company on the flight. Marie-France and Buzz will be on the same flight."

Yvette gritted her teeth. The thought of spending almost twelve hours in a confined space with the woman did not thrill her.

"Denis, I have friends in Paris. Do you mind if I change my flight to the next day so I can visit them?"

"I am sorry, Yvette but we will need to keep the arrangements. There is business at the Consulate that needs our attention."

Chapter 41

Return to San Francisco and de Passioné Estate.

The flight from Paris was uneventful. After landing in the early afternoon, Denis and Yvette said farewell to Marie-France and Buzz. Marie-France advised Yvette she would be in contact to discuss the wedding. Buzz left to rent a car to drive to the de Passioné Estate in Napa Valley.

At the Estate, they freshened up. Buzz decided to spend the evening with Marie-France. His business problems could wait until the morning. He was tired from the flight.

"Marie-France, tomorrow I will drive out to my skydiving and flight training business. Cynthia Honeysucker has informed me of some important matters that I need to attend to. Do you wish to come with me or stay here to rest after our trip?"

Marie-France considered the situation and decided she did not wish to leave Buzz alone around that Cynthia Honeysucker.

"I would love to go with you. Maybe you can take me up for my first skydive if you have the time. What should I wear to do that?"

"I am sure we can find time to take you up. Just wear jeans and a long sleeve blouse. You will be fine. If I cannot take you up, Cynthia is a qualified skydiving instructor and I'm sure she would be happy to assist you to make your first dive. I will call her now to have one of the pilots available to take you up."

"I would feel safer with you taking me on my first dive."

"Don't worry. Cynthia is experienced and will ensure your jump will be safe."

At the suggestion of Cynthia Honeysucker being in control, Marie-France seethed inside and puckered her lips in distaste. Her dislike of the woman was immense. She was determined Cynthia Honeysucker would never be in a position to entice Buzz.

They were both tired after the trip from Paris and decided on a light dinner before retiring early for the night.

"Buzz, what would you like me to have the kitchen prepare for us?"

"I would enjoy a lobster roll. I ate too much in France."

"I will speak to the kitchen and find us a suitable white wine to enjoy with dinner."

Buzz yawned. Tiredness was creeping over him. The thought of the business matters facing him caused anxiety.

"Tomorrow morning, I would like to leave early. I will not retire late this evening."

A look of disappointment clouded Marie-France's face. She had visions of passion and love while they were alone. She left to not only speak to the kitchen but also to change into something she hoped would allure Buzz into her bed.

Minutes passed before she returned with a bottle of smoky chardonnay and two glasses.

"Buzz, this is one of our best white wines. It is a de Passioné vintage named le panache de dieu. (The Plume of God) One of the best wines we have ever produced. My late husband, The Marquis, was so proud of this wine. Let me pour you a glass before our dinner"

Marie-France handed Buzz a glass and bent forward to pour the wine in a suggestive manner whereby her pronounced cleavage was inches from his nose. Her overt move was in vain.

"I am so tired. It is unusual for me to tire this easily. I hope I am not becoming ill."

"Relax and after dinner, I will put you to bed. I am sure you will be fine after a good night's sleep."

Their dinner was served and they ate in silence. Buzz seemed distracted and aloof.

"Marie-France, I am going to retire. Hopefully, I will have more energy in the morning."

"I will escort you to my room. I will sleep with you tonight in case you need anything during the night. I will be there."

Buzz smiled and nodded. He did not resist.

As they were leaving the living room, a servant called to Marie-France.

"There is an officer from San Francisco on the phone wanting to speak to either you or Claude."

She impatiently picked up the phone and listened as the officer described recent developments linked to the recent shooting of Claude and the strange issues that had followed. The officer ended the call with a request for her to contact Claude and convince him to return to California. She agreed.

Before retiring, Marie-France checked the time. With the time difference between California and France, it was too late to attempt to contact Claude with the update from the San Francisco police. She decided to phone him when they awoke in the morning.

Before falling asleep, she attempted to understand what the police officer had told her. Certain of the information had been withheld from her by Claude and Barry and therefore it did not make sense.

She lay next to Buzz and thought of the things Claude had explained to her. Finally, she drifted into a deep sleep.

The sound of activity of servants working on the lower level floor awoke her and signaled the arrival of morning. Sunlight filtered by the branches of the high trees outside her room flickered on the wall. She reached her arm across to Buzz. He was gone. She sat up quickly and looked around the room. His clothes and shoes were gone. In panic, she checked the time and jumped from the bed remembering Buzz's desire to leave for his business early and hoping he had not left without her.

After throwing on her voluminous gown she raced down the stairs to find Buzz sitting with the kitchen staff and enjoying a coffee.

"Good morning sleepy. Are you ready for a day of action? I have called ahead and arranged for a pilot to take you up for your first skydive. Cynthia will jump with you. It is a perfect day for a jump. There is no haze, the sky is cloudless and there is no wind. Ideal conditions for your first jump."

"I was hoping that you would take me and not Cynthia. A pre-marriage event"

"I cannot. It seems there are going to be some challenges for me to deal with at the business. I will certainly take you in the future."

Marie-France glanced at the old clock on the kitchen wall. She calculated the time in France before leaving for the salon to call Claude.

She listened as the phone in France rang for a long while. It was finally answered by a servant who she did not know. He advised her that Claude was working in the vineyard and offered to send a message to him to return the call.

Thirty minutes passed before she received his call and told him of the police officer's call and request that he return to San Francisco without delay.

Claude thanked her and made small talk for a while. He listened to her excited enthusiasm regarding her first skydive and wished her well.

When the call was complete, Claude sat and analyzed the information she told him, before reaching for the phone and calling Paddy O'Regan.

Paddy answered in a gruff voice, exaggerating his fake Irish accent.

"Paddy, what is going on? Marie-France called me and told me one of your officers has requested I return to California."

"Top of the day to you as well. You forgotten your manners? I shouldn't be telling you anything. Seems to me our relationship is one of me assisting you."

"So my shamrock. Are we feeling a bit sensitive today? Has that Irish whiskey put you in this delightful mood?"

"There's too many bloody FBI, Interpol, and others climbing through the case now. Trying to get information and understand our local involvement is frustrating. I tell you, boyo, it's time for me to retire. This is too annoying. There are arguments over jurisdiction and what laws apply in the different countries. I'm surprised anything gets done."

"Paddy, why do they want me to return. Surely the French security police could handle it and work with me here."

"No, Claude. There has been a break in the case and again more information has been found that indicates you have some critical item. I suggest you return voluntarily as there are those here who want you arrested."

Chapter 42

During the drive to the business, Buzz seemed distracted and abnormally quiet. Marie-France attempted to start several different conversations but each died after a few sentences. He seemed deeply troubled.

She sat and watched out the window as they drove by farms and orchards, and found herself at peace in the California countryside. Her thoughts wandered to the coming weeks and months ahead, until the wedding.

Buzz slowed the truck and exited the highway into the parking lot of a truck stop. There were semi-trailers from Canada, Mexico, and multiple states parked there. Some were idling while their drivers were inside eating a meal or taking a shower. The place was busy. Groups of drivers sat around the cheap white laminate tables eating and talking. There was an almost club atmosphere.

On his way to order them coffees, Buzz waved to a couple of the drivers he knew. He returned and sat across from Marie-France and looked directly into her eyes.

"My dear, I am worried. It is nothing you have done or said, but I am wondering about getting married and how it may change us. In France when we were sailing the canals, it all seemed romantic and made sense. Now we are back here, I am questioning whether I made the correct decision."

"Buzz, nothing has changed. I am still the same person."

'No, it's not you. It is me. In the last few days, I have been having vivid memories of my former wife. I feel responsible for her death.

I loved her very much and I am surprised I still feel the pain of losing her,"

"But Buzz, you said she was killed during that war."

"Yes she was, but I was an American soldier and hated by the rebels. If she hadn't married me they would not have killed her. If I marry you and something bad happens to you I am not sure I will be able to handle another loss."

Marie-France reached over the table and took his hand.

"Buzz, You are a good person and strong. We cannot foresee the future or control fate. It would be foolish to change your life when these things are beyond your control. I too had to find a way to handle the loss of my husband, the Marquis. I knew he had many other lovers, but he brought vitality and satisfaction to my life."

"You are right. I will try to keep those thoughts out of my mind. Now, finish up. It's time to get you to the airfield and up in the sky for your first jump."

"Buzz, I would prefer that you accompanied me. I am uncomfortable with Cynthia Honeysucker. She does not like me. Have you told her of our plans to be married?"

"No. I was going to tell her this morning."

"I am not sure that is a good idea. Please wait until after I jump to tell her. I don't want her to do anything that may upset me. I sense her hostility toward me, and it's because she desires you."

"She is a professional instructor. I hardly imagine she would compromise her instructor's license over something like finding out we are getting married. I will not be able to take you. I have a serious meeting scheduled, besides I had arranged a pilot and booked off one of the planes for you."

They continued to the airfield. Upon arriving, a tall, lean, and tanned man in his thirties wearing aviator sunglasses and a flight suit walked up to their truck. Buzz introduced him to Marie-France as Jeff, the pilot for her jump.

As they stood talking, the office door opened and Cynthia Honeysucker emerged dressed in white coveralls.

"Good morning, all. We have a nice day to go up. I need to take Marie-France to the hangar and explain the equipment and procedure. Immediately after we will leave for her to experience the thrill of skydiving. I suggest she use the bathroom before we leave."

Buzz wished her the best of luck and headed into the office. Cynthia walked with Marie-France to the hangar where parachutes used for the jumps lay out on the floor waiting to be folded for use. Cynthia explained the equipment and the procedure.

" I will be jumping with you. We will climb to an altitude of 10,000ft. At 8000ft, I will attach the harness to the back of yours and we will then be coupled together. My harness has a MicroSigma parachute attached which is the best one for learners. After we are suited up, Jeff will climb to 10,00 ft. We will level off and the door will be opened. I will guide you out of the plane. There is a small step below the door. You will stand on the step and I will come out of the pane and gently push you from behind. There will be a lot of noise and a wind rush. Don't panic. You can expect some turbulence when the door opens and this is normal. After we step out and start the fall, we will free fall to 5000ft and hit a speed of 120Kph. During the fall the wind will blank out any noise. I will open the parachute at 5000ft. and we will slow to a speed of 30Kph. The jump will take seven minutes from the time we jump from the plane. It is safe, but some things can happen. If I signal a problem, please do not struggle or panic. I am trained to handle most situations. Let's go."

Marie-France was excited and headed off to the washroom. Her adrenaline was pumping. She followed Cynthia to the plane and crawled in.

The little Cessna 182 rocked side to side as Jeff started the engine. The engine caught and roared into life. Jeff spoke into the headset and received clearance for take-off. The plane taxied along the bumpy runway and the nose lifted as the engine raced. They lurched into the air. As they climbed, Marie-France looked out and down to see Buzz standing outside the office watching them. The Cessna shook and swayed until they had cleared 2000ft. as the thermals buffeted the plane.

They remained silent until Jeff announced they had reached the altitude to attach the harness. Cynthia was all business.

At 10,000ft. she assisted Marie-France to the open door and out onto the step. Minutes later Marie-France felt a slight nudge and they tumbled away from the plane and accelerated down toward the ground. Marie-France felt exhilarated as the wind rushed past her. It was an experience she could not have imagined. She felt a tug as Cynthia deployed the parachute and their pace of descent slowed. Cynthia controlled the lines and maneuvered them toward a landing area where a staff member was waiting to drive them back to the office.

Back in the office, Marie-France chattered excitedly. She was like a teenager on a first date. Buzz looked on amused. He was pleased to see she had taken an interest in flying and now, skydiving.

"Buzz, I want to train and be able to jump solo. Will you help me to achieve this?"

"You will need to take a course before you can jump solo. Depending on the level you wish to be qualified for, there are nineteen different levels of training. The first six to eight hours are spent on the basics and the equipment, what to do in the case of a malfunction, wind and landing procedures. It is a detailed course. Are you sure you want to do this?"

"Yes. When can I start?"

Cynthia had stood and watched and listened to their conversation. Buzz turned to her.

"Cynthia, I have an announcement to make. Marie-France and I will be getting married."

A thunderous look crossed Cynthia's face.

"I think your mental state is deteriorating as you age."

She turned and left the office without congratulating them or further comment.

Part 11

Revelations

Chapter 43

de Passioné Estate, Napa Valley, California.

The news that there had been a major development in the case was sufficient enticement to convince Claude to return to California. It was a time of the year in California that Claude did not particularly enjoy. The weather was often rainy and accompanied by cold winds.

He had waited several weeks before contacting Paddy O'Regan to advise him of the date he was returning. Again, Paddy had warned him to be careful as Interpol and other forces were anxious to speak with him and he could be arrested at any time. Claude did not encounter any problems on his trip to California.

Back in his office, he scanned the mail on his desk and set aside letters addressed directly to him. One letter, in particular, caught his attention. His name and address were written in blue ink and precise cursive. The writing style was perfect. Claude took a letter opener and carefully opened the envelope. He withdrew a light blue page and unfolded it. He gasped when started to read. It was a letter from his ex-lover, Misty Moon who had been arrested and charged with many serious crimes.

He read the letter in silence and when finished, read it a second time. The contents shocked him. He glanced at his watch and decided it was early enough to phone Barry in France.

The phone was answered by one of the servants who advised Claude that Barry was in a meeting with two men and had requested no interruptions.

Claude asked that Barry be told to call him back without delay when the meeting concluded.

Hours passed before Barry returned the call.

"Well, Claude my boy, it seems the French intelligence have stumbled onto something related to the shooting. They were here for hours and asked many questions. They were particularly interested in any travels you had with Misty Moon but seemed far more interested in Crystal Moon. I didn't have much to tell them, other than that night she arrived here and the tale she told. They are convinced you may have something in your possession those gangs want. I tried to find out more but they were very guarded in what they said."

"Barry, this morning I received a letter from Misty Moon. She extended apologies for getting me embroiled in this investigation. In her letter to me, she claimed her innocence in any criminal activities and claims that soon there will be a revelation made that will clear her of any charges. I am confused as her husband has been detained due to his involvement with these gangs."

"Do you believe her?"

"I am confused. It is time for me to visit with Paddy and understand what the current situation is. I will take this letter. He can share it with the other investigators working the case."

"I suggest you be very careful. For investigators from different countries to be pooling their resources and the secrecy surrounding the investigation means it has to be something major. I am planning on returning to San Francisco next week. I will stay with you for a week before leaving with Yvette to take my long overdue vacation in Australia. Yvette has been able to arrange a month's leave. I will be traveling around Australia visiting relatives and showing her the country. Everything here at the vineyards is under control and the managers we hired are doing excellent work. I am comfortable leaving the operation in their capable hands."

"It seems your involvement with Yvette is a lot more serious than I had realized."

"To be honest mate, I can't say I've been with anyone like her. Seems we have some things in common. Just have to see how it goes."

"Sounds to me as if the rough diamond is getting polished. Soon I won't know you. Maybe some of her French refinement and manners will rub off on you."

"Not much chance of that happening. You can't change an old dog's habits."

After the call, Claude reluctantly called Paddy O'Regan to arrange a meeting in San Francisco. Paddy suggested a coffee before they met with the others on the case. He looked out the window at the driving rain and gusty winds. He did not look forward to driving the beige Chrysler that the security company insisted on him using, but thought that in the bad weather it was a better option than his Ferrari 250LM.

Claude went to his bedroom closet and took his heavy raincoat, as he recalled the cold winds that blew in off the San Francisco Bay. He had not worn the coat in a long while.

As he was about to leave, the phone rang. It was Buzz.

"Claude, it's Buzz. I have decided that Marie-France and I will stay out here at my home as this weather that came up so quickly will make driving too difficult. We will see you in the morning."

"Buzz, I am just about to leave for a meeting with the investigators in the city. If the weather continues like this, I will stay overnight in the city."

Overhead lightning flashed and thunder roared. Claude looked up at the dark skies and the heavy clouds rolling by. It reminded him of the storms he had experienced during his stay on the tropical South Pacific island of Rarotonga.

In the garage, he removed the heavy raincoat and settled into the Chrysler's uncomfortable seat that had been modified with a bulletproof back and a quick-release pivot that could be activated in the event of an armed attack. It was not a car that Claude particularly enjoyed driving, but he understood the need for it.

The drive into San Fransisco was difficult. Surface flooding covered parts of the highway and semi-trailers threw up clouds of blinding spray. Claude checked his watch and decided to drive slowly as he still had adequate time to have a coffee with Paddy O'Regan before attending the meeting at the precinct.

He drove over the Golden Gate bridge and worked his way through the city to the Fisherman's Wharf area until he found a parking lot near the wharf. He declined the lot attendant's offer to park the Chrysler. He did not want the fact that it was an armored vehicle known.

He parked the car at the rear of the lot in a less visible location. He pulled on his raincoat and started off to meet Paddy. He passed tourists huddled under umbrellas, even though the rain had eased. . The biting cold wind swept in off the water. Claude pulled up his collar for protection. He hurried along past Alioto's restaurant and past the street merchants selling freshly steamed crab toward the Coastal Café and Bar where he had arranged to meet Paddy.

He swung open the café door and was greeted by a rush of warm humid air laced with the rich aroma of freshly brewed coffees and found Paddy sitting at the bar enjoying an Irish coffee.

"Paddy, good to see you after some time. Should you be drinking that while on duty?"

"Jesus, are you my conscience now? It's my break, and the weather is typically that of fall and winter. Lousy, and I'm sick of all the fucking interference back at the station. I can't wait to take my Colleen and get the hell out of here. Now, tell me what has happened since we last spoke."

Claude slid onto the stool beside Paddy and next to an attractive blonde woman. She seemed interested in Claude and flashed him a welcoming smile. Claude nodded to her and sat. He decided to calm himself and ordered a whiskey with his coffee.

"Not too much has happened Paddy. I spoke to Barry and he had a visit from French Intelligence claiming there was an item of interest at the Chateau. So far, I have not had any more visits or calls. It is baffling. You told me that there has been a big development. What is it?"

"Your old flame, Misty Moon has negotiated a deal. She has turned and is providing important information. I think you will be shocked to learn what she has told us."

"When did this happen? I received a letter from her today. I have brought it with me."

Claude slid his hand into his jacket pocket and removed the letter which he then handed to Paddy.

Paddy drew on his cigarette, sipped his Irish Coffee, and slowly read the letter before emitting a low whistle.

Chapter 44

Fog rolled in off the bay. The late morning sky remained leaden and cast a gloomy feeling over the city. It seemed that Paddy's mood matched the weather. They stood to leave the little café.

"Claude, I caution you that there are conflicting interests amongst the various officials you will be meeting. I suggest you only provide the minimum of information. Do not volunteer any more than what they ask."

Claude nodded and pulled on his heavy coat for the trip to the precinct.

As he was turning to leave, the blonde handed him a business card.

'If you ever want company here in the city, please call me. I love your French accent. It sweeps me away."

For a fleeting moment, Claude was tempted to abandon the meeting and pursue an afternoon of delight. He decided to follow up on the opportunity.

"I am here alone in the city. Would you like to meet later? We can have cocktails and then maybe dinner."

The blonde smiled and extended her hand to him.

"My name is Veronica. I would love to have cocktails. Where should we meet? What is your name?"

"My name is Claude. I will be at the lobby bar of the Hyatt. I hope to see you there."

"Claude. I love the Frenchness of you. I will be there at four this afternoon."

Her green eyes scanned Claude's physique, while Claude studied her figure and wondered what reconstruction had been performed to produce such a fine full figure.

Paddy gently tugged Claude by the shoulder.

"Come on lover boy. We have a meeting and can't keep those opinionated pricks waiting. If we are late you will hear them whining for miles."

Claude flirtatiously reached out and shook Veronica's hand.

"I will see you later at the Hyatt, mon Cheri."

As they walked out of the café, Claude chuckled.

"Well, Paddy. It seems I will have a busy afternoon and evening."

Outside the café, misty rain had returned. The cold drizzle was whipped into their faces by the wind off the bay. Claude dug his hands deep into the pockets of the coat. He was surprised to find something small and sharp deep in the pocket. He tried to remember when he had last worn the coat and whether he had put anything in the coat pockets.

He removed the item and unsure what it was he showed it to Paddy.

"Claude that is a USB memory stick. It is used to store computer information. Maybe your accounting or computer people may have handed it to you and you put it in your pocket without remembering."

"No that's not possible. I very rarely wear this coat. It would be almost a year since I wore it."

"When we get back to my office, I will have one of our techs look at it and tell you what it contains."

Claude thought no more about it and slipped it back into his pocket.

They continued their walk back to the police precinct. Crowds on the normally busy sidewalks were sparse due to the weather allowing Claude and Paddy to make good progress. The rain increased and fell heavily as they reached their destination.

Paddy ran up the stairs and pushed open the old oak door. A few feet behind him, Claude followed. Inside they removed their coats. Paddy asked for the USB memory stick and took it into a small secluded office on the main floor of the precinct. He went to one of the techs and handed him the memory stick. The tech took it and looked at it.

"What is this? Where did you get it? What is on it?"

Paddy explained the origin of the device and advised the tech they had no idea of its content. The tech frowned.

"In that case, I will not put it in any of the main computers. I will put it in the one we use to scan for viruses and malware. Then after we are sure it's clean I will put it in my system."

The tech walked over to a desk and started a computer. After it booted up, he entered several passwords then inserted the memory stick. The scan took several minutes and showed the device was clean. He removed the stick and returned to his desk where he inserted it into his computer and opened a software program. Within minutes characters and numbers appeared across his screen. The tech frowned.

"The files have been formatted and are not in English. It appears to be Chinese. Let me go and get someone who can read this."

The tech returned with a young uniformed cop who leaned over and read the screen.

"The information needs to be in the correct format, but yes it is Cantonese. There are names and telephone numbers and addresses. Some items appear to be codes. I can't help much more. If you want to understand more you will need to get Forensics to assemble the information in the correct format."

Claude pondered the situation. Chinese again. Suddenly he remembered when he last wore the coat. He had been on a date with Misty Moon before she was to return to Hong Kong. He recalled how she had wrapped her arm around his waist. It was now clear. She must he slipped the USB stick into his pocket. His curiosity arose as he wondered what the contents would reveal.

While waiting for the forensics member to arrive, Claude explained his thoughts to Paddy.

"I think we now know what the gangs have been looking for. They knew you had this memory stick. It must contain some very important information."

There was a knock at the door and a tall gangly member of the forensics group entered. He introduced himself and explained he was the head of the department who handled any computer-related crimes.

He sat at the desk and scanned the screen. Finally, he turned to Paddy.

"I think you need to formally get forensics involved. The fields of information are incomplete as they have used software that locks and conceals linked data. That software is extremely rare and expensive. I suggest whatever is on that memory stick must be of significant importance to go to such lengths the protect it."

Chapter 45

After requesting assistance from Forensics to retrieve the information, Paddy and Claude trudged up the stairs to the conference room to join the meeting. Fifteen men sat around the table and an older woman who Claude had previously seen on television granting interviews. He recalled those interviews dealt with major crimes the FBI had cracked. There was one other person he recognized, the humorless FBI Agent Wayne Steel.

When Paddy and Claude were seated, the FBI woman stood to address the meeting.

"For those of you who don't know me, my name is Dagmar Stryker. I am the Chief of Liaison for International Cooperation between US departments and our overseas counterparts. The reason for us to meet today is to provide an update on the progress of a major International crime investigation. In addition, we will be asking Claude de Passioné to disclose certain information, as we now know he is the focus of several gangs here, in China and Europe. During their respective investigations, our foreign counterparts have found consistent evidence that points to Claude de Passioné. While he may not be directly involved in any criminal activity there is reason for us to believe he is aware of certain facts and the gangs are determined to silence him before he shares anything with us."

Before Claude could react, Paddy leapt to his feet.

"Excuse me, but before we go any further there has been a development in the last few minutes."

Paddy continued and described the memory stick, where it was found, and the strange contents that were now with Forensics.

Dagmar Stryker appeared annoyed.

"I think you should have provided that item directly to the FBI. It is far too important for some local geek to mess up. Where is it? I order it be given to our agents immediately."

Agent Wayne Steel was on his feet and eager to obey her command.

Paddy seethed at the inference that the local police were incompetent.

"Unless you get an official order to release the item to you, it will stay where it is."

The small purple veins across Dagmar Stryker's forehead swelled as her temper arose.

"I have never encountered such insolence from a local flatfoot. Who do you think you are? I have the authority and the power to demand anything that may be of consequence to this case."

The men around the conference table exchanged looks and were enjoying the heated exchange. Their eyes focused on Paddy as he confronted Dagmar.

"Quite simply madam, it is just an article handed to us by a citizen, in this case, Claude de Passioné, and may have no bearing on your investigation. We accepted it to determine its contents. If it is of importance, then yes the information will be shared."

"We have received certain information that ties in with what you have. We have had significant developments. The Chinese were pursuing Wendy Wong, or as you may know her…Misty Moon. After an intense investigation by the Chinese and our agents in

China, it has been established that she is not the head of the notorious gang. Her sister, Crystal Moon had assumed Wendy's identity to disguise her involvement in crimes and had also created false evidence that incriminated Wendy Wong. She was working in conjunction with Wendy Wong's ex-husband. During the investigation, Wendy Wong admitted to hiding critical information with Claude de Passioné. She would not provide further information as she was using this while negotiating with us to drop several charges against her. We do have evidence that she participated in many criminal activities. Lawyers for her have been bargaining for exoneration and a new identity for her in the States in return for her disclosing where she hid the information at the de Passioné Estate. They claim her life is in danger if she remains in China. I believe that is the information contained on the USB memory stick."

Claude sat in disbelief. He thought of the discussion Barry had with him after Crystal Moon had gone to the Estate and why she had tried to determine if he was dead after the shooting incident. It was apparent to him she had hoped he was dead and the information that Wendy Wong had stolen and hidden at the Estate would never be discovered. He was angry that both he and Barry had been fooled by Crystal Moon.

Around the table, the representatives from the International agencies peppered Dagmar with questions. She deflected most of them or suggested that a later meeting be scheduled after the memory stick information was decoded.

Mild arguments arose regarding the jurisdictional control of the investigation. It was obvious that Dagmar Stryker had no intention of relinquishing control. The Interpol officials from the Netherlands were insistent they be included in all activities undertaken or discovered by the FBI.

Claude leaned and whispered in Paddy's ear.

"I do not see what value I am here. I would like to leave. I have other matters I wish to look after."

"Ms. Stryker, Claude wishes to leave. Do you require him to stay any longer? I don't think he has much to contribute until we know what is on the memory stick."

"We need to interview him. He had met with Wendy Wong on many occasions. We need to understand what happened, where he went with her, and what was discussed. If he agrees, he can leave and we will send agents to the Estate to conduct those interviews."

Paddy was about to reply when there was a loud knocking at the door and the Head of the Forensics division entered the conference room accompanied by the computer tech Paddy and Claude had met earlier.

"Excuse us, but we have been able to crack the password and decipher the files. I believe you will want to see the data. I have requested a projector and will show you what is contained on the memory stick. For safety and security reasons we have made backups of the memory stick."

Dagmar watched as the computer tech fidgeted and set up a laptop. Minutes later another tech arrived with a projector that was then hooked to the laptop. The lights were dimmed and after typing in passwords and screen names and numbers appeared. The FBI agents stared at the screen. The text was in Chinese.

Dagmar turned to Paddy and politely asked if there was an officer at the precinct who he trusted and could translate Chinese for them. Paddy nodded and excused himself to find the officer.

He returned ten minutes later with an older man who he introduced.

Dagmar stressed the importance of confidentiality to the man and signaled the computer tech to switch the laptop back on. Again the projected image lit up on the conference room screen. There was silence while the Chinese man read the characters on the image.

"This is a directory of some sort. It is in Cantonese. It is a list of names of different gangs and their leaders and members. The numbers are for telephone/cell phones. There are also bank accounts and people in the banks who work with people from the gangs. It is a complicated list. Please scroll down so I can see more data."

The tech scrolled down and figures flew up the screen. After several pages he paused. The Chinese officer read the screen and whistled.

'It is a very detailed document. It has the names and information on each gang by each country that the infamous K-14 gang operates in. There is also some information on the drugs, money laundering, and human trafficking networks in Asia and Europe. This is a manual that contains enough data to implicate many."

Dagmar arose and requested the projector and laptop be turned off. She dismissed the Forensic personnel. After they left, she addressed the group.

"We will adjourn now. I will set up another meeting after we have a full translation of that directory. I will employ the best special agents to join us and make the translation a bureau priority. This meeting is ended. You will be contacted regarding the resumption of the meeting. I will try to get this done within the next day or so."

The men around the table grumbled amongst themselves.

Claude addressed Dagmar.

"I have a question. You mentioned Wendy Wong's ex-husband. Do you know why she participated in his criminal activities?"

"What we know from the Chinese intelligence agents is limited, but we do know they were not married. He used her to cover up his criminal activity with Crystal Moon by confusing and fooling others into believing Wendy was in control. She cooperated as he had threatened to kill and torture her. We will know more after we have the opportunity to interrogate her. She is on a government aircraft on her way to America as we speak."

Claude shook his head and turned to Paddy.

"The revelations of today explain why I have been targeted and pursued. What will happen next?"

Dagmar spoke before Paddy could answer.

"Claude you will be briefed privately after we review the contents on that memory stick and plan what actions will be taken. I suggest you still be very careful until then. You are free to leave now."

Claude glanced at his watch. It was only half an hour before his planned rendezvous with Veronica.

"If you will excuse me I have some important business to look after and need to leave now."

Paddy looked at Claude and suppressed a smile, knowing the real reason for the hurried departure.

Chapter 46

Veronica sat alone in the Hyatt lobby bar ignoring the admiring looks of the men at the bar. She had just one single purpose in mind. She glanced at her watch and decided she had time to refresh her hair and makeup before Claude arrived.

Claude was walking through the entrance to the lobby bar as she returned from the powder room. Seeing her, he waved and headed towards her and then escorted her to a table near the pianist.

When they were seated, a cocktail waiter approached to take their order and offer some canapés courtesy of the Hyatt. Claude ordered a bottle of Prosecco and settled back in the high-backed chair to enjoy the company of Veronica. Before concentrating his attention on her, he looked around at the other patrons looking for anything unusual. He saw nothing and dropped his guard. It had been a long time since Claude had felt freedom. Now that the memory stick had been discovered he hoped the gangs, intent on its recovery, would cease their pursuit of him. He sighed and focused his attention on Veronica and imagined what lay ahead.

"Veronica, I am curious. What business are you in?"

"I own and operate a movie theater here. Unfortunately, the times have changed and it is no longer a lucrative business. I am looking to sell it or convert the business to something more popular. I have been consulting and meeting with restaurant owners to convert the building to a tourist-focused restaurant and use the upper space for a high-end fashion retail business. I will miss the movie business, but it is time to move on. Tell me about yourself, Claude."

She sat in silence and was intrigued as Claude described the de Passioné wine and vineyard businesses in France and California.

Hours passed as they sat making small talk. Claude looked at his watch.

"Veronica, it's getting a little late. Can I invite you to join me for dinner?"

Veronica purred at the invitation.

"I would be delighted."

Claude signaled one of the waiters and requested a dinner reservation in the Eclipse Bar.

Over dinner, they continued their conversation. Veronica asked many questions about the wine business. Claude had ordered a lobster salad, while Veronica took a Crab soufflé. Their conversation ebbed and flowed. Tiredness crept up on Claude. Even though he listened to Veronica, her words were lost as his thoughts strayed back to the meeting at the precinct and the revelation of the contents of the memory stick.

Claude studied Veronica's face and profile. She was a beautiful woman. He wondered why she was at the bar and alone. He thought that such a beauty would have been accompanied by a companion. He was confused.

"Veronica, you are such a beautiful woman. Why are you alone?"

"I have known men and lovers. I have never found someone I would be content with. My life is simple yet the men I have met are striving for things that do not interest me or portray the life I wish to lead."

"Surely you must have had relationships that could have grown and provided you with an interesting life."

"Claude, I should be asking you the same questions."

He sat back in his chair and was silent for several minutes.

"Veronica, let us go back to the lounge and I will explain some things to you."

Claude escorted her to a quiet corner in the dimly lit lounge. There were only a few patrons at the other tables.

"I will answer your question. I did have a woman I loved dearly. On the day I was to propose to her, an accident happened and she was killed. It has been hard for me to remember the life I had with her before the accident."

Veronica leaned forward and reached her hand out. She gently dropped her hand onto Claude's knee and slowly caressed his leg as she moved it up toward his thigh.

Claude attempted to remove her hand but before he could grasp hers she dropped it onto his masculinity. She raised her eyes and looked directly into his and held his stare while slightly smiling at him.

"I can sense a sorrow in you. Now I understand why. You have never recovered from your loss, but you must move on in life."

A waiter approached and Claude ordered them after dinner drinks.

He sat back in the comfortable club chair and focussed on Veronica.

"Things have been happening recently that I would like to tell you, but due to their sensitivity, I cannot. I have inadvertently become caught up in some nasty business. I am not involved, but it has affected me. I have been worried about my mother, the business, and my friends. I hope soon it will all be over."

Claude raised his arm and looked at his watch.

"Veronica, it's getting late and I have a long drive ahead of me to go back to the Estate."

"Claude, the weather is bad and there has been a lot of fog. I suggest you stay the night in San Francisco. You are welcome to stay at my place tonight. I will make you comfortable."

"You are right. I am tired and the weather is bad. I am going to book a room here at the hotel."

Veronica smiled. Her plan was working. Soon she would have Claude.

"That is a wise decision. To be honest, I am worried about driving home to my place. Maybe I should also book a room as well, or I could spend the night with you."

Claude studied Veronica. A night of passion with her intrigued him, but he was feeling fatigued and worried.

"Veronica, there will be another time. I am exhausted and I will need to leave very early tomorrow morning. Let us plan to meet again next week."

Veronica's face hardened as did her attitude.

"Don't bother Frenchie. Fuck you. Obviously, I'm not good enough for you."

She stood up quickly from her chair, grabbed her coat and spun on her heels, and briskly walked to the exit.

Claude sauntered over to the front desk and booked a room. He then rode the gondola-shaped elevator car up to the top floor. The bell boy opened his room and Claude crashed onto the bed and fell into a deep sleep. When he awoke, it was ten in the morning. He stripped and took a quick shower to freshen up. He was about to leave the room when an idea entered his head. He went to the room desk, picked up the phone, and dialed the French Consulate.

He waited patiently before Denis Ricard came on the line.

'Denis, it is Claude. I am here in the city at the Hyatt. I stayed last night after a meeting and didn't want to face the driving conditions to return to the Estate. I am about to go for a late breakfast and was wondering if you might be able to join me."

"I would be delighted to. Give me thirty minutes to complete a few things here and I will meet you in the lobby."

Claude reflected on last night's dinner with Veronica. He wondered what she had hoped to gain other than the obvious sexual encounter. He decided that it too was just one more of the strange things that were occurring in his life. His thoughts wandered to the previous relationships he had in the past. None had affected him or stayed in his mind than the time he had spent in Rarotonga with Atarangi. Even though it was now three years since he had seen her, he still vividly recalled her soft voice, charm, and beauty. Had it not been for the untimely death of his father, The Marquis, he would have stayed in Rarotonga longer and been with her. He dismissed the thought and gathered up his possessions to meet Denis.

The elevator was empty and dropped to the lobby floor without any stops. Claude walked out and saw Denis sitting across the lobby. He headed straight to him.

"Denis, good morning. I am pleased you could join me. Let's find a table in the café here."

"For me, it is a pleasant break from the office. Since Yvette went on her vacation with Barry, I have had to do a lot more administrative things. I need to take some time off to clear my brain."

"That is why I wanted to meet with you. There has been a major development in the criminal investigation regarding me. It seems like some important evidence has been found and a key witness is working with the authorities. That means I am now able to have some social life back. Things a very quiet for me at the Estate with Barry in Australia with Yvette, and Marie-France staying at her future husband's house while she is receiving flying and skydiving lessons. It is a bit too quiet. I was wondering if you want to drive up for the weekend in the beautiful British Green Aston-Martin. I will take my Ferrari and we can tour a number of the vineyards. You can stay at the Estate."

"I do need a break, so yes, I accept your invitation."

"It has been so quiet with Barry gone. I forgot how dominant his presence is."

"I have had telephone calls from Yvette. She is enjoying her trip to Australia with Barry. She says she has fallen in love with Sydney. Barry has taken her to different beaches and bushwalking. I understand that they are now traveling to small towns in the outback. It sounds like a real adventure."

"I am hoping that Barry contacts me. I wish to update him on the most recent developments with the investigation."

"I am sure he will be in contact. When should I drive up to the Estate? Should I come Saturday morning or on Friday evening?"

"Come Friday evening and we will drive to the Mark West Lodge for a fine dinner."

"I would like that. I have some news for you. I will need to travel on French Consulate business to some of the French interests in the Pacific, starting with Tahiti. You have made me interested in visiting the Cook Islands and Rarotonga. I intend to question you for recommendations."

Claude sat back and again his mind drifted to the time he had spent there.

"I wish I could go back. There was special magic there for me."

"Maybe you should go back and be there to show me the island."

"I cannot. Marie-France has a wedding planned that I will need to attend and I have no idea when Barry will return. When will you be leaving?"

"I have not established a schedule yet. Maybe you should think about coming with me. I think you need to take some time for yourself. You seem tired."

"Denis, it has been over three years since I was there. I am sure things have changed and some of the people I knew have moved on. I appreciate your thoughts of a vacation, but I am not sure it will work."

Claude fell silent. His thoughts returned to the days he had spent on the beach and with Atatrangi's family and friends. The more he thought about those days the more melancholy he became.

Denis watched Claude over the top of his glasses. His training had taught him to know when a person was deep in thought and distant. Denis stayed silent.

Part 12

In the clouds

Chapter 47

The Descenders Skydive and Flying School, California.

Marie-France showed a natural skill for both the flying lessons and the skydiving. Every day she was ready to proceed with the next lesson. Cynthia Honeysucker was both amazed and annoyed at her progress. She had developed an intense dislike for Marie-France.

With all 19 levels of training complete, the day for Marie-France to make her unaccompanied dive was approaching. During her training, she had spent over eight hours with Cynthia Honeysucker who had explained the equipment, the landing process, emergency procedures, and the most common types of malfunctions, and how to react. Marie-France was confident.

As she was about to leave the hangar where the skydive operations were based, Buzz arrived.

"I understand from Cynthia that today was your last lesson and you received your certification. Congratulations. I guess you will go up with Cynthia for your first solo dive tomorrow."

"Buzz, will you come with me. It would mean so much for me to dive with the man who will be my husband."

"I cannot tomorrow. I have meetings all day in the city."

Marie-France pouted and displayed her displeasure. Buzz watched.

"I am thinking that since you are now qualified to dive alone, why don't we go now. I have the time. The day and the wind conditions are perfect. I can ask Cynthia to take the controls and fly us up."

"Buzz, will you do that for me? Yes, let's do it."

Buzz returned to the little office and spoke to Cynthia.

"Buzz, I cannot take you up. Remember we have inspectors from the State visiting this morning to review our operations to renew our licenses. I can see whether one of our other pilots is available."

"Please do that. I will not be gone for a long time. We will climb, do the dive and be back here within an hour."

"I will find you an available pilot. Remember it is crop dusting time and most are scheduled out."

"I will be in the hangar assembling our gear."

Buzz walked back to the hangar and selected their gear. They were joined by one of the young pilots Buzz had recently hired. He was good and had been a US Navy carrier pilot.

"Morning, Boss. Where will you want to do your dive?"

"I am thinking the drop zone near Castillo Vineyards. There is plenty of open space there and is easily accessible. I will need to have one of the guys drive down there to bring us back. Are you ready to take us now?"

"Whenever you wish we can go."

"Help me put the gear in the plane and we will be on our way."

The gear was loaded into the Cessna 182. Marie-France climbed in, followed by Buzz.

The Cessna shook as the propeller turned and the engine caught. It roared into life and the pilot taxied over to the main runway for takeoff.

They climbed steadily until the large grassy area that served as a drop zone came into view.

The pilot turned and announced he would circle into the wind to compensate for any drift during the drop.

Buzz was about to lift the harness and assist Marie-France. She put out her hand to stop him.

"No Buzz. I want to experience the rush of wind and freedom during the dive. I will wear the helmet, goggles, and boots, but I wish to dive naked."

Buzz looked at her and smiled.

"My dear that could be painful. There are parts of your body that will get pushed around by the wind and when the parachute deploys any loose skin could be trapped and severely pinched. If you insist on this, I will need to ensure your harness and equipment is tight against your body. We don't want any embarrassing accidents. I will jump before you to be on the ground to assist you with landing."

Buzz tightened straps and double-checked everything before suiting himself up. He reached forward and tapped the pilot on the shoulder to announce they were ready. The pilot banked and climbed while slowing the plane.

He pulled down his goggles and exited the open doorway. A minute later he was plummeting down toward the earth. He spun to look back and see a naked Marie-France fall from the plane. She free fell longer than Buzz had expected. He was concerned. She continued to fall at an alarming rate. Suddenly there was a burst of white as the parachute deployed. He watched as her speed slowed and she drifted down. Something did not seem correct. Her Parachute was angled. He then realized that she was experiencing a line twist issue which was causing her to descend faster and made it difficult to flare up and slow her landing. She was experiencing a parachute landing failure.

He watched in horror as the wind carried her away from the edge of the drop zone and over the vineyard where migrant workers were attending to the vines. They looked up when they heard her screams. Several fell to their knees and made the sign of the cross and prayed as they observed her rotund lily-white naked body hurtling toward them. With the line twisted, it caused the parachute to assume a shape resembling angel wings. The migrants all fell to their knees praying in the belief that the Madonna was descending from the heavens to bless them as the illusion of her as an angel fell from the sky above them.

Buzz maneuvered himself to land beside the area she was heading toward. He watched as she crashed a large mound of trimmed grapevine cuttings. The white parachute fluttered down and covered her. The was no movement. Buzz cursed and using all his strength turned his parachute towards the area in which she lay. He hit the ground hard and immediately snapped off his harness and parachute. He saw one of his employees parked off in the distance in a company van and waved the man to come and assist.

He raced to the crumpled mass of parachute from which a naked arm protruded. He pulled back the parachute and found Marie-France lying on her back smiling. She was covered in squashed rotting grapes. The juice from the grapes ran in rivulets down her face and decorated her breasts. The migrant workers stood in a circle watching.

"Oh Buzz, that was truly the best experience I have ever had. Let's do it again."

"No, we are not doing it again. Cover yourself up. Are you hurt?"

He pulled off his skydiving suit and pushed it to Marie-France. Beneath the suit, he was dressed in a light shirt and jeans.

"Get dressed. We are returning to the office."

Chapter 48

de Passioné Estate

Claude decided to end his work early. It was Friday and he was expecting his friend Denis Ricard later in the afternoon. He needed a distraction and decided he would take his Ferrari out of the garage where it had been stored while he had driven the beige armored Chrysler.

The Estate was eerily quiet. He had given most of the staff the weekend off and without Barry or Marie-France there he was lonely and he felt discouraged.

In the garage, he removed a car cover off his prized Ferrari and slid himself into the driver's seat. He cranked the ignition and the V-12 engine roared into life. A smile creased his face. He was always happy in his Ferrari.

With his spirits lifted, he returned to the house and heard the phone ringing. He ran to answer it. Barry's voice boomed through.

"Claude, you old bugger. I just thought I'd give you a quick call to let you know that Yvette and I are returning next week. We will have some news for you then. Is everything fine there?"

"Better than fine, Barry."

Claude told Barry of the developments in the investigation into the gangs and the problems the gangs had caused. There was silence as he relayed all the information. When he finished, Barry let out a whistle.

"It seems that your Wendy Wong created a lot of problems for you. What will happen next?"

"I do not know. The FBI and the Interpol authorities have brought her to America for questioning. I am unaware of anything further."

"I suggest you better get out of town then fella.'

"This weekend, Denis from the Consulate is coming up to the Estate. We intend to spend the weekend in our cars touring the different vineyards. It will be a nice distraction."

"Do you think the problems with those Chinese gangs are over? Even though the authorities have been able to gather evidence and information on their activities I wonder if you will be safe now."

"It is hard to say. I can only accept the words of Dagmar Stryer and her people. I am hoping that they handle things in such a way that I remain anonymous."

"I don't understand you, Claude. They must still suspect something. That visit I had from Crystal Moon was planned. Now, Wendy Wong is cooperating with them and you had a relationship with her. I am not convinced this is over yet."

"Barry, just spend your last few days in Australia enjoying yourself. I hope Yvette has enjoyed the trip. I know that Marie-France is eager for her to return and assist in planning the wedding."

"I can assure you that if there was a way for her to stay in Australia and miss that wedding, she would do it."

Claude laughed. He had sensed the friction between Marie-France and Yvette even though Marie-France had offered an apology of sorts.

"We will see you this week. Enjoy your trip through the vineyards."

As Claude hung the call, he heard the distinctive sound of Denis' Aston Martin DB5 driving toward the Mansion. He looked from the salon window to see the late sun glint off the British Racing Green car. Denis pulled to a halt under the Estate's portico. Moments later he climbed from the car.

"It was a great drive up here. The traffic out of San Francisco was light. I am looking forward to our weekend of touring."

"Come on in. I'm sure you want to freshen up and enjoy a relaxing wine or two."

Denis gathered up his bags and followed Claude into the house.

"Go and freshen up. I will go and select a wine from our cellar. Meet me back in the Salon."

Claude was sitting and waiting for Denis when the phone rang. He found it strange for someone to be calling late on a Friday afternoon.

"de Passioné Estates, Claude speaking."

The caller asked him to hold while she connected another party to the call. There was a pause before he was joined into a conference call.

The voice of Dagmar Stryker boomed through the phone.

"We are sorry to disturb you, Claude, but it is important. I am on this conference call with agent Wayne Steel. He has been leading the investigation and the interrogation of Wendy Wong since her arrival. She has told us that certain parties still believe you have information and need to be silenced. We are going to hold a press conference either tonight or tomorrow to announce we have the USB memory stick. Our partners in the countries identified on the memory stick have been advised and the contents shared with them as it relates to their particular jurisdiction. We are not releasing all the information to any single party. The FBI will assume full control of the ongoing activities. Where necessary we will coordinate the activities in different countries.

We believe that after we disclose the existence of the memory stick and the story of how it came into our possession, the gangs will cease pursuing you, but we cannot be certain. You need to be cautious.

You had mentioned you will be traveling out of the country for your mother's wedding. How will you travel?"

"Her future husband is a pilot and owner of an aviation company. He has indicated that we will take one of his aircraft and fly to Aruba privately for the wedding."

"It is important you keep us informed of the arrangements in case we need to intervene.

I have one final request. Agent Wayne Steel and I would like to meet you at hour house on Monday morning. Is that possible?"

"Yes. Why is this necessary?"

"Until then. Agent Steel and I should be there around ten in the morning. It will all be clear at that time. We should end the call now."

Claude hung up the phone. He turned to find Denis standing behind him. He had been listening to the conversation.

"Is there a problem? If it's not convenient I can return to the city."

"No, it is that those people confuse me. Now let us enjoy our time and forget that mess."

Chapter 49

Monday morning, Claude arose fresh and relaxed after his weekend touring the wine country of Northern California with Denis. He had discovered new exciting wines and had eaten well at some of the many restaurants in the region.

Showered and working in his office he heard the arrival of Dagmar Stryker and Wayne Steel. He hurried down the stairs to greet them and thanked the servant who had shown them into the salon.

"Good morning. Can I offer you some fresh coffee? I will have the kitchen staff prepare some."

He returned to the salon from the kitchen and found that Wayne Steel had laid several manila folders on the table in front of him.

Dagmar was uncharacteristically smiling.

"Claude, I take great pleasure in creating this subterfuge and bluff. Considering the seriousness of the situation I consider it essential. I will hand this over to Wayne to explain."

"Good morning Claude. I attended all of the sessions when Wendy Wong was interrogated. She has disclosed a lot of information. The list contained on the memory stick has proven to be invaluable. Wendy admitted that she stole the memory stick and planted it in your coat pocket. It was prepared by Crystal Moon. Wendy claimed she had reached a point whereby she wanted out of the gang and took the stick to protect her security. Crystal found out the stick was somewhere at your Estate and was determined to retrieve it or have you killed. Crystal is a psychopath. She had her sister tortured until she confessed to taking the memory stick and hiding it with you.

We now have a complete breakdown of a major drug distribution network. The individual leaders in each country are identified, along with phone and financial information, including bank accounts with passwords. All the shipping and transportation information is there. It is a gold mine. It is no wonder you were pursued by the gangs. We have learned of links that were unknown to us, in particular, the existence of a Rotterdam-based motorbike gang and their access through other motorbike gangs in neighboring countries. It is set up as a huge distribution network.

This morning, there is a planned press conference at which Justice Department, FBI, Attorney General, and other high-ranking political officials will attend. We will announce some of our findings, but they will be presented as findings made by the FBI in the course of investigating other crimes. We are respecting the need for your safety and privacy. There will be no mention of you. We intend to deflect all attention away from you and your family. Wendy Wong has agreed to provide evidence in closed court. We are offering her clemency and a new identity in another country. You will never be able to speak or meet her again. That is our price to protect you. I suspect there will be major news coverage of this in the papers and on CNN."

For the next hour, Wayne Steel and Dagmar Stryker discussed the situation and provided advice on proceeding. Claude was requested to enter into a confidentiality agreement.

As they were leaving the Estate, the thunderous roar of Buzz Kutz's rusty red old pickup announced his and Marie-France's arrival. Wayne Steel's face froze as Buzz screeched to a halt inches behind the government-issued Crown Victoria.

"Good morning all. Who do we have the pleasure of meeting this morning?"

"Buzz, this is Dagmar Stryker and Agent Wayne Steel of the FBI. They have been briefing me on certain matters relating to the strange happenings we have had happening here. It seems all is fine now."

Dagmar Stryker walked to them both.

"I believe that congratulations are in order for your upcoming wedding. Have you set a date yet?"

"We are hoping to have the event in about three weeks from now. I am waiting for my maid of honor to return from an overseas vacation."

"I wish you all the best. I hope you have a beautiful wedding."

"I believe I will. I am so looking forward to the day. I cannot wait to wear the tropical wedding gown I have chosen."

The FBI agents returned to their car and minutes later sped off down the long driveway.

"Dagmar, I have seen that Buzz Kutz before. I'll be damned if I can remember where."

"I too seemed to recognize him. When we get back to the San Francisco field office, we will mine the database and see what we can find."

Claude assisted Buzz with the little luggage they had.

"Are you going to be here a while or will you go back to Buzz's home?"

Marie-France turned to Claude and responded.

"No. I will be staying here with Buzz as we need to plan the wedding and make the necessary arrangements. I will be in contact with Carla de Cuba, our wedding coordinator in Aruba, to ensure everything is in order there. Have you heard from Barry and Yvette? I need her here to have the final fitting of our gorgeous dresses"

"Yes, I spoke with Barry just a few hours ago. They are returning next week."

"Good. That will give me time to arrange a surprise gift for her. I must leave you men for a few minutes."

Claude immediately cringed, wondering what Marie-France had planned, and remembered the somewhat hostile interaction that had occurred. He sensed a problem in the making.

" Barry and I will need to make reservations for the trip. How are you intending to travel to Aruba, Buzz?"

"I intend to take our new Cessna Citation Latitude jet. You are welcome to travel with us. It has the range to fly directly to Aruba without needing a refueling stop. I think it's best if we all travel together. I have been in contact with the Hyatt and we can obtain a wedding group package. I cannot confirm anything yet until we know Barry and Yvette will join in with us."

"I am sure they will, after all, Yvette is an important part of the ceremony. It only makes sense we all travel together. Go ahead and make the arrangements. Remember that Marie-France has requested our chef Jacques to prepare food at the wedding. I believe Jacques has been in contact with the Executive Chef of the Hyatt and the two of them have been working together in planning the reception foods."

"I had forgotten Jacques. Thank you for reminding me."

"How long will you stay in Aruba? I need to attend to some business back in France, after which I intend to take a vacation. I am tired. The stress of always being aware of the gang pursuing me has caused me a lot of worries. I need to get away from business for a while."

"Where will you take your vacation?"

"My friend, the Cultural Attaché at the San Francisco French Consulate is traveling on business to Tahiti. He has invited me to accompany him. I am seriously considering it."

"When is this happening?"

"After the wedding, and when Barry has returned and taken control of the Estate. First, I must return to France to receive an award from the French Government for the wines and the record exports that the de Passioné have achieved. It's a very prestigious affair."

Buzz listened attentively. He was about to leave when Marie-France entered the room. She had changed into new attire. Claude did not know whether he should laugh or cry. Buzz broke the silence.

"Marie-France, you look splendid. Where did you get that stunning outfit?"

Claude looked in disbelief. Marie-France was draped in dark brown wooden beads that hung over a large floppy purple and black tie-dyed blouse, tight artificial crocodile skin jeans, and knee-high black patent leather boots. Carved wooden earrings in the shape of African figures dangled from her ears.

Marie-France beamed at Buzz's comment.

"I'm pleased you like it. It is my traveling outfit for Aruba. I think the Aruban people will love it."

Chapter 50

Slowly, the weeks passed at the Estate. Barry returned from Australia with Yvette. Almost every day sensational news articles detailed the massive bust of the international crime ring.

Claude became increasingly impatient while waiting to attend the function in France. He was unsettled and found it hard to concentrate on the family's business affairs.

Marie-France and Buzz were preoccupied with the wedding plans. Everything for the wedding in Aruba seemed to be progressing according to plan. The day arrived for Marie-France to visit the bridal gown boutique with Yvette for the final fitting. She called the private number Yvette had provided her.

"Yvette, We need to visit the boutique to try on our dresses for my big event. When is convenient for you?"

Yvette thought to herself silently. "No time is convenient."

"I have time this afternoon. Will this be the last visit?"

"Yes. We leave for Aruba next Monday. I hope you will be ready."

"Marie-France, Is Barry available? I would like to speak with him."

"He is in the office with Claude. I will let him know you are on the phone."

She left to find Barry, who was sitting with Claude. They were both laughing at a joke Barry had heard during his Australia visit.

"What is so funny?"

"It's a man's joke. Don't worry."

"Barry, I have Yvette on the phone downstairs. She wishes to speak with you."

Barry quickly left the office and ran down the stairs.

"Yvette. Is everything alright?"

"Not really, Barry. Marie-France wants to go to the boutique this afternoon to try on those horrible dresses for her wedding. I wish there was a way for me to cancel. I am not looking forward to this. I am certain she has planned some nasty surprise for me. Can you come to the city this afternoon? We can have an early dinner. You can stay at my apartment for the night."

"Let me speak with Claude and call you back. He leaves for that award presentation in France tomorrow, so we will need to come into the city for him to take the flight."

Barry ended the call and went back to the office to speak with Claude.

"I need to be in the city in the morning. The Air France flight leaves mid-afternoon. I will need to be at the airport before noon, so why don't we both go together and stay overnight. You can drop me off at the airport in the morning. I will ask Buzz to take Marie-France for the fitting."

Barry was delighted with the suggestion and called Yvette to advise her.

Claude spoke to Buzz who was delighted to take Marie-France to the boutique and the prospect of a night in the city.

"I will call my friend, Denis, and ask if he is available for dinner. You and Buzz have your partners and I am sure you both wish privacy and to be alone for the evening. I won't be having a late evening as that trip to France is only a two-day trip and I want to be refreshed when I leave. I will no sooner return, then it will be time to leave for the wedding in Aruba."

That evening, each couple left Claude and went for their dinners and entertainment. Claude met Denis at Alioto's for a dinner of fresh fish. He looked forward to the Alaska King Crab dinner.

Over dinner, Denis advised of his travel plans for his trip to Tahiti.

"Claude, I will be leaving in just over 2 weeks. You will be back from the wedding in Aruba. Why don't you join me? It will be a nice break for you. As I am traveling on official business, I can assure you we will receive first-class treatment in Tahiti."

Claude thought about the idea of a trip to the South Sea. He fondly remembered his earlier trips, and especially the time he spent in Rarotonga. He made up his mind.

"Yes, I think I would like to join you."

"Excellent. Send me your passport information and I will have our travel planners arrange for us to be booked together. We can arrange financial details later. This will be a great trip for you."

After dinner, Claude returned to his hotel and found Barry and Yvette enjoying a nightcap in the hotel lobby bar. The lighting was dim and only a few people were seated in the bar.

As he approached he looked at Yvette. Her eyes were puffy and tired.

"Yvette. Are you alright? You do not look happy."

"Claude, with all respect, your mother is a real nasty bitch. The dress she has had made for me is horrible. It is bright orange and I look like an oversize pumpkin on Halloween. I cannot wear it."

Claude thought about the situation before answering.

"Yvette, she has her own style. I suggest you put it on right before the ceremony and then remove it immediately after."

"But she is having photos taken. I do not want to be seen in that sack she has had them make. She has done this on purpose. I am not stupid. I know when I see revenge. I am thinking of becoming ill and unable to go to the wedding."

Barry decided it was time to intervene and offered his solution.

"I suggest you go as planned. Take something nice to wear and the dress she has had made. Just before the wedding have an unfortunate accident that damages the dress beyond repair then wear the one you like. That should make things corker. Problem solved. Now let's have some fun deciding on the accident you can have."

Yvette immediately brightened up and her mood changed.

"That's why I love you, Barry. You are a grown-up rascal."

Claude shook his head and stood up to leave.

"I'm not sure I want to know anymore."

Barry was laughing heartily.

"Strewth, Mate. Got to have some bloody fun with all this nonsense. She's off her fucking rocker anyway."

As much as Claude did not appreciate Barry's comment, he knew it to be true. He wondered what Buzz possibly saw in her. She was eccentric and past middle age, but extremely wealthy. Buzz was also very wealthy. The whole relationship confused him. Claude walked away after saying goodnight.

Part 13

Betrothed

Chapter 51

Finally, two days before the wedding arrived. Buzz had the aircraft readied for their morning departure. He filed a flight plan which took them to Miami and then onto Aruba. He checked the plane thoroughly and double-checked the fuel load and consumption figures. He decided to take on more fuel in Miami to be safe.

In the office, he gave last-minute instructions to Cynthia Honeysucker. Her mood was dark. She detested losing Buzz to Marie-France who she had decided was a hussy, regardless of her wealth.

Buzz walked from the office and spent time speaking to his co-pilot. Other workers were loading the party's luggage onto the plane.

With everyone onboard, Buzz instructed the co-pilot to start the engines. There was a low whine that rose in pitch as the speed of the spinning turbines increased. They taxied out to the runway. Buzz radioed San Francisco air traffic and relayed his flight info and waited until he received clearance.

The co-pilot revved the engines and released the brake. The Cessna accelerated sharply and within a minute they were airborne. Claude was impressed with the roominess in the plane and how quiet it was. The co-pilot climbed rapidly to reach an altitude of 38,000 feet per the approved flight plan. Once they reached altitude, the co-pilot throttled back to a cruising speed of 600 miles per hour. Buzz calculated that with the tailwind, they would arrive in Miami in just less than five hours. He allowed an hour in Miami for fuelling before continuing on the two hours thirty-minute flight to Reina Beatrix airport in Aruba.

The flight conditions were perfect. Flying across the United States there was no turbulence. Along the way, Buzz passed off from each air traffic control center. The flight conditions were perfect and Buzz was happy.

Approximately an hour out of Miami, they hit turbulence over the Dominican Republic. The Cessna bounced as it lost and regained altitude. Buzz called Miami tower and requested a change in altitude, which was granted within a minute. They continued over the deep blue ocean until the radio crackled welcoming them into Aruban airspace.

Marie-France craned her neck to look out the window. In the distance, she could see the shape of the small Aruban island. As they approached and dropped in height, she saw the pure white sand beaches.

Buzz took the controls for the landing. He had been given a flight path that took them over the sand dunes at the north end of the island and then on a southern path past Malmok and Palm Beach. Buzz followed the controller's instructions and turned left past the capital of Oranjestad and dropped down onto the airport runway. He applied the reverse thrusters and the plane shuddered as it quickly slowed. He was advised to taxi to an area and await Customs and Immigration.

The formalities were performed quickly and the Immigration staff were thrilled that Buzz and Marie-France had chosen to marry in Aruba.

The airport's contracted aviation company advised Buzz that they would tow the plane to a storage location. Buzz was given contact information and instructions to follow before they would be able to fly back from Aruba.

Yvette loved the warm wind that blew. She loved the heat. After they crossed the tarmac, they were escorted through the main terminal and found taxis waiting to take them to their destination.

On their way from the airport, they drove by Governor's Bay and through the capital, Oranjestad, with its majestic Dutch-inspired buildings. Two large cruise ships were docked and the traffic crawled as tourists crossed the narrow road in pursuit of souvenirs and other items. Marie-France was delighted to see some of the world's leading fashion and jewelry stores.

Barry had stayed very quiet the whole trip. Claude found it unusual.

"Barry, you are very quiet. Are you not well?"

"I'm fine. I just enjoyed the trip on the plane. The first time I have flown on a private plane, and now I'm looking at all the different buildings and things here."

They continued in the taxi for another five minutes until the driver turned sharply and swooped into the banked entrance to the Hyatt Hotel. A doorman walked briskly to the taxi and opened the passenger doors. He extended his hand to assist Marie-France and then Yvette.

The entrance to the lobby was imposing. The hotel staff hurried to help them with luggage and guided assistance to the front desk. A female concierge approached Buzz who informed the woman that they were there for a wedding. She advised the party to wait and left to get a manager.

Minutes later they were escorted to rooms on the top floor overlooking Palm Beach and the Caribbean. Marie-France and Buzz were taken to a special bridal suite.

So far, the wedding plans were unfolding perfectly.

Barry stripped into a bathing suit, T-Shirt, and flip-flops to head to the beach. Still tanned and looking healthy, Yvette changed into her bikini to join him. With frozen cocktails in hand, they splashed into the warm waters of Palm Beach.

Claude found himself alone and feeling lonely. He looked out the window from his room and watched couples and families enjoying the beach. Barry was now occupied with Yvette, and Marie-France and Buzz were wrapped up with each other and their plans. Claude decided to leave the hotel and browse the local stores.

He walked along the Palm Beach road behind the hotels until he reached a small restaurant. He was hungry after the day's travel and decided to eat early.

The restaurant was not busy and he was taken to a table that looked out to the Caribbean. The waitress was charming and somewhat intrigued by the handsome customer. She provided a menu and inquired what he would like.

"I have been traveling all day and I am thirsty. Do you have a good beer you can recommend?"

"Would you like to try our local beer? It's called Balashi. We have it in the bottle and ice cold."

Although Claude drank beer very seldom, he decided to go with her recommendation. He was not one for fancy tropical drinks.

Thoughts ran through his mind. The romances he had when younger had all crumbled. His one serious love was killed by the hippie college girl in her Volkswagen Kombi van the day he wished to propose to her. A feeling of increased gloom grew. Claude decided there was no one for him. Friends, and now his mother all had romances and partners. Claude felt bitter that he was alone.

He looked across at the waitress and guessed she was in her early thirties. She was extremely attractive but Claude had no desire to try and engage with her.

After a while, she returned to take Claude's order.

"Is there anything you see that you would like to order?"

"No. Can you recommend a nice local dish for me?"

"I suggest you try our Keshi Yena. We make it here. It's delicious. It is like a small chicken casserole. There is a bottom layer of a light garlic tomato sauce and the shredded chicken is mixed with nuts and prunes. The dish is then covered with Gouda cheese and baked. You won't regret trying it."

"That sounds nice. I will take your advice."

Claude enjoyed his ice-cold beer and the Keshi Yena. When he finished he asked for the bill and gave the girl a large tip, but she had hoped for more of Claude than just a money tip.

"Thank you, sir. Please come back. My name is Lucinda and it will be my pleasure to look after you."

Claude smiled and made his way back to the Hyatt.

Chapter 52

Back at the hotel, Claude walked into the lobby and found Marie-France and Buzz sitting and talking with a woman. Books and papers were scattered on the table in front of them. Marie-France beckoned Claude to join them.

"Claude, this is Carla de Cuba our wedding planner. I have been speaking with her over the phone, but now it's nice to meet her personally. Carla has everything set up for our sunset wedding tomorrow. I am so excited. Carla, this is my son, Claude."

Carla smiled as her eyes took in Claude's physique and handsome face.

"It is nice to meet you, Claude. I did not see a name for a partner for you at the wedding. Did I miss something?"

"No, I am here alone. I will not be able to stay for long in Aruba as I have other commitments. It was nice to meet you, but I am tired and am going to go and retire early."

Claude left for his room. Even though he was tired, he showered and collapsed into the luxurious bed. Sleep came easily.

In the morning he awoke to a bright sun and clear blue sky and checked his watch. He decided to call Barry for an early breakfast. The hotel operator connected him to Barry's room. The phone rang and rang unanswered. Claude decided Barry and Yvette had already gone for breakfast. He dressed quickly and proceeded to the breakfast restaurant. It was a beautiful location styled to look like ancient ruins. An outside patio overlooked a pool with a cascading waterfall. Black swans swam in the pool and large koi fish swam lazily looking for food.

Claude looked around but did not see Barry and Yvette. He decided to ask the waiter whether they had been at the restaurant for breakfast. Claude described them and the waiter shook his head. Claude was puzzled, but then decided they must have gone for an early morning walk on the beach.

For the next two hours, Claude walked both Palm and Eagle Beaches in an attempt to locate them. He was concerned, knowing that Marie-France had arranged hairdressing and makeup appointments early afternoon before the wedding.

He returned to the hotel and encountered Buzz enjoying a light breakfast accompanied by a large decorated Bloody Mary. Buzz was in an upbeat mood.

"Care to join me. The Bloody Marys here are great. Let me get you one."

"Buzz, I have been looking for Barry and Yvette for the past few hours. I am concerned. It's unlike Barry to take off and not inform me. If Marie-France finds out they are not here she will go beserk. Carla de Cuba, the wedding planner had things planned today. I hope they show up here soon."

"I wouldn't worry. Marie-France has herself far too occupied than to be looking for them. I will not say anything to her."

Together they sat and enjoyed their drinks. As Claude was about to leave he noticed Barry and Yvette walking through the lobby. He rushed over to them.

"Where have you been? I have been looking everywhere for you."

"I hired a driver and had him drive us around a bit. We went down through San Nicolaas to an area called Baby Beach. Took a swim there. It's an interesting little island."

"Is Yvette ready for the appointments the Carla de Cuba has set up today? Are you ready?"

"I'm as ready as any bloke would be to watch someone get hitched. Ask me, it's a bit of a load."

Buzz chuckled.

"It's not exactly going to be a wedding without some humor. I have a little surprise in store for everyone."

"Buzz, we are going to need your help. Yvette tried on that Orange dress that Marie-France had made for her. It is bloody horrible. Looks like a potato sack. In Australia, Yvette had used an Australian natural suntan product that was meant to promote a tan but turns her an orange shade when she is in the sun. When she wears that dress and with her skin color, she looks hideous. Like a giant pumpkin. She tore the dress off in a fit and it is damaged beyond repair. Don't worry though. She has brought another tasteful outfit. All should be good. I need you to tell her this."

"I will, but be ready for her tantrum. Remember we are all meant to meet a little later for a pre-wedding lunch."

Buzz excused himself. Yvette left to shower and clean up after her swim at Baby Beach. Barry ordered a double round of Balashi beers and settled in for a chat with Claude.

"Barry, things seem to be getting serious between you and Yvette. Is it just a friendship or more?"

"Now that you ask mate, I should tell you that we got engaged in Australia. We wanted to keep it quiet for a while. I'll let you know if anything changes. Yvette is worried about her position at the Consulate if it becomes known. She has another year or so to go on her contract."

"I guess I should congratulate you. Have you thought about how this may change our business partnership?"

"While Yvette loved Australia, she has decided to live in California after her contract with the French is complete. I don't have any plans to move from California, so I don't see any changes happening. What about you, fella? Any damsels you've got hidden away?"

"No, Barry. Seems I'm going to be a bachelor for some time."

For the next hour, they sat talking before Claude recommended they go and dress for the luncheon.

Shortly before noon, Marie-France, accompanied by Carla de Cuba and Yvette entered the patio restaurant and joined Claude and Barry for the lunch. The hotel provided a complimentary magnum of champagne. Several guests at other tables extended congratulations.

Marie-France was ecstatic to be the center of attention. Waiters circled and ensured glasses were filled and plates of food were swiftly delivered. The conversation was light and bubbly. A happy atmosphere prevailed.

Claude watched in amazement as dishes containing crudités, meats, and seafood were presented.

Marie-France was unaware of the resentment that Yvette harbored. She had yet to be told of the destruction of Yvette's dress. She believed she had exacted her revenge on Yvette by selecting that horrible orange dress.

In silence, Yvette watched Marie-France devour food as if she was a vacuum cleaner. Yvette looked at the ring of shrimp that Marie-France was attacking. She noticed one of the shrimps Marie-France was eating had a bright yellow-orange color in its tail. A sure sign the shrimp was bad. Yvette was torn between telling her and just leaving the situation as her act of revenge. Yvette smiled as she thought of the consequences of eating bad shrimp.

Carla de Cuba briefed them on the last-minute arrangements. All seemed to understand and were happy. Marie-France was purely effervescent.

After the luncheon concluded, everyone retired to their rooms to sleep, except for Claude who decided he would spend time resting poolside, until it was time for the wedding. He looked at his watch. Four more hours until six-thirty when the sun would set as the wedding proceeded.

After a while, Claude went to his room, changed into his bathing suit, and returned to the pool. He watched over couples and families enjoying the pool and the warm, sunny afternoon. Feelings of loneliness returned.

Chapter 53

The sun slipped down toward the horizon in the west. The sky was dotted with clouds that assumed and reflected orange and pink from the sun's setting rays.

On the beach, the white arbor was brightly decorated with roses and other flowers. Soft music played. Seating was arranged in front of the arbor on the pure white sand. Guests were slowly arriving. The wedding officiate stood to the right of the arbor waiting for the arrival of the bride and her maid of honor. Buzz stood beside the officiate. He was dressed in his best country and western gear with a silver and turquoise bolo tied around his neck.

Suddenly the music changed to the Bridal March and Marie-France, dressed in her turquoise dress, started her walk down the beach to the arbor, accompanied by Yvette who wore a shimmering light green dress. Claude, as best man stood dressed in his white linen suit. It was a fairytale scene.

Curious onlookers on the beach congregated a little distance back from the wedding party and guests. Some clapped and called out wishes to Marie-France as she slowly navigated her way to Buzz.

Buzz took Marie-France's hand and recited the words spoken by the wedding officiate. The wedding was over in minutes. Buzz took Marie-France in an embrace and kissed her for what seemed the longest time. The DJ played some joyful music. The guests mingled and champagne was served by white-coated waiters and waitresses.

Eventually, the guests and official members of the wedding were directed to tables set up on the beach. Tiki lamps burned as the wedding reception started. Various friends gave toasts to the cheers and clapping. Buzz remained seated and silent. The twilight started to fade at which time Buzz stood and went to the DJ. He took the microphone and addressed to guests.

"I thank everyone who came to our special event today. I won't speak long, but I have a special treat for my wife and you all. When I first met Marie-France it was at a country line dance where I called the words to one of the favorite tunes. I would like to repeat that now for you all and especially my wife."

The music started and Buzz started to whistle and call the words to the 'do-si-do'. He paused to allow the harmonica section to play before resuming. The guests started clapping to the tune and line dancing. The mood was infectious. The music was too much for the assembled onlookers on the beach who started dancing on the sand. Within minutes, over fifty were dancing. Girls were jiggling in bikinis and men in speedos and board shorts were gyrating. Buzz finished the song with loud and long applause. Many of the onlookers called for more. Buzz was only too happy to oblige with more songs, and his impromptu beach party continued for the next hour, as more beachgoers joined in.

Buzz looked up to see some of Aruba's local police standing at the entrance to the beach watching. Some were smiling and clapping.

The festivities ended late. Buzz was exhausted. Marie-France started to feel nauseous. The shrimp was hitting and hitting hard. Her wedding night was destroyed by frequent vomiting and diarrhea attacks.

In the morning, Claude joined Barry and Yvette for breakfast. He had stopped to invite Buzz and Marie-France to breakfast but quickly changed his mind when he saw her pasty white face.

Yvette enjoyed the moment as Claude told them of the problem.

While they were eating, Claude turned serious.

"Barry, I have made a decision. I am very tired as a result of the threats from the Chinese gangs and I am also somewhat despondent. My friend Denis will be traveling to Tahiti and invited me along to see the island. I need a vacation and intend to go with him. I am asking you to assume responsibility for the California and French vineyards and wineries. It has been years since I took some time for myself."

"Do you know when you will leave?"

"I will call Denis upon my return. I believe he is eager to leave as soon a possible."

Part 14

South Seas

Chapter 54

Papeete Faa'a International Airport, Tahiti.

It was four-thirty in the morning when Denis and Claude's flight landed in Tahiti. They had left Los Angeles at eleven in the night. The eight-hour flight had been without incident.

As Claude stepped from the plane, the heat and heady aroma of the tropics filled the air around him. He breathed in the soft air and scent of the frangipani as they walked from the tarmac to the airport terminal. Native girls dressed in costume offered leis to the visiting tourists much to their delight.

After retrieving their luggage and passing through Customs and Immigration, they exited the terminal. A driver was waiting to take Denis to his hotel.

"Did you have a good trip, Sir?"

"Yes thank you. I am traveling with my friend. He is staying at the Intercontinental so he can join us for the ride."

The driver loaded their luggage into the trunk of the Peugeot wagon and in the breaking light of dawn drove to the Intercontinental.

At the hotel, they checked in and decided to catch a few hours' sleep, and agreed to meet for lunch before exploring the island.

Exhausted, Claude fell into a deep sleep and was awakened in the morning by the unique tones of the ringing phone. Wearily he answered to hear the voice of Denis.

"Time to get up and let Tahiti know we are here. Come on down. I am in the bar sampling a few exotic drinks."

Claude arose and headed to the shower. He was amazed at the selection of cosmetic products supplied by the hotel. He selected a vanilla soap and ginger shampoo and soaked himself to wash off the exhaustion and grime of traveling. After showering, Claude dressed in a lightweight white cotton shirt, linen pants, and lightweight brown leather loafers.

He found Denis at the bar. They decided to take a light lunch at the lagoon side restaurant before relaxing on the beach and in the pool that afternoon.

In the restaurant, Denis ordered seared scallops. Claude chose the poached salmon and a bottle of crisp chardonnay.

Claude watched Denis as they ate. He had a roving eye and was intently watching the pretty Tahitian girls.

"I am captured by the beauty of these women every time I visit Tahiti. I understand why Paul Gauguin painted these women with such detail and passion."

"Denis, maybe you should marry one. You are single and wealthy. What's stopping you?"

"I have my heart set on a French Canadian girl, Guylaine. She has captured my heart. I am hoping to marry her soon, but she is pursued by many men who want her hand. What about you, Claude? You are surely a prize catch for any woman. You have wineries, a nice lifestyle, seem healthy, and are good-looking. What is holding you back?"

"It seems I have never been lucky in my love adventures. I have met many women, some of whom I loved, yet fate intervened and the romances went nowhere. The fiancé I wished to marry died in that car accident and it seemed that events have always happened that destroy any relationship I had. The last one with Misty Moon turned into a disaster. Now that she has exposed information on the gangs and the crimes and the ring leaders, she wants to see me again. I think the risk is too high, even though she had been given a new identity and life by the FBI. So I will not see her."

"It seems you have had too much drama in your life. After all those revelations by her, you need to find some peace in your life."

"Denis, I was most at peace when I was in Rarotonga. I enjoyed the people and the way of life there. I also had one of the most romantic times of my life there. Unfortunately, too much time has passed since then. It was over three years ago. I did write to her for about a year, but I never received a response. Her name was Atarangi and she was beautiful, both as a person and physically."

"If you enjoyed it so much, why don't you make a trip there. It's only two and a bit hours to Rarotonga from here. I will not be going there on this trip as it was a New Zealand protectorate and not one of the many French islands. I would love to see it one day."

"Denis, I am not sure it will be the same for me after being away for over three years. I have lost all contact with the people I knew there. I would find it hard to return."

Denis steered the conversation away from the topic.

"This is not my first time in Tahiti. I will show you some of the island this afternoon. Tomorrow I must attend to official business."

They finished their meal and Claude wished to return to his room to call the Estate. On his way to the room, he passed by the hotel bookstore. Various newspapers were displayed at the entrance. He glanced at them and froze in his tracks. There amongst the French papers, was an English paper. The headlines screamed **'MAJOR INTERNATIONAL CRIMINAL RING BUSTED'**. A large photo of Dagmar Stryker headlined the story. Claude grabbed up a paper and hurried into the store to pay. He went to his room to read the article.

The article was long. Claude sat and carefully read the whole piece. His anonymity in the case had been guaranteed and respected. Dagmar had controlled the press interview and stated that because of an Asian informant, they had been able to recover a dossier of information containing names, phone numbers, gang affiliations, banking information, ports, and transit routes. There was no mention of the USB Memory stick or Claude. Dagmar had carefully created a diversion that claimed all the material was obtained during their investigation after receiving information from the informant.

Claude sensed relief and found his mood lightened as the stress of wondering whether the investigation he had left behind would implicate him. The FBI had kept their word. He wondered if it would be enough for the gangs to give up their pursuit of him in their efforts to find the USB memory stick.

He thought back to the visit of Crystal Moon and the lies she had told Barry. He needed to contact Paddy and the FBI to determine whether she had been arrested during the raids that had been made. He looked at his watch. With the three-hour time difference between Tahiti and San Francisco, he would still be able to reach Paddy.

The phone rang at Paddy's desk until answered by his assistant.

"It is Claude de Passioné. I need to speak with Paddy. Is he available?"

"No, he is at a press conference with the FBI representatives. There is another local press conference afterward. I can leave a message for him to call you."

"No. I will call him at his home later. Please tell him I called and to expect the call."

Claude returned to the lobby to find Denis waiting impatiently. He had changed into tropical holiday wear and looked every bit like a foreign tourist. Claude laughed.

"Claude, I have hired a driver to spend the afternoon with us touring some of the points of interest on the island."

The driver, who was dressed in a bright yellow shirt, khaki shorts, and flip-flops, was waiting outside the lobby and upon seeing them jumped from his old Cadillac convertible and opened the door.

For the balance of the afternoon, they were entertained with tales of the Tahiti and yesteryear, peppered with local folklore. Claude wondered how much was fact and how much was fiction.

The sun was setting when they returned to the hotel. Both Claude and Denis decided to shower and rest a little before meeting for dinner.

Two hours later, they met for dinner at the overwater Le Lotus restaurant. Claude was impressed by the restaurant and the menu. It reminded him of some of the meals served in the restaurants in Paris. He was happy.

"Denis, I phoned the detective in San Francisco. He provided me with some excellent news. It seems the one person who I feared was behind the troubles has been captured. That is a huge relief."

The conversation drifted to their cars and wine. There was a lull of several minutes until Claude spoke.

"You are right, Denis, and I have made a decision. I was happy in Rarotonga and should not be concerned about a return visit. I have decided to go and find the people who I knew there. I have nothing to be ashamed of or hide from. I have booked a direct flight on Air New Zealand for tomorrow. Maybe when your business here is complete you can join me there."

"I would like that, but when I am finished here I need to visit Noumea and New Caledonia. It will depend if I can take time off before returning to California. I will do my best."

That night, Claude retired happily.

Part 15

Finding Peace

Chapter 55

Rarotonga, The Cook Islands.

The drive from the Rarotonga International Airport to the Takitumu Villas was quick. At the Villas, he was greeted by Nana who he remembered from his previous visit. Upon seeing Claude, she rushed from behind the reception desk and hugged him.

"Welcome back. I am so happy to see you. Where have you been? We missed you."

"I needed to return to France due to the death of my father. It became necessary for me to become involved in the operation of our family business. I did send letters here to Atarangi and her family but never received a reply. Are they all right?"

Nana diverted her eyes from Claude and shuffled uncomfortably.

"I have not seen much of the family. I believe Atarangi has been working at the perfume factory. Come let me take you to your villa. I know you loved the villa on the beach so that is the one I reserved for you."

Claude sensed her discomfort when asking about Atarangi and decided not to pursue the topic.

Nana led Claude from the reception area down past a giant pool and garden area containing tropical plants. Koi fish swam lazily up to the edge of the pool seeking food. Within minutes they arrived at the pure white sand beach and walked along to Claude's favorite villa. The villa was deceptive. The exterior was decorated as a grass hut, but inside there was a large Jacuzzi, a modern kitchen, air conditioning, and a bedroom equipped with a king-size bed over which a tropical fan hung. Claude's memories flooded back reminding him of his earlier amorous time in the villa with Atarangi.

Nana placed the keys on the kitchen counter, before turning to Claude.

"Is there anything you want, Claude?"

"No, I will just take a walk and then take an early dinner."

Nana stood silently looking at Claude. She seemed anxious. Claude sensed she wished to say something.

"Nana, you seem reserved. Is there something I should know?"

"It is awkward for me to tell you of some things."

"Please, if it is something I should know, then tell me."

Nana hesitated and twisted her hands together before speaking.

"Claude, I realize that you needed to depart in a hurry on your last trip due to the death of your father. There are people you were close with here who feel you betrayed them. Some are angry. You may find that certain people will stay away from you."

"But I did send letters and never received a response. I don't know why anyone would be upset at me."

"I am certain you will find out in time. Now I must go back to the desk. We have more guests due to check-in."

Nana left Claude alone. He unpacked his clothes, wondering what her comment meant. He changed into a pair of shorts and a light shirt and decided to take a walk along the beach.

The beach was empty except for several local men in the lagoon spearfishing. Claude stood for minutes watching as they plunged the long spears into the water and then pulled them up with a speared fish flapping and struggling. The speared fish were then dropped into a large flax basket.

He continued his walk along the beach toward an outcrop of rock that designated the end of the beach. He noticed a sandy track leading from the beach and up through some dense vegetation. Curious as to where it led, Claude decided to follow it. The track wound its way up to the sealed road that lead back to the villas and into the village.

On the corner of the track and road, there was a shack with a sign above it reading 'Mikey T's Pastissereie and Bake Shop.' A small group of local women stood at the window counter. As he approached, Claude smelled the aroma of freshly baked items. It was then he realized he was hungry. As he walked up to the counter, the local women fell silent. There was a noticeable lapse in the laughing and chattering. The women looked at him in an unsmiling manner as he approached. The normal warm and friendly Rarotongan greeting of Kia Orana was missing. Claude was aware that he was not being welcomed. The women disbanded while he stood at the counter.

Inside the little bakery, Claude watched as Mikey withdrew hot trays from the ovens and placed them on wooden counters. She turned to Claude.

"Good afternoon. What delight can I tempt you with?"

"I am not sure yet. Let me look at the selection."

"Take your time. Everything is good. I haven't seen you here before. Are you just visiting on vacation?"

"Yes. I was here years ago and have always wanted to return. I do not remember your bakery though."

"No. I started my business a year ago. The local people have a sweet tooth and love my baked goods. I have had to adapt my baking for their tastes. I had to learn to use things like coconut, mango, pineapple, passionfruit, and papaya in my baking. I have enjoyed learning to do this."

"If I might ask, where are you from?"

"I am from Canada. My name is Michele and my mother was of French Canadian descent. I learned a lot from her about baking and cooking. She was a master in the kitchen and prepared marvelous meals and baked treats."

Claude surveyed the glass display case before making his selection.

"I will take one of those small pies, two of the palmiers, and a local lemon and sugar crepe.

Mikey took a small white box into which she carefully placed his purchase.

"Where are you staying? How long will you stay here on the island?"

"I'm staying at the Takitumu Villas. That is where I stayed on my last visit. I have no idea how long I will be staying as there is some business I need to finish."

Mikey frowned, wondering what business he could possibly have. She looked out over the counter and was surprised to see that all the locals had left. It was unusual as the shack had become a favorite meeting place for them to have coffee and treats.

Claude took his purchases and turned to leave.

"Thank you. I am sure I will be seeing you again. There are many pastries here I would love to try. I will see you later."

Claude walked back along the beach to the hotel. He watched as a group of young children ran on the beach and splashed into the water. He listened to their excited squeals of laughter and thought of how ideal it was for a child to grow up on the island.

Back at the hotel, he sat on the beach in front of his villa and enjoyed his pastries. He gazed out over the blue Pacific ocean and reflected on his earlier trip to the island. His thoughts wandered to the times he had spent with Atarangi and her family. It was then that Claude decided he would find Atarangi. He needed to know why the locals were avoiding him. At Mikey T's shack, he had seen a couple of women he had met on his previous visit. They had turned their eyes away from him. It troubled him. He recalled Nana's words… 'you will find out in time'. Claude decided it was time to confront Nana.

Chapter 56

In the lobby, Nana was working with a small tour group who had just arrived. She saw Claude and waved a greeting. He walked up to the desk past the tourists.

"Nana, I must speak with you. Can we meet later?"

Nana was flustered and fidgeted with some papers that provided her a distraction.

"Claude, I have a church meeting I must attend. I will not have time today. Maybe tomorrow."

Recognizing that he had been stalled, Claude decided to attempt and find out what the problem was. He returned to his room and phoned a rental company to rent a moped.

After the moped was delivered, Claude set off in the direction of the perfume factory that was owned by Atarangi's family. He sped along the road which circled the island. Thick tropical vegetation lined either side of the road. Colorful birds flew from the palms at the sound of Claude approaching on the moped. It was late afternoon and the sky was lit with clouds reflecting the light orange glow of the setting sun.

He arrived at the perfume factory as it was closing. He dismounted and walked down the frangipani lined path and into the factory where he recognized several members of Atarangi's family. Some turned and left but the brothers stayed. He was greeted in a cool manner. It was unlike the friendship he had experienced before.

"I am looking for Atarangi. Is there something wrong?"

The brothers exchanged glances and the older spoke.

"She is not here. She has gone to visit relatives on another island. You should leave her alone. You broke her heart after you left. You shouldn't see her. You are not welcome here by our family and friends."

"I do not know what I have done to be treated like this. Can you explain?"

"It is not for us to explain. We wish you would just leave the island and never return."

"I cannot think of anything I did to harm anyone here. Please tell me."

The brothers turned and walked away.

Saddened, Claude returned to the moped. He decided to drive and circle the island before returning to the hotel. The views of the beaches and water were stunning. He loved Rarotonga and vowed he would find out what trouble was attributed to him, though he could not think of anything.

He circled the island and arrived in the main township of Avarua. He slowed and cruised past the few stores with tourists looking in the windows in search of souvenirs. As he was about to leave the outskirt of the township, he passed by the Punanga Nui outdoor market. A few stalls were manned but almost all of the vendors awaited Saturday when it became the social event on the island and most islanders attended and intermingled with the tourists. Claude slowed to look at the market. As he drove past the entrance he spied a woman he believed was Atarangi. He spun around and raced back to where he had seen her. There was no trace of the woman. He parked the moped and walked into the stalls. A few women were packing up their artwork and jewelry before retiring for the day.

Claude asked several if they had seen Atarangi or knew where she could be found. Each question he asked was met with a blank stare.

Frustrated and despondent, Claude returned to the hotel and went to his villa. He was hoping that news of his presence on the island had reached Atarangi and she had contacted the hotel with a message for him. There was no message. He knew she was aware he was on the island.

The sky darkened as night fell. Claude ordered a light meal from the restaurant that he could take to the beach. He sat alone eating and deep in thought. Again, like the mystery of the gangs pursuing him in California, he was dealing with another less dangerous unknown.

The more he thought of the situation, the more he became determined to solve the puzzle. The reactions of the women at the outdoor market convinced him they knew far more than they were prepared to admit. As he sat on the beach in the dark he formulated a plan.

The next morning, Claude went early to Mikey's Patisserie and Bakeshop for fresh croissants and coffee. He returned to his favorite place on the beach. He mused about the day ahead and decided that for the two days until the outdoor market on Saturday, he would play at being a tourist. The thought of that made him laugh. There wasn't much he hadn't explored before with Atarangi.

Determined to look the part of a tourist, Claude visited Rarotonga's version of a department store. The selection was dated which suited Claude fine as he didn't want to create a fashion statement. He purchased a floppy sun hat, sunglasses, white socks, cargo shorts, a t-shirt emblazoned with a 'Visit New Zealand' logo, and some Roman sandals. He was convinced that when dressed in the clothes he would pass as an Australian or New Zealand tourist.

Back at his hotel he dressed and set out to join in with a tour operated by one of the small local companies. He needed his new clothes to look used before his Saturday objective of finding and surprising Atarangi.

He dressed and admired himself in the bedroom mirror. With his floppy hat angled like an Australian military hat, the t-shirt, and the long grey cargo shorts he looked every bit a tourist. In his mind, the final touch was the best. The open-toe Roman sandals worn with high white cotton socks finished his disguise perfectly. He chuckled thinking that Marie-France would approve.

Claude left the hotel and traveled to Avarua where he had noticed a tour company. As he parked his moped he noticed a small group waiting outside of Tiki Tours. He went into the office and was advised that the group would be hiking The Needle. Rarotonga's most famous hike. Claude was advised the hike was rugged and not for everyone. He decided to take the hike as he was bored and needed some adventure.

The small group was led by a guide named Mana. They walked along a road leading away from the exit of the outdoor market. As they passed the market, Claude again noticed the two women he knew to be friends of Atarangi. They were carrying boxes that he assumed contained the jewelry and other items they sold at their stall. The women glanced over at the group, but there was no indication they recognized Claude.

Mana chated to the group along the way. He described the hike ahead and warned them of the rugged conditions and the climb ahead. He promised they would have a view of the island from the top that would make the trek worthwhile.

They walked for a while on a paved road and Claude wondered why the guide had claimed the hike to be arduous. Finally, they reached a path overgrown with grass and plants and started their trek and climb to the Needle. The path was muddy and slippery. There were no handrails to support them. Roots of vines fell beside the track and the members of the group used these to pull themselves up as they climbed. There was a shout and Claude turned to see a young woman who had lost her footing crash across some rocks. Mana ordered the group to halt, while he went back to assist the woman. Within minutes Mana had her back on her feet. Fortunately, she was uninjured.

They continued on the climb. Each member of the group was covered in mud. Sweat dripped down their faces and soaked their clothes. Despite their condition, the group was in high spirits.

After an hour of pulling themselves up on root ladders, they reached the top of the huge rock from which the pinnacle, or Needle, rose to the sky. Claude looked around at the view. It was indeed magnificent. He looked out to the bright blue sea off the coast. He was tired, thirsty, and hungry. He cursed that he had not brought any water or food.

Claude wandered over to sit alone on a rock. He was not alone for long. Two Australian girls who found him interesting joined him and offered nuts and some water. He thanked them and they engaged in small talk. The girls were staying in Avarua and planned to attend a dance party that evening and invited Claude to join them. It was obvious to Claude they had more in mind than just dancing. He explained he had friends arriving that evening and would not be able to join them. Their disappointment was evident, and they invited Claude to join them for lunch and beach time the next day.

Claude was tempted but then thought of the problems he had just left behind. He decided he did not need any more issues. His goal was to find Atarangi.

While the group sat and refreshed, Mana idled over to Claude.

"Lucky thing we are doing this today. "

Mana pointed out to the west and some low cloud.

"That looks like a big storm forming. With the heat and high humidity, it will be a severe one if it makes it here. The winds are not blowing so it will probably take a couple of days before it arrives. Climbing the tracks up here after heavy rains is almost impossible."

Claude looked out to the clouds on the horizon. He would never have guessed a major storm was forming.

The group reassembled and started their descent. The conversation amongst them was quieter on the descent. They arrived back at the little tourist office mud-splattered, tired and happy.

As was leaving, the two Australian girls, Beth and Marion approached him.

"Would you like to join us tomorrow for a beach day? We are just going to hang out by the pool and take some walks on the beach."

"Thank you, but I have already made some plans."

The girls looked disappointed as they walked away.

Claude's interest was however piqued. The thought of spending the day on the beach with two scantily clad beauties was tempting him. He began to change his mind but then thought of his plan to find Atarangi.

Claude started the moped. As he pulled away he decided to stop at Mikeys Patisserie and buy some treats to enjoy while he lounged at the pool. He was ravished after the hike and could not wait until dinner.

Chapter 57

Upon entering the villa, Claude found an envelope had been slid under the door. He placed the envelope on his desk and went to strip off his muddy clothes and take a shower.

Dressed in clean clothes, he took the envelope and opened it. There was a message and a telephone number to call Denis in Tahiti.

Claude punched the numbers into the room phone. He listened to the phone ringing in Tahiti. After a while, Denis' voice came on the line.

"Claude, thank you for calling back. I was hoping to visit you in Rarotonga but now with my schedule revised by the powers in France, I will not have time. After I visit the other Islands I am to return immediately for an important briefing. I hope we can meet up in France. Do you know when you will return to California? Will you stay there long before returning to France?"

"I have a few things here to look after. After this weekend I should know. I will tell you."

"I hope we can meet again soon. After France, I will go to Canada. I have decided to find Guylaine and ask her to marry me. She may have many other man friends but I intend to win her over. If she accepts, I will be asking you to come to my wedding, wherever that may take place."

"I am sure she will want to marry you. I look forward to being invited to your wedding soon."

They ended the phone call. Claude decided he would visit Nana and ask her directly why he was being avoided by his old friends and acquaintances.

He found Nana working in a small office off the main reception area.

"Nana, I need to speak with you. Do you have a minute?"

Nana looked at him uncomfortably and beckoned him in.

"It is evident that people here are not happy with me. I have no idea what I could have possibly done to create this situation. Please try to help me understand. Maybe then I can correct whatever has happened."

"Claude, I think you are a good person and would never wish to harm anyone. The community is aware that after you left, you did not attempt to remain in contact with the girl that you had been so involved with. She and her family had made every effort to include you in our community. You were invited to traditional events, including a hangi where you enjoyed the roasting of meat and vegetables in the firepit dug into the earth. You were included in social gatherings with music and dancing. You did not attempt to keep these friends. Many feel you took advantage of the girl, her family, and your friends. They are insulted by your behavior. People believe you are a selfish individual who uses people to get what you want."

"Nana, that is not true. I wrote many letters to Atarangi and told her what was happening in my life in France and California. I asked her to share this with her family and the friends I had made. I do not understand."

Nana looked at him for the longest time without speaking, and when she did it stung like a whip.

"Claude, I do not believe that Atarangi would lie or hide those letters from others if they even exist. I suggest you go now and leave me alone. I think it would be best for you to leave the island as soon as you can. Some of the men in her family are very upset at what you did. You may be in danger. Now, go."

Claude left feeling alone and discouraged. He was no further ahead in finding the reason that others were avoiding him. He considered the invitation of the Australian girls, Beth and Marion, and was now determined he would meet with them. He recalled the resort where they were staying and decided to take his moped and visit.

He found the girls lounging at the pool and dropped down beside them on a chair underneath the shade of the palapa.

"Claude, what a nice surprise. Let me call the boy. What will you drink?"

Claude considered the question. After his talk with Nana, he was upset and decided a strong drink would calm him, and unlike his normal drink of wine, he ordered a 151Proof Mai Tai.

After several Mai Tais, he stripped off his shirt and jumped into the pool. Beth and Marion were quick to join him. The drinks had loosened the trio up. Beth laughed as she removed her bikini top. Marion followed minutes later and they both wrapped their arms around Claude who was feeling the impact of the five Mai Tais he had drunk.

Marion shrieked with laughter as Beth attempted to remove Claude's shorts. Minutes later a shout from the pool attendant ended their raucous fun as they were informed to cover up and leave the pool.

Claude rebelled and removed all his clothing. He climbed the stairs from the pool and to the delight of the girls stood at the edge exposing himself.

The pool attendant returned with the resort security. His clothes were fished from the pond and as the security man held him, Claude was ordered to dress. Other guests were observing and laughing at the scene. Too drunk to maintain his balance, Claude stumbled and fell back into the pool naked.

A second security man arrived and quickly took in the situation before he and the other man jumped into the pool to remove Claude.

He was roughly pulled from the pool and wrapped in towels before being dragged into the resort. The girls lay on their loungers still laughing.

The burly security officer returned to them.

"You may not be staying here much longer if you pull another stunt like that."

His stern comment drew further laughter from the alcohol-impaired couple. Shaking his head he walked off to attend to the situation with Claude.

In the security office, Claude sat incoherent, wrapped in pool towels. The security guards watched as he slumped on the couch and fell asleep. They decided to leave him there until he sobered up.

Time passed and darkness was descending when they decided to transport him back to his hotel.

"Where are you staying? We will take you back there."

"I am at Takitumu villas. I have my moped. I can drive."

"You're not driving anywhere. We will deliver you back. I know about you from friends here on the island. You are undesirable. Better you leave the island soon."

They escorted him out to their pickup truck and placed his moped on the tray at the back. Claude attempted to climb into the truck but stumbled.

"No, you don't. You can sit on the tray with your moped. I don't want to be cleaning up your vomit."

They bounced along the road until they arrived at Takitumu. The security guards unloaded the moped and assisted Claude into the lobby. Nana was at the desk and shook her head when she saw the state Claude was in.

"Thank you for bringing him back. I will look after him from here. He is a decent person but I think he is having a hard time. Don't worry. I will see he is safely escorted to his room. I don't think we will hear too much from him tonight."

The security guards laughed and left after wishing Nana good night.

Nana wrapped her arm around Claude and awkwardly walked him to his villa where she lowered him onto a bed and covered him with a sheet before she left.

Nana returned to her office knowing the torment that Claude was experiencing.

Chapter 58

Claude woke the next morning in a haze. His head ached and the room seemed to be spinning. He crawled from his bed to the bathroom and barely made it to the counter before he vomited. As he turned to leave the bathroom, the urge to return and vomit again hit him hard.

He returned and collapsed onto the bed. He touched his forehead. It felt cold. He tried to recall the previous night but could not.

In an attempt to start his day, Claude opened his beachfront front doors. And walked out into the day. The brightness of the pure white sand blinded him. He looked at the sky and was surprised to see it was purple and not the deep blue he knew.

He walked out to the beach and collapsed onto the sand. He tried to recall the previous night and day. Slowly the events flowed back into his mind. He recalled the Australian girls and the party he had with them. He groaned as it was not something he would normally have done.

Claude returned to his villa and dressed in his best island clothes and then left to visit Nana and apologize for his behavior.

Nana was at the reception desk and smiled as she saw Claude approach.

"Good morning Mr. Claude. You must have had quite the day yesterday. Please don't worry or feel embarrassed. I know things have been difficult for you. Once in a while, we all go crazy. It is alright with me. You didn't hurt anyone or destroy any property."

Still partially inebriated, Claude found his way to a table on the courtyard next to the pool and ordered a black coffee. As he sat drinking his coffee, he was joined by Nana.

"Claude, something you said has disturbed me. You claim that you sent letters here after you left. Is that the truth? Who did you send the letters to? Did you mail them to a mail depot address or a postal box? As you may be aware our mail is not delivered to our homes."

"I sent them to Atarangi Puretu. I sent them to the address she had given me for the family's perfume business."

"How many letters did you send? Can you remember? Did you keep sending even though you never received a response?"

"I stopped sending after about a year. I assumed that either the letters were lost or the address was wrong. I never considered that Atarangi did not want to respond."

Nana frowned and considered the information Claude had shared.

"I suggest you have a quiet day today. I noticed your clothes were dirty after your hike to the Needle. I will have housekeeping launder them for you as today is the day we wash everything after most guests checkout and in preparation for the week ahead and the arrival of new guests tomorrow."

Nana stood to leave, but before she did she spoke to Claude.

"There is something I am going to check about your mail story. Now I must go. Fridays are busy days here. I need to leave and check some things. I will return later today. Please stay out of trouble today."

Although severely hungover, Claude was hungry. He had not eaten dinner the night before, and the pastries he had enjoyed hardly satisfied his need. He went into the dining area and ordered a ham and cheese omelet with a side order of toast.

After he finished eating, Claude changed into swimwear and found a shaded area on the beach. The food helped to reduce the impact of the hangover. He lay on a lounger and drifted off to sleep.

It was several hours later when he was woken by Nana. She was accompanied by a man that Claude recognized to be Rongo, a brother of Atarangi. He stepped forward and shook Claude's hand.

"I must apologize for our treatment of you the other day. Nana has helped us understand what has happened. We should never have treated you this way. I will make sure others in our community know what happened."

Claude was confused. He looked at Nana and shrugged.

"Claude, when you told me about the letters and that you sent them to the perfume factory it made me think. At the factory, there is a person who has wanted Atarangi for years. He has created trouble in the past. He is the one who retrieves the company mail from the mailbox of the company. This afternoon, Rongo confronted him about missing mail, and with his brother, they searched his desk and cabinets. They found a box containing the letters you sent. It was carefully hidden amongst some old files. There were other letters and orders in the box with your letters. Rongo and the family will deal with this man. It seems you have told the truth and they want to make things better for you. The man at the factory was determined that you would not have any contact with Atarangi."

"It is not necessary. I understand. Maybe now I can find Atarangi and speak. I miss her."

'I suggest you wait and see if she comes to you. Other matters exist that are best discussed by her."

Again Claude was confused by the information. No one wanted to tell him why Atarangi would not welcome a visit from him.

He was about to protest Rongo's suggestion that he wait till Atarangi contacted him when a tropical rain started. They ran from the beach for cover in the hotel's lobby area. The rain was heavy and fell in sheets reducing visibility.

"It is late so there is no point in me returning to the factory this afternoon. Let me buy you lunch and drink. It is the least I can do now we know what happened."

"I am not sure about the drink. I overdid it yesterday and I have suffered today."

"I will order you a beer that is made by my family's brewery. It is very refreshing and I suggest it will help you recover from yesterday."

Nana left them and together Rongo and Claude selected to eat on the sheltered patio where they watched the rain cascading off the roof onto the lush gardens.

Rongo ordered two of the beers produced by the family brewery. The lunch menu consisted of fresh mango rubbed lamb chops, fresh snapper, or a mélange of fruits.

Rongo ordered the lamb chops and Claude decided on the fruits.

"When I visited the perfume factory, you told me that Atarangi was visiting another island. When will she return?"

"She is visiting relatives on the island of Aitutaki. She is meant to return on this evening's flight. I am not sure whether she will be able to travel as a huge storm has been forecast for either tonight or tomorrow morning."

"I wish to meet her, especially now I know my letters never reached her."

"Claude, there are things that you need to know. It is not for me to speak of these things. You must hear them from her."

"What is it? Is she married or with someone? Please tell me."

"No. It is Atarangi's business and decision."

"Where can I find her? Does she still live in the same villa?"

"No. I will ask her to come and see you. You should leave it that way."

After lunch, Claude returned to his villa. He found his 'tourist' clothes clean and neatly folded at the end of his bed. He smiled as he planned to use them in the morning.

Chapter 59

Claude woke early in anticipation of the day ahead. He opened the door to go and visit the restaurant for coffee and a light snack. He remembered the Saturday outdoor Punanga Nui market with its numerous food stalls. It seemed that almost all Rarotongans congregated at the Saturday market and that it was a community event. In addition to the food, there were women selling souvenirs and jewelry to tourists. Claude recalled the atmosphere of the market. He had loved visiting it.

As he walked to the restaurant, Claude looked up at the sky. It was threatening. Dark, almost purple, clouds hung in the sky. There was no wind. The clouds were not moving. He had lived through heat storms in Rarotonga before and remembered how fierce they could be. The threat of a storm was not going to deter him from his goal of visiting the market.

Claude ordered a croissant and coffee and sat outside to enjoy them. He watched the sky. It was still. Nothing was changing, so he decided to take his moped and head to the market.

Even though it was early, the market was busy. Smoke from wood-fired grills drifted across the grounds. The aroma of roasted meats and other delicacies filled the air. The market had an almost carnival atmosphere.

Dressed as a tourist, Claude wandered through the market, stopping at stalls to admire local art and handicrafts. He found a food vendor selling roasted wild boar on a home-baked roll, filled with sweet pickled vegetables. Claude could not resist.

As more people arrived at the market, the heat and humidity increased, but did not discourage the new arrivals,

At the rear of the market, a huge stage had been set up. Musical instruments were placed in clusters on the bare wooden stage floor. There would soon be music and dancing.

Claude continued to walk through the stalls, stopping and talking to various vendors. He loved the market.

As he reached the end of a row of covered stalls he saw the two women he knew were close friends of Atarangi. They sat behind a table with a display of black pearls, silver, and other jewelry. He approached slowly. At first, the women did not recognize him and attempted to entice him to buy. but the disguise only lasted less than a minute. Looks of shock filled their faces. One stood and attempted to cover something behind her. She was too slow. Claude gasped. Standing in the rear of the stall near some boxes was Atarangi. She was every bit as beautiful as Claude remembered. He walked forward.

"Atarangi, please can we talk."

She stayed motionless and did not respond.

"Please. I spoke to Rongo. He can explain. I need to see you and talk."

Slowly she moved forward to the front of the stall.

"Claude, it has been a long time. I am not sure we still have feelings for each other. Many things have happened. My life is no longer the life I had when you met me. It is best to just remain friends. I spoke to Rongo last night. He was anxious to talk to me after my flight arrived. I now understand why I had not heard from you. I was heartbroken for over a year. I thought I would never see you again.

Many of my friends and relatives helped me during those times, but unfortunately, many now think badly of you."

"Atarangi, I came back here because you have stayed in my mind. I can not forget you or your kindness. I have never met anyone else like you. Please don't send me away."

She stepped around the table and stood close and in front of Claude. She wrapped her arms around him and rose on her toes to kiss him. As she did huge claps of thunder roared overhead. Giant raindrops started to fall. Seconds later intense bolts of lightning lit up the sky. There was a deafening crack as a bolt hit a nearby tree and a strange odor drifted through the grounds.

People ran for shelter as the rain pelted down and the lightning crashed. Thunder shook the ground.

Claude held Atarangi tight and they moved into the shelter of the covered stall. The sky flickered a bluish-white as lightning illuminated the market. Claude was startled as a small voice called 'Mama Mama' and a little girl rushed from the back of the stall and snatched Atarangi's dress and clutched it.

"Claude, she is scared of the thunder and lightning. Please come under the cover."

"Who is this? She called you Mama. Were you married? I don't understand."

"No Claude I never married. There has been no man I have met who is like you. I still love you. Her name is Rangimarie. She is our daughter."

"I don't understand."

"Claude, she is just three years old, I did not tell you at the time, but I was pregnant when you left the island."

Claude looked at the child. He admired her beauty. She had the same large soft brown eyes as Atarangi. Her hair was long and curly.

"What does her name mean. It is a nice name."

"In Maori it means peace."

Tears welled in Claude's eyes. He dropped on his knee on the wet and muddy grass and turned to Atarangi.

"Atarangi, I came here to find you and ask you to marry me."

She was stunned.

"Yes, of course."

While still kneeling, Claude reached for Peace and hugged her.

The two women in the stall clapped and laughed and picked up a ukulele. She played the two women sang a song in harmony. It was a bizarre scene. Atarangi with a child clutching her skirt, the two women singing to the music, rain pelting down, thunder crashing overhead, and flashes of lightning.

Claude turned to the woman and held up his hand to stop.

"I didn't bring a ring. Do you have a nice ring I can wed Atarangi with?"

One of the women reached under a pile of boxes and removed a tray upon which sat an exquisite black pearl ring. Claude reached for it and slid it onto Atarangi's finger.

Claude looked at her face. Tears of joy streamed down her cheeks intermingled with the Rarotongan raindrops.

"You have made me happy Claude. I had always hoped this day may happen."

"I am thrilled to have you for my wife. Where should we marry?"

"I think right here. We met here and you have returned."

"I have returned and not only do I find you, but I have also found Peace."

--------------------------------------**FIN**---------------------------------